W0254268

The Book of
Eastbay

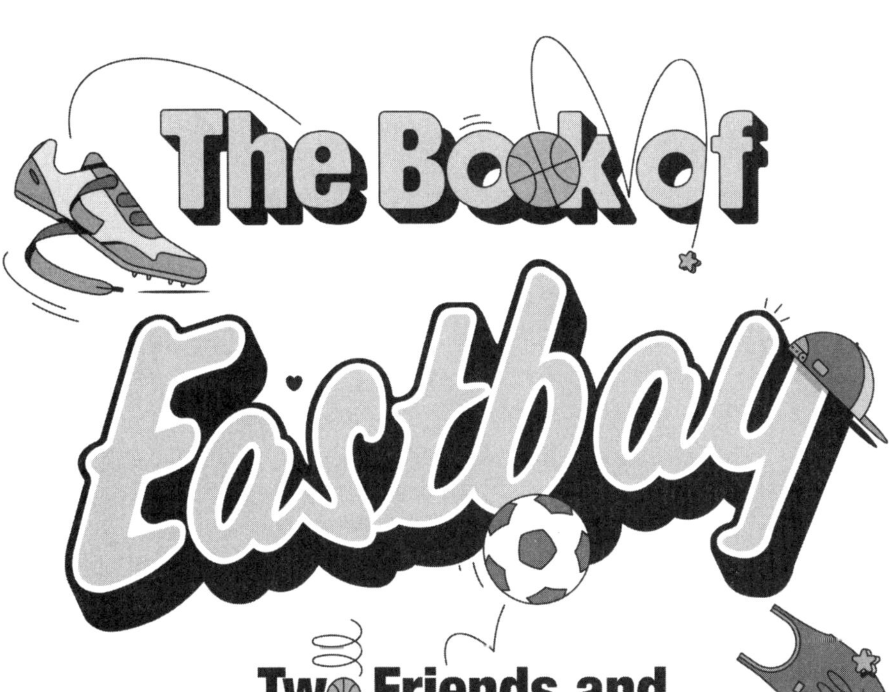

The Book of Eastbay

Two Friends and the Catalog That Changed the Sneaker Business Forever

ART JUEDES & RICK GERING

HARVARD BUSINESS REVIEW PRESS
BOSTON, MASSACHUSETTS

HBR Press Quantity Sales Discounts

Harvard Business Review Press titles are available at significant quantity discounts when purchased in bulk for leadership development programs, client gifts, or sales promotions. Opportunities to co-brand copies with your logo or messaging are also available. For details and discount information for both print and ebook formats, contact booksales@hbr.org or visit www.hbr.org/bulksales.

Copyright 2026 Art Juedes and Rick Gering

All rights reserved

Printed in the United States of America

10 9 8 7 6 5 4 3 2 1

No part of this publication may be reproduced, stored in or introduced into a retrieval system, or transmitted, in any form, or by any means (electronic, mechanical, photocopying, recording, or otherwise), without the prior permission of the publisher. Requests for permission should be directed to permissions@harvardbusiness.org, or mailed to Permissions, Harvard Business School Publishing, 60 Harvard Way, Boston, Massachusetts 02163.

This work depicts actual events in the lives of the authors as truthfully as recollection permits and/or can be verified by research. Occasionally, dialogue consistent with the character or nature of the person speaking has been supplemented. All persons within are actual individuals; there are no composite characters.

The web addresses referenced in this book were live and correct at the time of the book's publication but may be subject to change.

Cataloging-in-Publication data is forthcoming.

ISBN: 979-8-89279-069-7
eISBN: 979-8-89279-070-3

The paper used in this publication meets the requirements of the American National Standard for Permanence of Paper for Publications and Documents in Libraries and Archives Z39.48-1992.

For our children, Jessica, James, and Jenna, and Elizabeth and Tommy, our greatest pride, who encouraged us to do this.

And for our wives, Barb and Susie, our best friends, who never once wavered.

As the song goes, "You fill up my senses
like a night in the forest . . ."

Contents

PART THREE

Growing Fast

PART FOUR

Growing Up

PART FIVE

Getting Huge

Foreword

Dreams Made Tangible

I still remember the joy that washed over me every time the *Eastbay* catalog landed in our mailbox. As a kid growing up in Brookfield, Wisconsin, I inhabited a world where sports were everything. I was a Brookfield Central High Lancer through and through. In football, I played offensive line, defensive end, and I even did some placekicking. In track, it was discus and shot put. But no matter the sport or the season, that little brick of glossy pages always felt like a portal into a bigger world.

You didn't just flip through it—you devoured it. Every shoe, every cleat, every piece of gear felt like a discovery. And there were pages and pages, inviting you to discover your favorites and circle them. Read the funny and inspiring notes peppered throughout. *Eastbay* opened you up to a universe of sporting goods you didn't even know existed. And the athletes and sneaker enthusiasts who got it, *got it.* We all felt like we were in on something cool, something that bound us together.

Before I ever stepped onto an NFL field for the Cleveland Browns, before being selected third overall in the draft, before I earned a scholarship to the University of Wisconsin, before I knew what my future would look like, *Eastbay* gave me something just as important: dreams made tangible. For me it was the first evidence that there were tools to help you achieve greatness—and those tools were within reach. Those *Eastbay* pages didn't just sell products; they fueled passion, curiosity, and the belief that if you laced up the right pair of cleats, you could go after something bigger.

For kids like me all over the Midwest—and across the country and even the world—*Eastbay* was more than a catalog. It was culture. It was aspirational. It was the spark.

That's why this book matters. It chronicles the people who built something iconic—something that shaped generations of athletes long before social media, influencers, or online drops existed. Art Juedes and Rick Gering weren't just entrepreneurs; they were storytellers, visionaries, and champions for every young athlete chasing a dream.

It helps that this book is a heck of a read, too. You'll learn, for sure, but you'll conjure fond memories of a different time, long before the internet, when you'd rush to the mailbox, hoping the catalog was there. When a delivery truck bringing your new gear felt like magic. You'll be inspired as you read about how these two friends started the business and then grew it, eventually achieving their own sort of greatness. I couldn't help but see parallels in Art and Rick's story to the stories of the athletes they were serving, including my own. To read about their singular focus on their mission, their perseverance in the face of major setbacks, and the great teamwork it took to achieve what they did. All of it resonated deeply with me.

Most of all, I could relate to the fact that Art and Rick always showed up. I take great pride in playing 10,363 straight snaps in the NFL. It reminds me that I was there for my teammates and, no matter what else was happening, I wanted to show up for them. Put in the work. That's what Art and Rick did. They put in the work every day for two decades.

I'm honored to help tell their story. Because if you're holding this book, chances are you were like me—a kid dreaming big, dreaming often. And you felt that rush of possibility when you cracked open the *Eastbay* catalog and saw your dreams made tangible, right there in those pages.

—Joe Thomas
Pro Football Hall of Fame
College Football Hall of Fame

The Book of
Eastbay

Prologue

We Had No Idea

In early January 2022, a CEO stared out the window of a fourth-floor office in Midtown Manhattan, contemplating the most emotional decision of his career. In fact, circumstances had made the decision for him; it had been headed this way for years. But he knew he was the one who had to voice the decision, which meant that first, he had to accept it.

With New York City sprawled before him, full of noise and hustle and honking and ambition, the CEO of Foot Locker, our dear friend and former colleague Dick Johnson, reflected on just how high and how far this business had taken him—had taken all of us. Decades later and thousands of miles from where it all began, he stood for an extra moment, remembering, holding on to the gratitude. It eased the pain.

He sighed a heavy sigh, then strode to a conference room, where he said the words out loud to his team: "We're shutting down Eastbay."

For those of you who saw the Eastbay wordmark on the cover of this book and were immediately flooded with nostalgia for your youth, you know what that means. For those of you who don't know Eastbay as well, it was the business we started in 1980 to sell sneakers to young athletes, which grew to become *Eastbay,* a catalog that turned out to be extraordinarily special, to us and to millions of kids. Perhaps you came to this book because you love smart, inspiring stories about entrepreneurs, or you're fascinated by the sneaker industry, or maybe you just want to bask a while in nostalgia for what life was like and what business was like in the '80s and '90s. In any case, welcome.

We are Art and Rick, by the way—although over the years we've used more colorful names for each other, too. A lot of good things have happened to us since we met, as babies in the hospital. Many of these things we chalk up to sheer luck, but the fact that we have stayed friends for more than seven decades is not one of them. For all we've managed to accomplish, this may be the thing we're most proud of. No matter how often we fought—and we've fought *a lot*—we always figured things out. We always stuck to our unspoken agreement: the business would go before the friendship would go. There's only one time we can think of when we both disagreed so strongly that we couldn't find a solution, so we decided to flip a coin. But we'll get to that.

Our story is actually three stories. The first is a story about friends who became accidental entrepreneurs, living some ninety miles west of the frozen tundra of Lambeau Field, in the cold, wintry land known as Wausau, Wisconsin. We sent a letter to thirty-five track coaches in the area, asking them if we could stop by their schools, show their athletes some shoes, help them find the right ones. We were just two guys trying to build something from nothing through hard work, a healthy dose of delusion, and, we hoped, plenty of dumb luck.

The second story is one about transformation, first of our business. Somehow the thirty-five letters to area coaches led us decades later to taking nearly 400,000 pictures of shoes and producing up to sixteen thick catalogs per year—each with the iconic Eastbay wordmark and some magical, zany, or deeply inspiring cover. At its peak, some forty to fifty million copies of *Eastbay* were sent all over the world every year, eagerly snatched from mailboxes everywhere, from the heart of New York, Detroit, Los Angeles, Tokyo, and every big city, to ranches in Wyoming, farms in Indiana, suburbs in Florida, and dusty towns in West Texas. Wherever they were, kids would pore over those pages, in awe of the sheer volume of sneakers, and the colors, and the sizes. They'd dog-ear pages, circle their favorites. Even if they couldn't get them, they could dream about getting them. Maybe they had to mow some lawns or babysit to save up. Eventually they'd call to place their order. And then, miraculously, just a few days later—that was instantaneous in the 1980s—the shoes were at their doorstep.

It's hard to fathom how we got from the first story to the second. It certainly wasn't planned. We just *felt* that what we were doing was right, no matter what anyone else told us, and plenty told us we were crazy, or wrong, or unwelcome. And that's part of the second story, too: the role we played, often unwittingly, in the transformation of the shoe business more generally, and of the culture of young athletes, and of sneakers as fashion and as identity-shaping artifacts.

Polly James was a multisport high school athlete when we first hired her (then named Polly Weiland) to just do whatever needed doing. She stayed with us for a long time, in many, many roles. When we talked to her for this book, she told us, "Eastbay is kind of folklore to so many people. It's kind of a unicorn. It just doesn't happen every day. And we were in the middle of nowhere in people's minds. It wasn't an easy place to get to. Some salespeople would come through and then go back to their companies and tell these mythical stories about Eastbay in this little town. 'You wouldn't believe these guys. There are people running all over the place in this office, in these warehouses, they're pushing all these packages out the door.' It wasn't the most organized and highbrow kind of place. So, there was kind of this urban legend—this sneakerhead legend—that kind of grew about who we were and what we were doing."

Journalist Bobbito Garcia, the author of *Where'd You Get Those?* and an icon of sneaker culture who was the first journalist ever to write about that culture, for hip-hop magazine *The Source* in 1990, later told us, "For sneakerheads, having something like *Eastbay* was equivalent to porn, basically . . . Because literally, it was insane to see . . . Sneakerhead culture had already formed . . . and the idea of trying to search high and low for sneakers that weren't available otherwise had already been established. What *Eastbay* did was create a cog in that ecosystem when they finally arrived. Once it got on my radar, it became dear. If you're in any other city [besides New York], basically, where sneaker culture wasn't bubbling just yet, then that's your bible. And for that, I think *Eastbay* really plays a role in the expansion of sneaker culture beyond New York."

To us, there's something beautiful about what Polly and Bobbito say about the connection and access that *Eastbay* created—at a time, remember, when culture and community didn't spread instantly. But we had no idea. Okay, maybe we had *some* idea. We had heard funny stories about kids getting *Eastbay* catalogs confiscated from their backpacks or right from their desks during class, and we had noticed multiple catalogs going to the same address. Now and again, a successful athlete would call on us. Shaq was a fan, as you'll find out.

But what we hadn't realized was just how deep the bond was that people formed with *Eastbay*. While we certainly tried to create something that was special to athletes, especially young athletes, we had no idea that the catalog meant so much to them, and how much it would come to mean to this other burgeoning community of sneaker enthusiasts who now are part of a worldwide, multibillion-dollar industry. Even today, we're still learning about the magical connection so many had to *Eastbay*.

How could you not know? People have asked since then.

Mostly because we were so busy working. That's the third story—the story of perseverance. There was not a single year at Eastbay without drama of one sort or another, much of it existential. Almost every year felt like it could very well be our last before we accidentally bankrupted ourselves. Even though Eastbay grew in giant leaps, we're not sure if we ever felt like we knew exactly what we were doing. We just loved helping athletes get the right shoes, and we set out to do it the best ways we knew how. Our strategy was simple: if we thought something might work, we threw everything we could at it until proven wrong (or until lawyers told us to stop—more on that, soon, too). And a lot of times, that meant botching it before we got it right. We broke so many rules because we didn't know the rules.

We always felt like these guys with this simple idea flailing about in the middle of nowhere, and often big industry players treated us that way, despite the fact that we were, in many ways, ahead of them. We were making bets—on inventory, on digitization, on customer service, on content strategy—that foretold how business would transform in general. We understood the customers in ways other industry players didn't seem to grasp.

We're not trying to brag. We weren't smarter than anyone else. Much of Eastbay's success was based on instinct, timing, luck, and, frankly, stubbornness. We started the company on a simple idea, one that guys who wear suits to work (we never did) would probably call a *mission* or a *North Star*. We just called it the plan: Give young athletes access to good shoes they couldn't get anywhere else at prices they could afford. That's it. And, stubbornly, we never really stopped doing that.

That simple idea wasn't a strategy we dreamt up in some business session or based on advice from an entrepreneur's handbook. It came from our own experiences as kids and as athletes. We both played multiple sports. Rick was a track star, fast as wind on the prairie. Art's game was baseball, and could he hit. We had always loved the feeling of putting on the perfect new pair of shoes. There was some magic in tying up that track spike or baseball cleat or basketball shoe that made you feel faster, made you feel like you could jump higher, or just made you feel like what you had on your feet *looked cool*. Stepping into the right pair of new shoes can make you feel like a new person, a better athlete. That's what we wanted to give to people, because growing up, we knew how hard it could be to get that feeling, to find that right pair of shoes, and to afford them.

We believe—we know—our commitment to this one idea is the source of the deep and loyal connection athletes and, we'd find out later, sneakerheads felt toward the *Eastbay* catalog.

Eastbay was the proverbial lightning in a bottle, and we felt the heat and energy, the buzz from it every day for twenty years. It became a blessing beyond words, and a story that we now find hard to believe. It's a story about friendship and business, about failing and succeeding. It's about luck and smarts and always showing up. It's about what happens when you surround yourself with great people—and what happens when, no matter what you do, you know *why* you're doing it.

All good things must pass, and Eastbay did, too. That's part of our story as well. When Eastbay shut down just a couple of years ago, many people encouraged us to share our story. It was not an easy decision for us—we worried we'd forgotten more of it than we could remember. But then we enlisted the help of many of those who were there with us. We spent many hours interviewing them and amassing notes from their memories, and this gave us a newfound energy for telling the story. You will hear their voices throughout this book, and you'll hear from fans of the catalog, from sneakerheads and athletes, because we can't tell the story of Eastbay without all of them. You'll meet an array of characters who colored in the years.

It was a lot of years, and it was a lot of years ago, too. Once we started this book, we realized that getting the timeline right and aligning events was trickier than we expected it would be. There were so many memories weaving together and overlapping, and not everyone remembered them the same way. Everything in this book happened, and all the people are real. We worked hard to verify and align events and dates, but please forgive us if we slightly misplaced an event in time. One more note: In order to tell our story together, sometimes we need to refer to ourselves in the third person so as not to confuse you. Thank you for understanding.

We hope you're inspired by our story. Maybe you'll learn from it. Mostly, we want you to enjoy it. We sure have.

We were on a walk with our wives down in Florida, when Art's phone rang. Dick Johnson, still holding on to the gratitude, called us the minute the news of Eastbay's closing was made public.

"I'm sorry," he told us. "I kept it going as long as I could."

We told him that there was no reason to be sorry, that it had all become more than we ever dreamed. Dick chuckled. "That is the truth," he said. "It's been a great ride."

PART ONE

Starting Out

1

Thanks for Reading

It was an amazing ride we took, a ride that started on a Thursday in June in 1952, when Art was born at St. Mary's hospital in Wausau, Wisconsin. Rick followed him two days after that. In the hospital nursery, Rick ended up in the bassinet right next to Art's. Brothers-in-arms, taking on this sudden, bright, cold life together.

But then our parents wanted to go home, so they ripped us apart, and that was that.

The end.

Thanks for reading.

2

Welcome to the Middle

Just kidding.

We did part after our stint as newborns, but two years later, by sheer happenstance, Rick's family moved three doors down from Art's. Our parents hadn't known each other before that, and they had no idea we'd turn into something like Butch and Sundance meet *Dumb and Dumber*. No one saw this whole *Eastbay* thing coming. But any success we've had—business, friendship, life in general—starts with where we came from and how we grew up. You know that quote in *The Sandlot* about how at some point in your childhood, you and your friends went outside to play together for the last time, and nobody knew it? We never had that last time.

Wausau, Wisconsin, and the endless acres of pastures sprawling beyond its borders throughout Marathon County probably had more cows than people—about 40,000 people back then. It had one of the biggest high schools in Wisconsin at the time, and the Lumberjacks were notoriously good in a lot of sports.

It was a good town, in a good area that is about as middle as it gets. Wausau lies in the middle of the state, which is in the middle of the country. It sits between Minneapolis and Chicago. It's also located sort of in the middle between L.A., two thousand miles that way, and New York, one thousand miles the other way.

And we never went anywhere like that. While this made some things seem more difficult than we wished they'd been at the time, with the benefit of hindsight we now see this as one of our greatest strengths, both for ourselves and for building the Eastbay business.

Long before we opened a shop downtown, we were just kids screwing around in a neighborhood along Wausau Avenue, a noisy two-lane street with humble one- and two-story homes. The stretch of road we lived on was nestled into a small valley that kept us hemmed into a two-block neighborhood, at least until we could sneak away on bikes. It was a middle-class development, with some gravel roads and places still without streetlights. High school kids drag-raced a quarter-mile strip of road there to see who could hit Highway 52 first. That's a good metaphor for how a lot of kids talked about Wausau—how could they get out as fast as possible?

Highway 52 was busy enough that you had to look both ways and dodge traffic to get across it. It separated us from the rest of town, so in a lot of ways we felt like it was us versus the world—the world being downtown Wausau. We were on the underdogs' side.

Rick was the first kid Art remembers meeting in the neighborhood. Art lived in a small white house between 8th and 9th streets, with Rick's red brick place a few houses down on the corner of 9th and Wausau Ave. Making our way around the neighborhood meant cutting through various neighbors' yards and breezeways, ducking below windows so as not to get caught. There were no paths to follow except the ones we made.

But it was a good place to grow up, where people were nice and, for the most part, lived by the Golden Rule. It was the sort of place that both required and gave room for imagination.

Our family ties were strong. Neither of our families had much money, but if we were poor, we didn't know it. Rick's dad, Cliff, who worked for Kraft Foods, would cut the mold out of outdated food and cheese he could bring home from his grocery accounts. We scraped by the best we could. Art's mom was a homemaker and, later, a housecleaner. Art often helped his mom clean other people's houses. His dad, Art Senior, owned a great old-fashioned neighborhood place, Bud's Bar, a few blocks away, and just past that was Athletic Park, where Art Senior played and inspired Art's passion for baseball. Art had three older sisters, Ellen, Barb, and dear Joan, a special-needs child whose laugh made even Wausau's cold, gray days seem warmer and brighter. Once, we were racing our bikes and Rick crashed and broke his leg. Joan saw this and, though she rarely ever ran, in this moment she did, running back to Rick's house to tell Rick's mom that Rick was lying in the road. We still don't know how she got there so fast. How we learned to treat Joan, and appreciate her, would reverberate through our relationships for the rest of our lives.

At the Gerings', Rick's mom, Dawn, stayed home with him. He was an only child in the early years but would eventually have four younger brothers: Doug, Tom, Jim, and John.

On our first day of kindergarten, Rick's mom got permission to transfer Art from a different school to Ms. Cawley's class in the school Rick was in. We don't know how, but one of our working theories is that Rick's grandma lived across the street from the school, and they all believed that we needed extra adult supervision and wanted Grandma available for reinforcements.

The town was growing, and had run out of space for us, so our kindergarten class of thirty was stuck in the high school with two thousand teenagers. We did not behave. The details of our crimes are fuzzy, but we know that we sometimes got kicked out of class. The high school kids regularly passed us in the hallways. *Hey, Art. Hey, Rick. Out here again? Need a cigarette, kid?* We made friends with them quick. *No, Ms. Cawley, that's not* our *cigarette box on the floor.*

Neither of us remembers any other kindergarteners getting kicked out of class. And it was never just one or the other of us. We always got kicked out together. Our parents never had to ask us about it, either. We were too clueless to lie, and Rick's grandma and Ms. Cawley were closer than we knew.

Art was raised Catholic. Rick's dad was a devout Baptist, but his mom was Catholic, and he was raised Catholic when he went to school. Had he not been, we wouldn't have attended grade school together at St. Michael's. That church has changed now, but back when we were kids, it was impossible to miss the massive brick steeples towering above the neighborhood as though built by God himself. St. Mike's took up nearly a full block. We knew a short cut through an alley to get there, but we were told not to take it because of the busy street it dumped on to. We took it every day anyway.

One of the moments we both looked forward to most as kids was our First Communion, a literal rite of passage—and we knew we'd get presents. Two nights before ours, Art's dad was rushed over to St. Mary's

Hospital. Art went to visit him the next day; his father didn't look good. When Art went searching for his sisters, he found them in the hospital chapel, where they were praying and crying. Art wasn't sure what was happening, and nobody explained it to him. Soon, someone took him home.

The next day, he went to St. Michael's for our First Communion. When he sat beside Rick in the church—whose idea was that?—Rick was thrilled. Another opportunity to goof off. But then Art said, "I think my dad died last night."

3

Making the Nuns Pray Extra

He was right about his dad. Something went wrong with his dad's liver, and by the time doctors found answers, time had run out. His family had tried to shield him from it so that he could enjoy his First Communion.

It would have been impossible for this not to have changed Art. He knew it made his mom, Evelyn, worry deeply—she was suddenly alone with four children, one with special needs. His Uncle George stepped in to help. Art remembers that at the funeral Uncle George said to him, "You're the man of the house, now." Art was seven.

It probably brought us closer together, too, as the Gerings became a second family to Art. Over the years it would be Rick's dad who taught Art things like how to tie a tie and ride a bike, and when Art got confused about kids on his baseball team talking about wearing a cup, it was Rick and his dad who explained to him what that valuable piece of equipment was.

We spent most of our childhood outdoors. In Wausau, you felt safe wherever you went. Parents let kids out of the house at eight in the morning and said come home when the streetlights come on. And we had all the typical kids' dustups. Art's first bike was a hulking green thing that must have weighed seven hundred pounds. It had rock-hard tubeless tires that could probably crush rocks. One day out riding, Art was going so slow on this thing that Rick pulled up to pass him. Art's tubeless tire got stuck in a rut. He fell over, and Rick rode right over him and just kept going. Years later Art would joke with Rick that, "You never threw me under the bus, but you rode over me with your bike."

Art's mom made chicken and dumplings, and pork and sauerkraut, things Rick's mom never made. Sometimes Rick would just show up at dinnertime because he'd smelled something good from outside. When we were hanging out, Rick would stay around until he knew what Art's mom had cooked and then decide whether to go back to his house for dinner or not. On the other hand, Rick's mom made legendary cookies, and the jar was always full, and Art could smell those from outside, too, and find reasons to go in and nab some.

We were on our own quite a bit. The way we spent most of our time is best summarized by one of our favorite movie quotes, from *Armageddon*: "I bet they're just sitting there, thinking shit up."

Around the corner from our houses was a steep hill, a choice spot for our neighborhood go-kart races, which came only after our go-kart construction wars. We'd all rummage through each other's trash to find makeshift parts—two-by-fours, old wagons, ropes, horseshoe nails, and the *pièce de résistance* of every go-kart, the parts that would make or break your race: wheels. The older kids always seemed to get the good wheels first, taking tires from old lawnmowers and baby buggies. We'd find ourselves making do with lame, wobbly roller-skate wheels. Still, we'd patch together a box that could hold a kid and roll, and we'd drag it up the hill. There we'd line up the go-karts and give ourselves over to gravity. One of the go-karts we built always seemed to go sideways. We had to use our feet to steer the thing straight, which in hindsight gave us a vivid sense of how quickly kids wear out shoes.

Neighbors driving by or on their porches would yell and shake their fists. They were expecting us to crash and die, and they didn't want that happening on their lawn. Somehow, we survived. In retrospect, the go-kart races were a foreshadowing of our business operations, at least early on.

If we weren't hurtling down hills in death traps, we were playing Wiffle ball in Art's backyard. Like most kids, we adapted to the space. Home plate was right beside the kitchen window, so Rick always knew what Art was having for dinner. Center field was a cement wall with a fence on top. If you didn't get it over the fence in center, automatic out. If you hit it over a telephone wire running through the yard, automatic double. You got to hit until you made an out. Sometimes, Art would be at bat for two and a half days.

During the long Wisconsin winters, we would trudge a mile up and down two hills to an ice-skating pond and spend all day and part of the night there. Our parents didn't think anything about it. If you were too stupid to come in from the cold, that was your own fault.

In the woods near our house was where we did some of our best thinking, with BB guns, and tree forts, and rope swings over a stream. Unlimited apples and currants. Once we set a grass fire that got out of control.

Bike rides to school were out of control, too, fraught with racing, barreling through stop signs, and nearly getting hit by cars.

We were late to mass most mornings, since we had to stop at Loppnow's Market for candy. Our winter boot buckles would echo through the church as we trudged to our pew, past all the punctual kids. One teacher or another might wallop us on the sides of our heads. One day we really pissed off our fourth-grade teacher, who seemed cranky. Leaving for lunch in a no-talking line, Art said to me that she must have gotten up on the wrong side of the bed. Someone told our teacher, and that got us a personalized mediation session where we got another good yelling at and got slapped around some more. Santa wasn't real, she told us, but ghosts were, and if we didn't get our act together, then the ghosts were coming for us.

Our teachers and priests and various other authority figures struggled to keep us properly focused and motivated. Another St. Mike's nun told us that she worried not only for our souls, but also for the rest of our human lives, unable to see what sort of future they could possibly hold. She said she felt called to pray extra for us.

The older kids in the neighborhood always liked pushing us around. What we lacked in size and smarts, though, we made up for in tenacity and thickheadedness. We'd jump up and shove them back, usually to minimal result, and find ourselves thrown down to the ground again and again. But we got back up.

We figured out early that helping each other made life better, and in no time, we came to trust each other totally. That meant trusting that we'd back each other up in fights, or that we'd give each other good advice, or that one of us wouldn't hate the other's guts when we called each other complete idiots for whatever reason. We got good at telling each other when we were being dumb.

One time, Rick lucked out and got a Mickey Mantle baseball card. An older kid wanted it, and he knew an easy mark when he saw one. He told Rick to hand it over in exchange for a half dozen other cards of guys with names nobody remembers now. Rick was ready to do the deal. Art knew that the Mick was a special card. Rick just saw *more cards*. Lacking concrete evidence to support his claim about the Mick's long-term value, Art relied on a tried-and-true argument to change Rick's mind: "If you take that deal," Art told Rick, "I'll think you're an idiot forever."

We fought about it for a while until the lightbulb came on: More wasn't always better. Rick kept the Mantle.

As we got older, we played sports. Basketball. Baseball. Football. And just like the *Sandlot* kids, half our time "playing football" was really spent flirting with girls at the nearby pool.

The lot we played football in sat at the top of a hill that overlooked Thom Field where the local high school teams played. We couldn't afford to go into the stadium, but our parents would let us go up to the hill on cold fall Friday nights to watch the high school games. We'd play our own game up there while the real game was going on down on Thom Field, and we would dream about playing under the lights ourselves someday.

We always tried to be teammates, knowing we could beat the older kids with our complementary skills. Art was bigger and stronger and could out-throw anybody, while Rick was slimmer and smaller and a total speed demon.

Baseball was a burgeoning passion for Art—in part for the memories the game brought him of listening to the Yankees on the radio with his dad, before First Communion, and in part because he was good, better than he cared to admit—certainly better than Rick. In baseball Rick drove Art nuts. Rick hit lefty and was so fast he could have made a decent living hitting to contact and beating out throws. But instead, Rick always swung for the fences, screwing himself into the ground taking donkey hacks. When he did connect, all his slight frame could manage was a looping fly ball to not-deep-left-center field.

"Just hit the damn ball on the *ground*, Rick!" Art would yell. "They're never gonna get you out!"

"No!" Rick would shout back. "I can hit a home run!"

In junior high, we got separated as Art went on to the Catholic school and Rick went to the public school. We never felt that separate at this time. Rick was around Art so much, some kids at the Catholic school assumed he went to school there. Sports were sparse where Art went, so when he couldn't play, he got into music, playing guitar in garage bands. Art exposed Rick to rock and roll, since it was forbidden in Rick's house. Rick returned the favor by getting Art blind dates.

The local YMCA had a room called Red Rail where kids would hang out after school and eat snacks and play music and dance. There were always girls at the Red Rail, so we hung out there, too, and flirted. We spent whatever money we could scrounge on banana splits at Woolworth's. Later, we'd get some of the money we spent there back.

Art was all in on baseball. Rick swapped his cleats for running shoes and became a star sprinter, and he was also a two-way starter at running back and defensive back in football, coached by future Wisconsin Hall of Fame high school football coach Wynn Brockmeyer. His senior year, Wausau beat the number one team in the state. Rick's mom and dad never missed a game or a meet.

One day our junior year, Rick's mom asked Art if he could go pick Rick up from the nearby ski hill. Art had never been there, but he said sure. He found Rick at the lodge hanging out with a group of girls, of course, and one caught Art's eye. He played it cool for a while but found a way to say hi. Her name was Barb. Soon enough they'd swapped phone numbers and made plans to go to a movie—much to Rick's surprise, who told Art he was swinging above his weight class here with Barb, who was the daughter of one of the most prominent surgeons in Wausau. She lived across the highway in the nice area of town, where the country club was. Barb would turn out to be one of the best things that could have happened to us.

So, small-town kids to our bones, pretty much all we knew about life was what we had there in our Wausau bubble, closed off from the rest of the world other than what we glimpsed through CBS and ABC, and maybe NBC if you were handy with rabbit ears and aluminum foil. But Wausau became one of our greatest strengths, because our isolation made the outside world inspiring and aspirational.

This was especially true in sports. The kids who played varsity sports in Wausau were the heroes we looked up to, even more than we did to pro or college athletes who we had little access to. Wausau High had play-by-play for football and even a PA announcer for track meets, Rick remembers, and the stands weren't empty for those track meets, either. When we got old enough to try out, we recognized you had to earn your spot, and we looked up to the kids who already had.

Anything beyond that we'd learn from papers and *Sports Illustrated* and the radio. Of course, everyone followed the Packers in football, and the old Milwaukee Braves in baseball. We would see games on television occasionally, but our families didn't have any extra money even to go to the local high school games, let alone college games, and forget about going somewhere like Milwaukee for a pro game. Yankees games on the radio gave us a crackling connection to a world that was hard for us to even imagine was real. Those teams in those big cities seemed to exist on distant planets; pro athletes might as well have been otherworldly members of a mythic species.

We had no idea that somehow the shoe company we would start would one day take us flying around the country to meet with real-life legends, some of the best athletes in the world. Indeed, Lady Luck would guide us right to the center of the sports world. Somehow, we'd land right in the middle of everything.

4

Six (or More) Years of College down the Drain

Eastbay was founded in 1980, but it really got its start in 1970, before the state track meet. It was senior year for Rick, and he was a star.

Wausau High gave kids shoes for sports, even track. The track we ran on was an outdoor cinder one, and the spikes they gave us were heavy, stiff leather—good for durability when you're passing them down year after year, but terrible for speed. Rick's school's indoor track shoes had red canvas uppers and gum rubber soles, and they provided good traction but no support and they squeaked so loud that runners always knew when you were gaining on them. Luckily, sprinters didn't have to run very far.

Good runners like Rick wanted something lighter and faster, especially for a state final, something Rick learned from Skip Kent, who graduated a year ahead of Rick at Wausau High and then became a college middle-distance runner at the University of Wisconsin who ran a 1:47.2 880-yard dash and was national champion. Rick knew from him about white and black Adidas sprint spikes with a proper sprint plate—the hard part on the forefoot of the shoe the spikes screw into that helps generate power. But he couldn't find them anywhere near Wausau. He has never forgotten the feeling of frustration at not being able to find those sprint spikes and then feeling so deeply invested in locating a pair that he went on a quest to find some down in Madison, two hours south.

He got the spikes he needed and performed well enough that a coach at UW–Stevens Point asked him to come run at the university.

We did indeed graduate high school, much to the nuns' shock and relief.

While Rick set up at Point, Art went to the University of Wisconsin–Eau Claire about a hundred miles due west of Wausau, putting us some two hours apart. Rick would visit Eau Claire more than Art visited Stevens Point, probably in no small part because Eau Claire, a big nursing school, had a five-to-one female-to-male student ratio.

Turns out Rick wasn't ready for college; all he cared about was running and having a good time. For the first couple of years, Art felt similar, minus the running. His junior year, Art sold a twelve-string Gibson for beer money. He worked his way through college earning money cleaning the dorm bathrooms, cleaning like he used to with his mother. One day a friend from high school saw him working the job and said he was happy to see that Art had found some work—he didn't suspect that Art was actually *in* college.

Mostly, we were having so much fun that Art took six years to graduate. Rick became a professional student, wondering why Art had been in such a rush. Rick kept changing his majors. He would drop classes a week before the final if it looked like he might get an F. And when he ran out of tuition money, he'd take time off to work and save up money for another semester. He liked this, though, because he knew he would likely end up being a teacher and coach someday, like Art, and that having these different life experiences between semesters would help him understand people better than a classroom would.

He worked some good jobs in those off times, too. He moved to Orlando for eight months in 1971 to work for Disney, which was launching Disney World, its second theme park. He hustled while washing dishes and waiting tables and could pull in $400 in a week.

He'd always come back to Point, though. During what would have been a good student's senior year of college, Rick was helping a friend look for some track spikes he lost prior to a meet. Another fellow sauntered up, asking "Which dumbass lost his spikes, and how can I help?" That's how Rick met the man we came to call Trebs: Don Trezbiatowski. Later, when Art was waiting for Rick in Rick's apartment, Art heard the door open and without looking, threw a bottle of beer for Rick to catch. Only it wasn't Rick. It was Trebs coming to get Rick for a softball game. Trebs just caught the bottle hurtling at his head and said, "Hey, buddy. I got a bat here! What are you trying to prove?"

And that's how Art met Trebs. In time, the three of us would somehow find ourselves deciding that we had what it took to go into business together.

Art graduated in 1976 and got a job as a physical education teacher while coaching basketball. That same spring, the UW–Stevens Point track team, as usual, had several athletes reach the NAIA national championships under legendary coach Rick Witt. Rick's and Trebs's eligibility had run out, but they still ran and worked with the team as student assistants.

After an arduous fifteen-hour van ride down to the NAIA championships in Arkadelphia, Arkansas, Rick got out of the van and sized up the field. And the thing he noticed, immediately, was everyone's track spikes. They were wearing spikes he'd never seen in his life, and in an array of amazing colors—blue and red and purple and yellow and green. They looked *good*—sleek, aerodynamic, technical. *Fast.* So thin that some of the spikes looked molded to the runners' feet.

They were breathtaking. He saw three different types of Adidas alone, one for sprinting, one for middle distance, and another for long distance. In Stevens Point, all we had was the sprint shoe, if we could track it down. Rick felt awestruck by the variety and frustrated by the fact that he never had these choices. He had to drive two hours to Madison for basic sprinting spikes once. *Most kids,* he thought, *don't have these options.*

A good friend of ours on the Stevens Point team, a shorter, skinny, marathon-running specialist named Dave Elger, won the NAIA marathon national championship that year. Afterward, while Elger and Rick and Trebs celebrated, they kept coming back to the same topic. All they wanted to talk about was all the different, cool shoes they'd seen.

Rick needed to know more. Where did they come from, and how could he get them in the hands of kids in Wausau and Stevens Point? Kids like we'd been, whose only choices had been whatever was in our local stores.

Nobody seemed to offer anything significant to more serious athletes. We didn't know much else even existed.

Rick knew the track-shoe landscape was changing. Schools that had once given kids shoes at the start of season—no matter how clunky they were—had gotten away from that because of budget cuts. Companies, he saw in Arkadelphia, were creating more specific styles for specific events. Many had new technology that radically improved performance from even that of a few years before.

Something in Rick felt set ablaze. He had no idea how to go about doing it, but after that event, he couldn't stop thinking about figuring out a way to start a business selling shoes like those to kids like us.

Rick and Don and Dave stayed on it. They'd run, drink, think, drink, dream, in what would become our standard brainstorming style. *How could we do it? Who would buy them? How would we get the shoes? How could we get them to kids?*

Two years after Arkadelphia, Art and Barb, the girl he'd met at the ski lodge, had graduated, were married, and were both teaching.

Rick continued helping with the track team at Point, taking classes and working another new job as UWSP Director of Recreational Services. There he figured out some of the basics of budgeting, hiring, firing, and managing. He once hired Art when Art was in grad school—on a contract basis, mind you—to help put together fiberglass canoes. We kept waiting to hear that someone had sunk. As far as we know, nobody did.

At a bar one night in Stevens Point, Rick met a woman celebrating her twenty-first birthday with friends. "There may have been table dancing involved," the woman in question—Susie—recalls. They hardly talked, but Rick says he asked if he could call her. She must have said okay, but Susie never gave him her name or number. The next day, someone on the woman's dorm floor told Susie she had a call. (There was one phone for the whole floor.) She picked up to hear Rick asking, "How is the birthday girl?"

"I did not remember him," Susie says, but Rick asked her on a date anyway, and she said yes. "When he arrived at my dorm to pick me up, my friends, not too discreetly, walked through the lobby"—to scout him—"and they gave me the okay. He never told me how he got my name and number until he was writing this book." Someone at the bar had told him Susie's name, and from there, he *may have* consulted a university database he had access to as part of his job.

Despite Rick's thick beard and general lack of prospects, he and Susie hit it off. He kept the beard for the first three years they dated, meaning Susie never even really saw his face for those years. And she still stuck with him.

And she stuck with him as he remained obsessed with figuring out how to turn this idea of getting better sneakers to kids into a business. Rick's mind was in overdrive. He started to see opportunity everywhere. There's this wider selection of shoes with new technology, at least in the bigger cities, but there's not much information about these shoes. We could educate people about which shoes were best for them, he thought. And we could sell all these shoes to kids at affordable prices. We knew what it felt like to want better shoes with no way to pay for them.

Partnering with Trebs and Dave was a good call, too. Dave was a great student and a driven athlete, of course, having just won the marathon. He knew how to work hard. Trebs had been a great runner himself, a big half-miler, and he'd been raised as a Midwestern farm boy, taught to be humble and get the job done, fully.

Rick called Art and raved about the idea, telling Art he planned to move back to Wausau and live with his parents while he built this thing with Trebs and Dave. And he asked Art if he would move back to Wausau and help them.

Rick's pitch left Art unimpressed. This was one of Rick's shakiest ideas yet. *What are you, an idiot? Selling shoes? How was this even worth trying?* Art's career was progressing well. He coached baseball and basketball and taught special needs P.E. in Union Grove, Wisconsin. Barb had a nice teaching job herself. Life was good.

Art got off the call and told Barb about Rick's wild idea to sell high-end running shoes in Wausau and how he wanted Art to move back there with him.

"Well," Barb said, "I actually think it sounds like a wonderful idea."

Wanting kids sooner rather than later, Barb also loved the thought of raising them in her hometown, around people and places she'd known and loved growing up. In her opinion, Rick's idea had potential. And as Barb talked about it, Art started to see it.

Barb's optimism was more the exception than the rule. Art wasn't alone in his skepticism. Barb's dad, who Art always called Dr. Molinaro, or Doc, didn't love it. "Move back to Wausau if you want to raise your kids there," he said, "but stay away from the shoe game, Art. Keep teaching." Doc Molinaro even brought in reinforcements. He invited his friend Bob Greenheck, a prominent Wausau businessman, to talk some sense into Art. But unfortunately for Doc, after hearing the pitch, Greenheck said Art should go for it.

It was Barb's endorsement that ultimately convinced Art. We know now, and Art will tell you, everything good in his life has happened because his wife first told him he should do it.

Art still hadn't told Rick or the other guys. Rick, meanwhile, needed to navigate one more pressing matter. If he wanted to invest real time into this shoe business, he needed to graduate from college. He asked Art to help him figure out what he needed to do to graduate. Art examined Rick's transcripts. "Rick," he said, "you already have enough credits to graduate in history *and* English."

"Really? When can I?" Rick said.

"About two years ago."

PART TWO

Starting Up

5

Cutting a Deal

We knew we wanted to sell athletes shoes but had only vague notions of how to do it. Our first idea was to buy into a sneaker franchise like Athlete's Foot or Athletic Attic. But even then, the franchise fee could cost around $250,000 ($1.4 million now), and that was before inventory. We were a schoolteacher and three kids fresh out of college. So, no franchise.

And, though we weren't thinking about it at the time, in retrospect it was an awful moment to start a business. Inflation was rampant, rising from 4 percent early in the '70s to 14 percent near the start of the '80s. Interest rates jumped from 11.5 percent to start 1979 to 15.5 percent by Christmas. The Soviet Union decided to invade Afghanistan that December. Some sixty countries were threatening to boycott the 1980 Summer Olympics in Moscow, creating dramatic tension heading into February and the 1980 Lake Placid Winter Olympics in New York.

If we had any sense, three young guys just starting out in the world would never have thought about starting a business in this moment, but it's better to be lucky than good. And we got lucky in 1979, when our friend Dave Elger—who had won the NAIA marathon in Arkadelphia—ran a 10K road race in Milwaukee. At the front of the pack with his fellow elite runners, all doing their usual prerace trash talk, Elger met a guy named Dave Hill. After the race, Hill told Elger that he owned Milwaukee's first and best running shoe store. Elger told Hill all about our plans and Hill invited us to his store in Milwaukee to see what he could do to help us. His store was called the Eastbay Running Store, named after a bay in Lake Superior near Hill's hometown in Upper Peninsula Michigan.

As 1979 turned over to 1980, marathon champ Dave Elger, displaying keen wisdom, decided that though he had brokered the meeting with Dave Hill, none of us in fact knew what the hell we were doing. He opted out. Rather than starting his career with a half-baked shoe business, Elger went on to get his master's in exercise physiology, and he began coaching (he's been marvelously successful with both). We're still friends, and we still applaud his sense of pragmatism and remain forever grateful he entered that 10K.

Art said he couldn't make the meeting in Milwaukee, so Rick and Trebs made the trek down to Eastbay and met with Hill. None of us was treating this as momentous. Nothing at the time suggested this was more than a learning opportunity with someone who knew what they were doing.

Rick's first surprise came as he and Trebs pulled up to the Eastbay Running Store and saw a blue Celica parked out front that looked a lot like Art's. And sure enough, Rick and Trebs entered to see Art already sitting with Hill. Barb had suggested to Art that maybe he should drive to Milwaukee for the meeting. Art knew what that meant. Rick remembers this as auspicious. *If Art made the trip, he must really think we have a shot at this.*

The meeting with Hill went so well that we raised an intriguing idea right there: Let's make a deal and go into business together.

We were too broke to open an Eastbay franchise store, but Hill could sell us shoes from his inventory at cost. We'd first get "fitting shoes" from him to show to kids at clinics that we'd hold at their schools. We agreed any discounts from the manufacturer Hill received for the shoes we ordered he would keep. Fortunately, we think Hill liked the idea of going directly to the athletes at their schools. He thought of us as salesmen for Eastbay and agreed to the plan.

All we needed was some cash to cement the deal. Art brought cash. He gave Hill a $4,000 check—everything he and Barb had saved. Soon after, Trebs would cut a check for $5,000 and Rick would add . . . $500. We decided he'd work off the rest.

That's what we started the business with. Our only other term was that if Art was serious about selling running shoes, he would also have to become a runner himself. He agreed.

Art jumped back in the Celica and returned to Union Grove so that he and Barb could finish the school year before moving back to Wausau for the business. Rick and Trebs stuffed cases of shoes, 108 pairs total, into Don's car.

It's no small irony that we had spent all that time in college and none of us had taken a single business course. We didn't know budgeting from Adam.

Looking back at how we started, we may not have had any formal schooling, but we'd learned a few things growing up trying to figure out how to do things like cross Hwy 52 and compete with the older kids. Selling shoes seemed like a manageable challenge.

We didn't cloud our minds with questions like where would we be in three to five years, what's our next big thing, what's our budget, do we need a strategic plan? One of our greatest strengths was focusing all our energy on short-term goals. Let's get some shoes and try to sell them at a clinic—just like in sports, where learning from one win leads to the next win and builds confidence and momentum.

If nothing else, we left Milwaukee that day ready to sell shoes and deluded enough to think we could. Trebs remembers thinking that he would have been thrilled if we eventually made $50,000 a year off this.

We had work to do.

6

Right Idea, Wrong Business Plan

Rick and Don hauled their cargo to our first world headquarters, which was also the warehouse and distribution center. It was a small space known familiarly as the basement of Rick's parents' house.

Half of the basement was a finished room, insulated and with a fireplace. The other half was raw basement, wringer washing machine and dryer shoved against a wall among an array of tools, fishing equipment, and other basement staples. The floors always felt vaguely damp and smelled like wet socks. A dank layer of dust covered everything. Small, grimy windows let a little weak, dirty light through.

Rick and Don artfully stacked the shoeboxes on an elegant shelving system composed of some two-by-fours they may have found in a dumpster, to keep the boxes away from the damp floor.

The number and variety of shoes stacked up down there got Rick excited. He knew that running shoe technology was changing fast, and track-and-field training in general was undergoing a radical transformation because of it. It wasn't long before this that Rick helped run some meets for kids who were serious about track, and he remembers kids showing up to sprint in old Chuck Taylor basketball sneakers. New technology and specialization were finding their way into the shoes of every varsity sport, from football to volleyball to wrestling. Coaches, who used to just pull a pile of fumigated shoes out of the equipment room each season, had little idea where to direct their athletes in this new world when the kids came to them asking what they needed for the 400, or the long jump, or for playing wide receiver or lineman. The best they could do was to send them to a shoe store, where the people working had as little understanding of the new shoes as the coaches.

Our plan was to fix that. We'd take the shoes directly to track athletes at nearby schools. They'd see options they didn't even know existed. We'd provide them with a clinic to help them find the right fit for their foot and the right shoe for their event, because we knew all that, and we'd offer the shoes at team-discount prices.

That was the heart and soul of the whole thing: Give kids options they'd never seen before at prices kids could afford; help them become better athletes.

We had a few thousand bucks in fit inventory and no additional overhead beyond our time, gas money, and the wholesale cost of the sneakers we'd buy to fulfill orders. We felt like business geniuses.

We weren't.

We sent letters to thirty-five local coaches telling them about our new company, which we called Eastbay Running Store, and offering them a clinic.

And then we prayed. We didn't know if we'd even get a response. But we did. One after another, the coaches replied and said yes, please come.

Eastbay began with the coaches, our first and best connection to the athletes. Coaches got what we were trying to do right away. They could tell we wanted what was best for the athletes, like they did, and we could answer the questions they hadn't been able to. In the '80s, the coaches would be perhaps the single most critical factor in the survival and growth of our business. As their yesses came in, we felt pure elation. This idea might actually work.

But at our first clinic, we immediately realized it probably wouldn't.

Trebs and Rick dusted off our cases of shoes in the basement and loaded them into the back of Don's red-and-black hatchback AMC Gremlin. They really had to cram them in there. At least Don, a responsible farm boy, kept his car in immaculate condition.

First stop, our alma mater, UW–Stevens Point. However things went, we figured this would be a nice warm-up, because we knew these coaches and athletes personally. Some had listened to us talk about this shoe business for months. We hauled the red and blue and yellow boxes bearing logos for Nike, Adidas, New Balance, Asics, Brooks, Saucony, Puma, and more into the gym. The men's and women's track teams gathered around.

Rick and Don, experienced runners, launched into their spiel, explaining the shoe specs, fit, flexibility, comfort, and support—but it was obvious before they were even done talking that the runners were impatient to dive in. They were as excited as Rick had been at Arkadelphia, only they got to tear into boxes, marvel at all the options in one place. And they couldn't believe the prices. When they found a pair they liked, they laced them up to try them out, take a start out of the blocks, take a spin in the shot-put ring, or see how they gripped on a track's tight corners. We figured people test drive new cars all the time, so why not test drive new shoes?

So far, so great.

Our plan was, once the athletes decided on a pair of sneakers, we'd take their orders and then head back to headquarters and relay the orders to Dave Hill at Eastbay in Milwaukee. Once we could get the shoes from Dave, we'd pack them up and drop them off on our way to another clinic.

The shoes we brought to the clinic were supposed to be a fit inventory, not the pairs that the athletes bought. But once they found a pair they loved, they didn't want to take them off. Not only that, they wanted to buy training shoes, too, even though we only planned on taking orders for competition shoes that day.

Rick and Trebs smiled at each other nervously. *Holy cow. What now?*

We sold them the shoes and figured we'd just have to call Dave Hill and get more. Two days later, the Stevens Point coach, Rick Witt, called us to order *more* shoes. *A coach called to order shoes. Hmm. Interesting.* Word had gotten around.

After just one test clinic, we felt great about the idea of going to the athletes, but we also knew we wouldn't be able to keep up with demand if we were selling the pairs we brought to clinics, and it would be hard to keep up just by ordering inventory on demand from Dave Hill. Trebs and Rick called Art to report on the clinic—and the dilemma. In what would become an Eastbay tradition, we decided right there to change our business plan so that we could sell shoes at the clinic rather than just take orders through the fit inventory.

The high school track season was coming up, and that would be our chance to test and adjust our method of doing sales on-site. Our first clinic was only three weeks away. Step one in the new plan was to stock up on inventory. We needed a lot more shoes if we were going to sell at the clinics.

Then we started planning.

Which shoes should we stock up on? How many of each size? How many shoes could we sell for the season? How many could we afford to have left over? How many fit in Trebs's Gremlin? How can we get shoes from Milwaukee fast but still have time to pay for the inventory? Could we leave the coaches with a list of shoes and have them call us with more orders?

We asked ourselves if we'd use any profit for wages or put it back into more inventory. Inventory won, hands down. We guessed on the sizes we'd need based on what was ordered for the UW–Stevens Point test clinic, minus half a size for high school athletes. We stocked the most popular and hardest-to-get shoes, along with a few specialty shoes for sprinting, shot put, high jump, triple jump, and long jump.

And off we went. For weeks, Rick and Trebs raced back and forth in the Gremlin, from clinic to warehouse/basement to clinic. Day after day, we were selling the hell out of those shoes, which was great. But we also kept running out of shoes. So did Dave Hill, back in Milwaukee. We were killing his inventory. He was having an especially hard time keeping odd sizes in stock, since we found we needed those, which was a surprising discovery.

Those early clinics gave us a good sense of the growing demand for sneakers and an early peek into something that the shoe companies hadn't quite figured out yet. Sneakers were not just for performance; they were becoming a way for kids to establish their identity. We saw it at every clinic, how the athletes lit up when they found the right pair. And giving that to a kid, giving them the opportunity to have shoes that made them feel good, shoes we wouldn't have even thought to dream about when we were their age, gave us an unexpected sense of joy and satisfaction. The sales told us we were onto something for sure. But the *feeling* told us more.

We just had to figure out how to keep going without going broke. All our revenue went back into inventory, which got complicated for Dave Hill. Getting shoes to Wausau was giving him headaches. We took up more of his time than his percentage of sales was worth, and despite our best efforts not to, we were disrupting his inventory every day and putting stress on his lines of credit. Honoring his word, Hill stuck to the terms of the deal we'd made, but he also told us early on that we needed to get our own lines of credit from the sneaker companies.

We set out to do that, only to learn that the shoe companies had no interest in giving *us* lines of credit. Shockingly, a couple of guys with an AMC Gremlin who were warehousing inventory in a basement wasn't appealing to them. Granted, the vendors probably didn't know *specifically* about the basement, or the car—but what they *did* know was that we didn't have the one thing they required to give out lines of credit: a physical retail location.

If we wanted to keep this going, we needed a store.

7

April Fools

It was time to move out of the basement anyway. After the team clinics were done, we knew the rent-free arrangement at Rick's parents' basement wasn't sustainable. The phone situation wasn't great either. If we didn't answer the Eastbay phone number we'd set up, the call went to the Gerings. Rick's mom loved to chitchat, but she was at a loss when a coach asked how much the Adidas Oregon weighed, and whether it could be used for training and racing.

We scoured greater Wausau for a proper storefront but ultimately decided that for a fighting chance at making any money, we needed to be downtown, a few long blocks of two-story brick buildings near the edge of the Wisconsin River. That's where the crowds from the city and the surrounding farm country would be, and although we knew nothing about retail, we figured that being where the people were made sense. We also needed something budget friendly. Using those two factors to triangulate our options, we were left with just one: two blocks off downtown's main drag, we found an old garage and showroom for a Jeep dealership.

The place was a dump. You couldn't see the door from the street, just big windows on a nondescript red brick building. To enter, you first had to walk onto a small, four-by-four landing where three options awaited you: One, walk right to an open driveway that led to an auto repair shop below us, but watch for cars barreling up the drive that could clip you. Two, take the door straight ahead that led to our landlord's law office. Or three, take the door on the left, which was ours. If more than one person arrived at the landing at the same time, you had to take turns to avoid collisions. We taped a piece of paper to our door with *Eastbay* scrawled on it, and that was how you found us for our first several weeks.

Inside, our store had all the ambiance—and aroma—of the glorified gas station it had been. Smooth, gray cement walls gave it a Brutalist feel. Tire streaks and other stains would require cleaning. We could smell the wafts of oil and smoke from the service garage. Nothing about it felt like it could inspire a sense of athletic greatness as you browsed sneakers. In the offices behind the showroom, it got bleaker. Army-green walls were interrupted by small windows that let in meager light.

At least, we thought, it backed up to a near-empty parking lot where we could tell customers to park, until we realized they were getting tickets by parking there, a spectacular backfiring of our first retail marketing idea.

But rent was cheap, we were in downtown Wausau, and, crucially, just down the block, there were two of our favorite watering holes: Market Square and Wally's Wonder Bar, both of which would return our patronage by becoming our softball team sponsors at different times.

When the clinics subsided, we spruced the place up as best we could, drawing on skills developed during our go-kart days. We built some storage shelves out of spare wood and lined the walls with pegboard and hooks. We scrounged some of those large wooden spools that hold commercial electrical wiring and set those up as shoe displays. We didn't have a cash register; we just stuck money in an old tin box (and we'd do that for the next seven years).

When Ralph Mirman, the owner of Mirman's Furniture Store next door, came by, his assessment was swift: "Nobody would have a clue you were doing any business out of here." Ralph was successful and always helpful, especially early on when he constantly dropped pearls of retail wisdom. "I do my best business after five," he told us. "Don't worry if they come to look and don't buy—if you're good with them, they'll come back . . . Put your hours on the door . . . People like to window shop . . . Those spiderwebs in the corner aren't helping . . . I like the newspaper and radio ads people, but only believe about half of what they tell you . . . One of my best days every year is the Sidewalk Sales day."

On April Fool's Day—of course—in 1981 we officially opened the Eastbay store in Wausau. Our expectations were low. For one thing, April's a tough month in Wisconsin, not quite winter anymore but barely spring.

Wausau is a city of hills, so the winter's sludge would flow through town, rivers full of salt and slush and sand and everything leftover from the dark months. People didn't flood the stores looking to shop.

Just as our first rent payment was coming due, the spring sports season was ending, and our sales slowed to a trickle. The clinics drove a few people to the store, but we struggled to drive anyone else to come in. Maybe it was the spider webs. Through the summer, the storefront barely paid the bills. Customers who'd wander in usually asked what our name meant. Surf shop? Sailing? Skiing? Scuba? Whatever they thought, they weren't getting hardcore runners, or performance-focused athletes, from the name or the place.

Doubt crept in. Maybe it all had been too much too fast, and we'd made a mistake. What provided us with the faintest glimmer of hope was the fact that, even though it was slow, every couple of days, we would get a phone call from a coach at some school where we'd done a clinic. A few of their runners had worn out some trainers. Another kid's tore. Their star sprinter wanted to train over the summer. Could you send a couple more pairs? We were happy to oblige. We also thought, in a hazy way, that we could make it easier for the coaches if we made a list of our shoes for them so they could just call and order them when they needed rather than call and ask about what we had.

With the summer slowdown, Trebs gained some legitimate skepticism about our business staying afloat. Plus, he was curious about life beyond Wisconsin. He told us he was moving to California and asked us to buy him out. Knowing the state of things, he was bighearted enough to say we could pay him back over time. We're not sure we could have gotten the money otherwise, and if not for his kindness we might have gone out of business right then.

With Trebs gone, it was just the two of us. We used those slow months to make a few decisions. We decided to add inventory for other sports while developing a plan to build the retail business, which would help us get lines of credit.

But there was only so much we could do when things were so slow. At some point, we also added one more thing to our daily routine, something that would end up being essential to any success we had going forward: every day, we decided, we'd find time to go for a run.

8

"I Think You Guys Are Toast"

Art followed through on his promise to become a runner, getting help from John Braasch, a former teacher and an excellent runner. Art and John began running daily around lunchtime while Rick watched the store. Before long, Art set his sights on marathons.

Only problem was that Art's time and distance improvements were the most productive things happening at Eastbay.

Our first retail customer was Jim West, a marathoner and our insurance agent, who probably realized that if we sold more shoes, he could increase our premiums. During that slow summer, he began to bring his running buddies around to the store, including a guy named Harry Colcord, whom you'll meet soon enough. They were all as eager and excited to get new and better shoes as the high school kids were.

The Wausau running community was small, passionate, and loyal, but it was part of a nationwide boom in running, spearheaded by legends like Bill Rodgers, Joan Benoit, Frank Shorter, and Jim Fixx. We spent that summer developing friendships with the local runners. The Eastbay store became a place for enthusiasts to hang out and talk running, brag about their times in recent races. Eventually those hangouts morphed into the Running Wild Road Runners Club. It included some incredible distance runners. Rick, a natural sprinter, began to suspect some of them were addicted to the pain of distance running. They liked pushing each other, seemingly in possession of superhuman oxygen capacity, breathing every three to four strides while Rick sucked in two breaths every stride. In retrospect, we were having some of the best runs of our lives with Running Wild. We all pushed each other hard on those runs.

We still see many of those folks, including Jimmy Lombardo, Doug Riske, Mike Matushak, Jim Neumann, Al Hlavacek, Jerry Smith, Jim West, and John Wilke. Wilke would turn a tiny town in Wisconsin called Phillips into an unlikely track and cross-country powerhouse. There are others who have gone on to the place where every run is downhill and the wind is always at your back.

One day, as we sat in the store trying to figure out how we were going to make any money, Rick's dad, Cliff, dropped by. He looked around, made a face, and let out a snorting grunt. He said, "You know, there's another big store like this that just opened down the street."

Oh, we knew. Barefoot Sports, a well-known Wisconsin franchise, had appeared five blocks away. Not only that, a block over from Barefoot there was Athlete's Foot. Three stores within six blocks were all selling sneakers in a town of forty thousand. Two of those three stores were well-financed with nice spaces and pristine reputations. The other one was ours.

"Yeah," Rick's dad said, nodding confidently, "I think you guys are toast."

It sure seemed like it. When the clinics weren't running, business was dead. Beyond friends and family and the running club, hardly anyone came into our store. A few kids who knew us from the clinics did. Everyone else was walking down Main Street two blocks over with no good reason to wander past us, and the rare passers-by that did find themselves near our doors would be frightened by rogue cars roaring up the ramp from the garage beneath our store. If they navigated *that,* then they walked in to find a store that was still kind of a dump.

However, if we managed to get to the point where we could talk shoes with them, those few customers that did come in could tell we knew what we were talking about with running shoes and with their feet.

We were discovering a rhythm that would define the first couple of years of Eastbay. Clinic season was busy, and we poured all our energy into it, writing letters to coaches, working on our shoe lists, and most important, getting our lines of credit established so that we could expand our inventory and branch into other sports. Then came the offseason and a lot of hanging around the store with the Running Wild folks, hoping for business to pick up.

To make ends meet in the early years we took on other jobs. Art coached as an assistant for a nearby varsity girls basketball team that later ended up winning state. The $1,500 Art got felt like a million bucks compared with the $5 per week we drew from Eastbay.

Rick had several side hustles. He repped some raw materials to footwear manufacturers for Dave Hill, and eventually became a sales rep for Sorbothane, a company that made foam insoles for shoes. Hailed as "a medical breakthrough" at the time, the material—per company claims—could absorb 95 percent of impact shock to the body and prevent shin splints. Somehow, someone at the company heard about our focus on fit and foot comfort at our clinics and offered the job to Rick. We didn't get rich off Sorbothane, but the commissions went right back into inventory and helped us learn how to take orders over the phone, and the connections we made in the footwear industry selling it would be invaluable.

Still, we manned the store as much as possible and stayed open until 9 p.m., no matter how dead it was. Most days, we'd play catch in an empty parking lot across the street with sightlines on the store. Other times, we'd go to Market Square, where we'd sit so that we could see our shop in case a customer showed up.

On the rare occasion that that happened, whichever one of us had less beer left slugged it down and ran back to the store. We were good friends with the bartender at Market Square, Johnny Lewandowski, so some days we got away with drinking for next to nothing. Sometimes we'd put a dollar bill down to pay, and he'd give four quarters in change. Later we found out that he'd been paying for some of our drinks out of his own pocket. Johnny was good, smart company, too. He'd been the smartest kid in school. He gave good advice about working with people in the service industry. "Breath mints," he told us. Lucky that we didn't choke on them running back to the store.

Sitting there, drinking beer and hoping a customer or two would walk into our store across the street, things looked bleak. Maybe the nuns had been right.

Then we got lucky again. Rick had known a guy named Jon Ulvilden from his days managing the UW–Stevens Point Rec Services Department, and they'd hung out at a local bar, the Yacht Club, sometimes. Ulvilden was an Adidas sales rep in the area—his dad was part owner of Adidas's Midwest distribution operation. Ulvilden helped us get a line of credit with Adidas, the biggest shoe company in the world at the time. With that credit we could stock up on the hugely popular Adidas Top Tens, basketball shoes, the iconic Superstars, and all the world-class track spikes, trainers, and specialty shoes without having to deplete Dave Hill's store.

Once Adidas did give us credit, the others followed. Nike extended a line, so we added Nike Dynasty Highs and Dynasty Lows, the company's latest entries, with mesh uppers, designed to compete with the dominant Top Tens. Were the industry the way it is now, these companies wouldn't have given us credit. We'd done less than $100,000 in sales total, including the clinics. But back then, the companies were rightly seeing that they were on the precipice of a new era in sneakers, and they were fighting like mad to stake out territory. They also liked our story of going directly to the athletes.

As 1980 turned over to '81, we went to do our taxes and discovered that our total profit for the year was zero dollars. We thought that meant we didn't need to file. Some serious gentlemen from the Internal Revenue Service reached out to tell us that we were incorrect in our assessment. Just a year in business, and we'd accidentally committed tax fraud.

Once the IRS realized it was dealing with clueless shoe salesmen and not criminal masterminds, its agents told us to file our taxes and fined us $500. We had to borrow $500 to pay the fine.

9

Top Ten

Just in time for the '81 basketball season, Trebs called. He was done with California, and he was moving back to Wausau. He wasn't looking to get his stake in the business back, but he wanted to work for us until he found a teaching job. It was perfect timing. With the track clinics restarting in January, we'd need someone to stay with the store while we hit the road again. We were thrilled to welcome him back. Just like that, we'd hired our first employee.

The lines of credit allowed us to expand our retail inventory to include several basketball shoes, so we sent another letter to coaches with a price list that included some of those, maybe a dozen shoes total. We had the Adidas Jabbar Hi and Jabbar Lo and the somewhat forgotten Osaga Ace Hi and Lo, and we had *the* premier basketball shoe of the day, a game-changer called Adidas Top Ten.

At the time, Adidas and Converse owned the hoops sneaker market. Shoe companies made three types of basketball shoes, and Adidas had a big seller for each type. For big men playing the post, Adidas had the high-top Nizza, basically a flexible, canvas work boot. (Kids today who watch 5-out offenses hurl up three pointers need to imagine a time when every team wanted to get the ball to a giant who camped down low and shoved his body back into a defender until a layup became inevitable—it's true!)

For slashing, cutting guards and forwards, Adidas offered the sleek, low-cut Campus. We didn't carry either of those. We did carry the shoe for the best athletes on the court, the superstars who could do it all—the Adidas Superstar, another low-cut shoe with a rounded toe and more support throughout.

The Superstar was the revolutionary basketball sneaker of its time, featuring a distinctive design of its rubber toe cap nicknamed "shell toes"—a design still popular today. It was the first option that was dramatically different from the ubiquitous canvas Chuck Taylors of the '70s.

But by the time we started Eastbay, Adidas was leaning on a new shoe, the Top Ten, to hit a hard reset on the basketball shoe market. The sneaker was designed, per its marketing materials, to be "positionless," worn by anyone on the court. It was developed by consulting with the Houston Rockets' six-foot-seven superstar forward Rick Barry, a dominant force at both ends of the court, capable of leading his team in both assists and rebounds on any given night.

But it wasn't Rick Barry's shoe. The concept of signature shoes for a single player wasn't much of a thing yet. Adidas put the Top Ten on the feet of ten of the league's best players, including Doug Collins, Bob Lanier, and Mitch Kupchak.

According to sneakerhead chronicler and legend Bobbito Garcia, the Top Ten's release in the late '70s ushered in a third era of sneaker culture. The first era was "the canvas one," the time of Converse Chuck Taylors and Jack Purcells, with their vulcanized rubber soles and light canvas uppers. The second era was "the simple/constructed-suede/leather-grips one," which included such shoes as Adidas Superstars and Nike Blazers, made from thicker, more athletic material, but with clean, simple designs and bold soles.

The Top Ten, as Garcia describes it, ushered in "the complex, bugged, super duty, high octane, moon boots period."

Its profile was unique, sleek, and athletic, like the best Adidas low-cut sneakers, but it also had a high-top extension that gave it a sense of strength. The part that rose above the ankle was usually in an opposing color to what was below. If you looked at it one way, it had the profile of a great Adidas low-cut for the fleet guards, just with this extra ankle wrap. If you looked at it another way, it was a modern, muscular high-top for a bruising big man. They had beautiful, soft, supple leather that formed to your foot, light and flexible, everything the Chuck Taylor was not, and they were barely half as heavy as Chucks. They were the first shoe we sold for more than $50.

Top Tens were more than just a sneaker; they were a statement that helped usher in the era when people began wearing sneakers as fashion and as a part of their identities. Wearing Top Tens at the time signaled an affiliation with excellence. *I want the latest and greatest. I want the shoe for players who do it all.*

We'd heard whispers about people collecting sneakers purely for the sake of owning them, but these weren't much more than secondhand stories, and we spent little time thinking about them. In his 2003 book *Where'd You Get Those?*, Garcia writes of this developing trend from the early '80s:

> Hunting for sneakers was a ritual shared with only select friends. It was almost a secret society. You'd see mad kids on the train all wearing the same shit, and then you'd see one kid who had some *magnetic* joints on. You'd become transfixed. He knew you were hawking him, but it was a form of respect. He had to have put as much effort into finding his sneakers and maintaining them as you had, and if you didn't have your flyest joints on to compete, you just took an L for the day.[1]

With our newly opened credit lines with Adidas and Nike and Converse, we had access to the top three brands for basketball. That meant that we were able to add winter basketball clinics to our schedule. (We added wrestling, too.) We doubled the number of clinics we ran. And because Trebs was back, we could have someone at the store, which meant we could expand our clinic runs further out, to towns within seventy-five miles of Wausau. This, we realized, was what would make us different. Athlete's Foot and Barefoot used to send kids a discount card—10 percent off if they came into their store—but that's all they would do. *You come to us.*

We went to *them*. We showed up at the athletes' schools. We made buying shoes a team activity and even a family event, inviting parents (often, the payers), who would buy shoes for themselves at the clinics. We showed our faces, made kids and coaches laugh, and shared our knowledge of what shoes would make them the best at what they did—and, maybe even more than that, of what shoes would make them feel the best about themselves, helping them find an identity as individuals and as part of a team.

The other companies would call the coaches, and sometimes their salesmen might visit the school, but other team dealers didn't have the same variety of inventory or the expertise we had. We knew how to talk to these coaches and athletes, because we'd built the relationships. They trusted us. And we'd been them, both as kids and as coaches.

And we'd experienced financial challenges like some of them, too. So we made it a point to meet or beat any price the kids could find at any other store. Now and again, if a kid really loved certain shoes but they didn't have the money for them at the clinic, then we would let them pay us later on, after they got a paycheck from their jobs. We would just say "Pay when you can" and they always did. We believed everyone deserved good new shoes, and we wanted to help them get just what they wanted. Maybe it dinged our cash flow in the short term, but it endeared us to the athletes and their families.

One drive after another, one clinic after another, we hustled. We bought a rusted black van that seemed two hundred years old, and we named it the Beast. It had no suspension. Maybe it was the stealthy black paint, or its overall forgettable nature, but something gave us the idea that we could never get speeding tickets in the Beast. It scared Susie's parents. Her dad, Chuck, skeptically asked Susie as the Beast pulled up, "How are you two going to make this work?" Susie didn't care. When Rick rumbled into a country club parking lot to pick Susie up for a date, a friend of her parents turned to her and said, "Are you still going out with that shoe man?" Indeed, she was, she informed them. Before long, Rick proposed, and she said yes. She'd be Mrs. Shoe Man forever.

The Beast was a godsend. We didn't need a smooth ride; we needed cargo space, and now we had that in spades. Finally, we could pack up with extra inventory. No more careful planning of what to pack and what to leave behind. It was a store on wheels.

The '81 track season was a blur. Track season was our busiest time of year, as it was for Dave Hill at Eastbay in Milwaukee. Though we had our lines of credit with Adidas and Nike, we still ordered some from him when we couldn't get enough from the companies directly, which was more often than we would have liked. We were still trying to get credit with companies like New Balance, Reebok, Brooks, Asics, and Saucony, so we ended up ordering plenty of pairs of those from Dave Hill, who had had enough of us. He said he'd call the shoe companies and ask if we could order using his credit but have the companies drop ship directly to us in Wausau. The invoices went to Milwaukee, and the shoes went to us, which was a bit of a headache. But that dramatically sped up the process of getting our own credit. At the time, the shoe-company sales reps were independent contractors working off commission. As we started ordering, they spread the word that there was a good customer up in Wausau. By early '81 we had lines of credit with most of the shoe companies.

Even a few years later, this wouldn't have worked, as shoe vendors started controlling inventory more tightly (and as they brought sales reps inside the company). At this time, though, we were extremely lucky that they had backup inventory and were arming up for a coming conflict among shoe companies as the companies staked out ground in what everyone thought was a market about to explode. The shoe companies were essentially financing our inventory learning curve, thirty days at a time, whenever we placed our orders.

As a show of faith to Dave Hill, we also told him that we would never sell shoes in the city of Milwaukee. That eliminated a chunk of Wisconsin high schools with a lot of people who would want shoes. This was significant, but we felt we owed it to him. Fine, he said, but he didn't seem particularly concerned. Whatever momentum we felt from the clinics, he didn't. He was frankly happy to get rid of us. Now we were truly on our own. He came up to Wausau to visit around this time, and he told Susie he didn't think we were going to make it much longer.

10

Four-Point Plan

The summer of '81 was better than the summer of '80. Clinics created a trickle of phone orders offseason that increased enough for us to establish phone lines—we took collect calls—reserved solely for taking orders.

But we weren't turning a profit. We always felt right on the edge of going under.

There was always stress, but we don't think we ever truly thought we would fail. How we'd make it, when we'd make it, what we'd have to do to make it, we didn't know, but we never doubted that we would. You may want to chalk this up to some kind of business genetics—the DNA of entrepreneurs makes them boldly impervious to failure—but we don't see it that way. We were confident for two much more specific reasons: One, we had experienced the reactions of the athletes to what we were doing. They loved that we came to them, and we knew we were connecting. We felt it. We just had to keep learning and figure out how to make a business on that connection. And two, we were fully supported by our family and friends. Barb made good enough money teaching to keep her and Art afloat, and Rick's parents gave him no grief about living with them. Susie was getting her master's and always supported Rick's ambitions.

Any of these people could have chosen to view us as the burden that we were in those extremely lean years. They could have told us what we were doing was completely foolish and impossible, and maybe irresponsible. For the most part, they didn't. Yes, Art's father-in-law, Dr. Molinaro, and his wife, Marilyn, thought Art was stupid for giving up his career in teaching to run a shoe business. And once at a coach's clinic in Madison, a couple of old friends from Wausau had perused other companies' booths before coming to our sad, disorganized space with some shoes tossed onto a table in front of us. They told us later they felt bad for us. Our friend Mike LaBarbera told us he thought, *Those guys ain't got a prayer.*

Family, friends, they had to wonder, but they never dissuaded us. Not once did Barb or Susie say anything to us like, *Maybe you should give up or find another line of work.* Not once did they ever make us feel bad, or small, even when we were bringing in $5 per week in our first year and $10 per week the next, while Barb was driving fifty miles each way, every day, to work, and Susie was still in school, inheriting her own long commute to work after she and Rick married in '83. It would take four more years for Art to make as much in a year as he would have if he'd just kept teaching.

At some point in those first couple of years, Art confessed some doubt to Barb. He was wondering if he should stick with it. They wanted to start a family, and he could be making good money teaching and coaching, both of which he loved. "Maybe so," Barb said. "But you know what that career will be, and you can always go back to it. You might not *know* what *this* will be yet, but you know what it could *become*, and isn't that worth believing in, at least for a little longer? Just to see what happens?"

So, we kept going. What a great joy, and fuel, it was for us to see them believe in what we were creating. How do you thank someone for that?

We spent the slow time coming up with as many options as we could think of to grow our business and draw customers into the store. We would try anything to stay afloat. We tried selling cross-country skis in the winter. We looked into importing bikes from Holland to sell. We talked endlessly about every aspect of the business, often talking in circles about our potential strategies. *Do we stay on the road? Should we scale that back and focus on retail? We want to grow the phone orders, and would scaling back slow down the phone orders? Or do we scale up our clinics? Would that mean we'd need to hire more people? Could we afford to hire more people? Is the Beast gonna make it?*

The only thing we were sure of was that whatever we did, we had to be different than the franchises. What could we do that Barefoot, Athlete's Foot, and another new retailer that had shown up in the new mall in Wausau, Foot Locker, couldn't?

We came up with a plan that included four primary things we'd do differently and better than our well-heeled competition. And believe us when we tell you, this is as formally as we've ever laid out this plan, right here.

First, we'd focus on *athletes and specific sports*. We began ordering unique running and other sports' shoes, looking at each sport as its own business. We'd order all sizes, widths, and colors, especially high-end and hard-to-find shoes those other stores wouldn't take on.

Second, we'd offer *expertise*. We had in-depth knowledge on the shoes and on feet, especially Rick. The other stores hired kids who knew nothing about running but could work the register. We didn't even have a cash register.

Third, we'd be *convenient*. We would go to the athletes. The coaches loved how easy we made it for kids to get a good shoe. It took the problem off their hands. We also expanded our inventory in other sports as much as we could, adding first basketball and then football, baseball, volleyball, and wrestling shoes. And figuring that more retail space could only lead to more sales, we opened a second storefront down in Stevens Point.

And fourth, we'd focus on *trust*. The other stores didn't understand coaches' needs, or the local running community, or how athletes wanted to be sure that when they bought a shoe it wouldn't hurt or diminish their performance. We treated athletes as athletes, not kids. When they came to the store, they got our full attention. Rick gave them every imaginable way to compare and understand shoes beyond simply how they felt on their feet or how cool they looked, and he would work hard to get them to pick the right shoe. Sometimes, kids would come in knowing exactly what they wanted, and even though Art knew another shoe might be a better fit for them (and Rick would tell them so), we would sell them what they asked for. Other times, kids would come in and say, "Hey, I've got thirty bucks, what's the fastest shoe you can get me for that?"

When people were debating between pairs of shoes, we told them to go ahead and try on a pair, take them for a quick spin around the block, just like we did at the clinics. They loved that. They'd run down the block, right by Athlete's Foot and Barefoot.

In retrospect it looks like a solid plan crafted by capable people, but we had no idea if it would work. Business had picked up some, but it was still slow enough that we got plenty of softball practice in. One afternoon around Valentine's Day 1982, we were out playing catch when a man pulled up to the store, looking rushed. He was nice enough but was vexed. *Why is there no one in the shoe store?* We told him we'd be right over.

We started the whole expertise routine, but he brushed us off, replying, "I just need some racing flats for my girlfriend." He was on his way to see her in Fond Du Lac, a small city at the foot of Lake Winnebago two hours southeast of us. She was a big runner, and he planned to propose by giving her the racing flats with the ring box tucked into one of them. We thought that was great.

That year we expanded to a hundred-mile radius for visiting schools, and mostly through the clinics we brought in about $250,000. Our inventory grew, but we still made zero profit.

At least our softball game was getting better. Our first year in business, we had been in the C League in softball, but business was so slow that we got a lot of practice in. We went undefeated and won the league championship that year and moved up to the B League the next year. Business was still slow, and we won the league again and moved up to the A League, where we usually got crushed. Most of those teams were built around a few hulks cranking out homers. We didn't have that, so we hit singles, ran fast, played good defense. We couldn't afford to swing for the fences and strike out a lot. Neither could Eastbay.

Late in the A League season, playing the best team in the league, we trailed by three with the bases loaded, and Rick coming to the plate. We swear we're not making this up. Rick decided to swing for the fences, but he took his eye off the ball and swung a mighty swing that mostly missed, catching just enough of the ball to send it dribbling weakly toward the pitcher.

Rick's speed so unnerved the pitcher, though, that he rushed his throw to first, which sailed out to the right field corner.

Rick tore around the bases and scored a walk-off, inside-the-park, bunt grand slam to win the game.

11

God Bless the Coaches

By 1983, three years into our venture, the four-point plan started to work. The clinics were humming. We had hired Rick's brother Tom and a guy named Tim Strohkirch—both great athletes—to do some of the clinics, which made us nervous at first. We had been doing everything, but when we started to grow, we had to build trust that others would handle the clinics well.

We started out a month before track season looking to hit six to eight schools a day. We'd send out the Beast and a new van we got after our brief attempt at selling bikes didn't work out, both loaded up with inventory. Sometimes we'd get one clinic in before the school day started. We always did a clinic at lunchtime at the first stop, tear off to do another before afternoon practice started at the second stop, then hit a third stop as practice ended. Then we did the same for basketball in the fall.

More clinics meant more calls and more customers coming to the store. Rick did the math later and thinks we were selling about seven pairs of shoes a day in the store. The phone order business was surprisingly constant. We added some office space behind the showroom and some inventory storage in the basement, below the store. We were hustling. We were *busy.* We found ourselves postponing our afternoon softball throwing. Art was training for his first marathon, anyway, and weekday bar excursions weren't part of his regimen.

Our store aesthetic remained as spartan and utilitarian as ever, down to the tin cash box. None of us thought about retail concepts like "people flow" and "emotional attachment" and those sorts of things that other stores seemed to know and care about. We entertained adding some improved lighting at one point until we learned it would cost more than $200. Too steep. Nearly every dollar that came in was sunk back into inventory, adding new shoes and restocking all the bestsellers and closeouts.

This hard-won success emboldened us. We set sights on the whole state (except Milwaukee). Wisconsin had just over four hundred high schools at the time, and we made it a goal to hit as many as we could.

As our business changed, so did the world around us. One of the harbingers of a new era took place during the NBA All-Star Game in Los Angeles in 1983, when Marvin Gaye sang the national anthem, the first Black man to do it. Gaye owned The Forum wearing dark shades and a dark-blue suit, and he delivered a rendition of the song unlike anything the sports world had ever heard before. Gaye delivered what Andscape writer Justin Tinsley later described as "the only time in history the national anthem closely resembled a rhythm and blues song . . . patriotic in its own soulful way, but it was simultaneously debonair, too. Each note left his vocal cords with the pizazz of a street crooner. Something special was happening."[1]

Then-Lakers coach Pat Riley called it "an almost-spiritual moment," and Julius Erving later described the performance by saying, "You knew it was history, but it was also 'hood."

Gaye's passion and soul signaled to us and to basketball fans the world over that the color and the culture of the game was changing. We loved it, and we were hearing whispers of shoe companies trying to come up with fresh and revolutionary designs to match the moment of basketball's new era. Adidas was number one in the world at the time, and it and Converse dominated the basketball market, but something was brewing in Beaverton, Oregon. We couldn't wait to see what might be coming next. We knew whatever shoes came out, we'd be able to sell them.

We had targeted all of Wisconsin, but we were already wondering if we could go even further. Coaches from other states we'd bumped into at Wisconsin coaching clinics had started calling us. We just had to figure out how to reach them. There was that glimmer of an idea that somehow there must be some way to scale the clinics. We *knew* what we were doing worked. We saw the connection we made with athletes and their parents. We saw the sheer joy kids got from seeing all the options and being able to decide for themselves the shoes they'd get. We just didn't know yet how to reach any athletes outside the Beast's range.

How can we do more? was the question we constantly asked ourselves. Or more specifically, *How can we do more and not fall on our faces and go out of business?*

All the while the phone was ringing. An order here from someone who couldn't make the clinic. A couple more there from a coach who gained a few new players.

One day, a coach called—God bless good coaches who always asked such good questions. "Hey, two of my best sprinters are also on the basketball team, so they couldn't be at your clinic," he said. "Could you send us a list of the shoes you've got? And do you think you could include some pictures?"

12

Birth of a Catalog

We had had a simple price list since 1981. It was typed up on standard letter paper. We made a couple dozen copies, threw them in big brown envelopes, and mailed them to the coaches prior to the clinics.

Word of mouth is hard to beat, and more coaches kept asking for the price list. Every time it yielded a healthy number of requests for clinics—and orders. We wanted to, but we couldn't keep adding more schools, especially now that we were getting interest from out-of-state schools. We were already grinding through fourteen-hour days, continually trying to speed between clinics without getting tickets.

And the coaches kept asking us to add more information to the list. Informally and organically, we added descriptions of the shoes and other information. The more data we added to the list, the more orders we received, and the more the coaches wanted us to add. Kids needed trainers and other shoes between clinics, too, and they had questions about style, fit, weight. Coaches called, relaying the questions: *What kind of traction on those New Balances? How light are the Top Tens compared with the Jabbar Hi? What Adidas shoe was best for training versus racing? What should I get if I can only afford one pair? Which were best at preventing knee pain and shin splints? What if the kid ordered a 10 but realized they needed a 12?*

It took virtually no time for coaches to grow weary of being the go-between in this business. It'd be great, they told us, if you just made a full-blown price list with all this information and sent it right to the athletes. They wanted the price list to become a kind of anytime clinic with the same information they were getting when we drove out to see them.

We had been thinking about this for a while, even back to that first clinic when Coach Witt at Stevens Point called with follow-up orders. From our side it wasn't a matter of whether we should do an expanded price list, but when and how. That flicker of an idea was now burning bright. This was the way to expand without extending our days to twenty hours; the way to sell more shoes without having to load up the Beast and haul boxes all over the region. This would enable us to reach states around us, and eventually—who knows?—maybe even the whole country. Why not, right?

But for as little as we knew about the shoe business when we started, we knew less about the catalog business. There weren't many established experts for us to learn from, either. Most important, anyone who was doing catalogs was sending them to adults. *Nobody* had a mailing list made up of young athletes.

We didn't know how to get a list like that. We didn't know how you make a price list with real pictures and good design and glossy pages and order forms. And as intrigued as we were, we didn't know if anyone would buy shoes through the mail. Why would they? Wouldn't they want to try them on first? And how would they pay? Credit cards were far less common then. We couldn't just trust they'd send us a check. How did cash-on-delivery work? And for anyone who did have a credit card, why in the world would they give us that information over the phone? That would be insane! At that time, you wouldn't give your best friend your credit card number, much less strangers at an unknown shoe company.

But we still sensed potential. We did have a few signals of an emerging catalog trend beyond Sears and J.C. Penney, both with their Christmas wish books that kids used to love to see arrive in the mail, so they could dog-ear pages with the things they wanted. Lands' End, the clothing retailer, had just started sending fifty-page, glossy, magazine-style catalogs around the country. J.Crew, too, though at the time it was called Popular Club Plan. Susie got that one. She gave us a wealth of knowledge on what made it work so well. We looked it over and couldn't help but be impressed by the presentation. *What if we tried to do some sort of scaled-down version of that?*

Rick, of course, was all in. Art was not a counterpoint to his enthusiasm this time. This didn't feel like a Mickey-Mantle-baseball-card trade to Art; he thought the idea was brilliant. We decided to go for it. It was another new business model, and a swing for the fences that would make or break Eastbay. We had put a store on wheels with the Beast and the clinics. Now we would put a store in the mail.

We weren't sure about the logistics, or the finances. We don't remember the specific numbers now, but we do remember that we figured out that between making the catalog and building a mailing list, it would require all our cash—and if it didn't work, then we would be out of business.

Today, you can design and publish a great-looking social media post in seconds on your phone. You can set up an online store in less than an hour. Some of you reading this will have a hard time believing how tedious it was back in 1983 to make a price list with pictures and, for that matter, to buy something without having a store nearby.

And our first effort was modest, to say the least. We started with a test we'd send to Wisconsin coaches, a black-and-white four-page price list, made by and printed at Presto Prints, a little shop owned by friends in Wausau. Presto managed the layout, design, and typesetting.

But first we hauled boxes of shoes to a photography studio. Shoe on a stool, casting an artful shadow. Snap. Repeat. They were impressive, professional shots, but we wouldn't know that during the photo shoot, because everything was shot on film, which was sent to a lab and returned as negatives, which we combed through with a magnifying glass, looking for the best shots. The winning negatives were then taken to the photo lab to be developed.

Meanwhile we had to write the copy to go with the pictures. We wanted these descriptions to be as close as possible to the hands-on customer service we developed at clinics, wanting them to carry that sense of knowledge and expertise. Ideally, we'd have pictures of all the shoes and lengthy descriptions, but space was tight. It was an arduous give-and-take process of which shoes to picture, and what information to put in and what to leave out. We mixed best sellers with lesser-known ones and made sure every brand was there. We were making best guesses.

> **Nike Pegasus.** New Nike air sole training shoe. Combines lightweight and flexibility of a racer. Midsole and outsole are extremely durable. GY-N. SZ 6-15. Suggested retail $44.95. **Eastbay Team Price $35.50.**
>
> **Nike Elite Classic.** Surprising support for a lightweight racing flat. The best racing/training combination for sprints and jumping events. BL/Y. SZ-3-14. Suggest retail $39.95. **Eastbay Team Price $30.95.**
>
> **Adidas Marathon Trainer.** Excellent shoe for those who need good stability. Excellent arch support with very durable outsole. Fits wide. Suggested retail $47.00. BL/SL. SZ 8-13. **Eastbay Team Price $37.95.**
>
> **Brooks Chariot.** Distance training shoe. Combines stability support and flexibility. Tri-density mid-sole offers excellent support for pronators. Suggested retail $59.95. GY/GY. SZ 8-12. **Eastbay Team Price $47.95.**
>
> **New Balance W555.** See photo in men's 555 section. Excellent training flat. Durable midsole and outsole. Combination lasted for both stability and flexibility. Suggest retail $55.95. TN-BL. SZ 5-10. **Eastbay team price: $43.95.**

In those four pages we included shoes from Nike, Adidas, New Balance, Saucony, Brooks, and a brand called Tiger (which later became Asics). We had photos of the Nike Lady Valkyrie, Lady Pegasus, Lady Yankee, and the men's Waffle Racer and Elite Classic, as well as specialty track shoes like the High Jump. We showed the Adidas Oregon and Boston Trainers. New Balance 555s. Brooks Chariot and Super Villanova. Tiger's X Ultra-T and Lady Explorer. And the Saucony Lady Dixon and Lady Jazz. Including women's running shoes would be one of the best decisions we could have made, as many of the retailers carried limited selections for women. Not only were we providing access to shoes for kids like we'd been, but also for others who were overlooked in sneaker retail.

That first price list was not a stapled book. It was a single 8.5-x-22-inch piece of paper that was folded twice, like a letter. It was designed the long (which is to say, wide) way, in landscape orientation. When it was folded up, all you saw was the Eastbay logo in yellow against a white background, our mailing address, and the bulk-rate postage-paid stamp with the Wausau postmark. An angled yellow hill appeared to rise from the fold at the bottom. And when you unfolded the list, you saw the full cover: the Eastbay logo, this time in white against the angled yellow column, and in massive black type, ***Track Shoes for 1983.***

Below that, we wrote a short letter. "As former coaches and athletes, we know the last problem you want is with footwear. That is where we want to help . . ." We deliberately repeated the word *service*—six times on the cover alone. "Ask any coach who has done business with us," we wrote. "Eastbay stands for SERVICE . . . Good luck this season and may a 1:50 800m runner transfer to your school. Yours in running." We added our signatures, and then in giant type: ***CALL COLLECT 715/845-5538.***

In all there were seventy one shoes listed in the price list, with pictures of seventeen (eleven men's shoes and six women's). We also featured a listing of running accessories, including Sorbothane, running suits and singlets, and some racing spikes. In just over a week, an arduously long and fraught week, we had gone from a hazy idea of what this could look like to holding a printed draft of our first mailing in our hands.

A few hundred copies in glorious black-and-white arrived at the store the next week. It would have been great to send these to kids, but that was still impossible—we had no list of young athletes to use. So, we again leaned on our earliest, best advocates: the coaches, of whom we did have a list. Knowing they'd be passing this thing around to all their athletes, we splurged on a heavy, glossy paper stock that would be more durable. We went to work writing by hand those coaches' names and school addresses on each catalog. We piled the price lists into huge mail bags and hauled them down to the post office. Then we waited.

A few days later, the phone started ringing. A lot.

13

Doers of Stuff

Within days we could exhale. The price-list gamble would not sink us. We had taken hundreds of calls for orders from Wisconsin, and a few from beyond. Within months it was generating meaningful business apart from clinics and the store, and it emboldened us that we could do a separate mailing for basketball and wrestling shoes. And we'd add an 800 number. No more collect calls.

We had to hire more people to take calls and fill orders. Our hiring process was as professional and polished as everything else we were doing. For example, Rick's younger brother Tom had come on after Rick's mom called and said Tom really needed a job. His fish management degree was useless after a new law gutted natural resources money.

"Yeah, Mom did the interview for me," Tom recalls, laughing. Tom didn't know much about our business, but he had been a member of the state-championship mile relay, so he knew running. Like so many others, Tom took the job as a bridge until he found work in what he'd gone to school for, and like so many others, he became an expert in the mail-order business and stuck around, fortunately for us.

And he remembers quickly becoming impressed by the reputation that we'd developed for being able to read a person's foot. "You were never trained in foot morphology," Tom says. "But you'd learned all about it. So, when you would sit down with somebody, you would really look at their foot type, their stride, and fit them into the best shoe for them. The whole thing was really predicated on customer service."

We were confident we could fit you with the right shoes. We were still figuring out how much inventory to buy.

If you want to know the differences between the two of us, bring up inventory. We both worried about having the right amount of inventory, because that was the whole business. Too little and you lost sales. Too much and you overspent. Either way you're losing money.

Rick's inventory-purchasing philosophy was to cut it close. If we estimated that we'd need, for instance, five hundred Nike Oregons, he'd say buy five hundred of them and then stock up on add-ons—running shorts, tank tops, and so forth.

Art didn't want to miss a shoe sale. If we estimated five hundred, he'd want to buy seven hundred and forgo the add-ons. We rarely disagreed on *which* models would be hot sellers, but we'd spend hours debating *how many* of those hot sellers we should buy, usually meeting in the middle.

In the game of business, inventory is a source of constant tension, but it can create real excitement when you make a good bet. And boy did we eventually get good at inventory bets, consistently hitting the right order size, or making a bet on a product that others didn't but that ended up being a big seller. In the early catalog days, Rick made a bet on Lycra tights for runners before that was a thing. Most in the industry thought it'd never work; men wouldn't buy tights. But Rick was right, we sold a ton, and we were ahead of the curve on it.

And if we missed and didn't sell something, we still had one final way to move it, at least once a year: Wausau's annual Sidewalk Sale Days, a Thursday-through-Saturday event for all the local retailers. We decided to create an event within the event: the annual Eastbay Running Store Tent Sale. All our excess inventory was stacked right there on tables out on the sidewalk, a towering reminder of our optimism, boxes upon boxes of shoes that we'd been certain would sell but that hadn't. Now available at a deep discount.

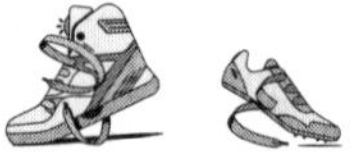

Not everyone we hired in the early to mid-1980s was related to us. We gave a job to a guy named Don Baptist, recommended by Rick's old track coach. We put him to work sweeping up the storage area, which had some shelves for inventory we hadn't really gotten around to using. One day we came down to see the inventory all shelved and categorized. "Who the hell did all this?" we asked.

"Almost like I did something wrong," Don recalls now. He would stay on and be a core part of those Eastbay years. He was like a human computer. He always knew exactly where all the inventory was in our chaotic warehouse situation.

The people we hired didn't just do the work; they did it better than we would've even thought to ask for. The people we chose would prove to be the most important reason Eastbay survived those early years. We were growing a family without even realizing it.

Polly Weiland came on when she was a junior in high school, and a multisport athlete at Wausau East High. She was bright and ambitious and, having grown up in Wausau, fully intended to leave town. "I couldn't wait to go to Madison," she recalls now. "I couldn't wait to live anywhere but Wausau. My dream was to go out to L.A. and live on the beach. That's all I wanted to do."

First thing she remembers is showing up to our Sidewalk Days tent sale, where someone pushed a small metal box at her. "This is our cash register."

She managed the till. If there wasn't a customer, she helped straighten tables and clean up around the area. We asked her back the next day. And the next. She remembers having a blast. "The days flew by."

After that, Polly worked part-time through the summer and then stayed to work weekends during the school year. She fondly recalls one of her first regular tasks, "Wally's runs" to the bar, which she remembers being a once- or twice-a-day thing, usually to get Mountain Dew and Junior Mints for Art, which she suspected he lived on. These Wally's runs offered her something else she came to cherish as well: getting to use a different bathroom than the one small one everyone shared at the Washington Street store.

The summer after she graduated, we hired her full-time. She didn't expect to stay on beyond the end of summer, when she'd planned to get out of Wausau and start college at the University of Wisconsin–Madison. When fall rolled around, though, Polly deferred her enrollment and started a two-year stint at a UW extension school in Wausau so she could keep working at Eastbay. "I was having so much fun," she says. "I loved working with sneakers, and sometimes it was hard to imagine they were really paying me for it. And I wanted to go into business, anyway, and here I was, seventeen, eighteen years old, getting to do all kinds of stuff that I knew that kids my age didn't normally get to do."

Before long, we trusted Polly enough to leave her the keys to the store when we went home. Sometimes we felt bad leaving her there with all that work, but later she told us how much she respected that we did that, leaving early enough in the evening to spend time with our families. That was one of the reasons she later told us she liked working for us. She also said that she appreciated how we tried to be generous even when we didn't have much to give. Her first year, we gave her a turkey to cook with her family at Thanksgiving. At Christmas, we gave her a small bonus, maybe fifty bucks. That's all we could afford. But apparently it meant the world to her. "I was so excited," she says now. "And my parents were excited for me."

Even after she finished the two-year program and started attending school in Madison, Polly stayed on staff and arranged her class schedule so that she was finished by Wednesday and could drive back and work full-time until classes picked up on Monday. "Hustled my ass off," she says.

It was a hard schedule to manage. One night, after one particularly long Saturday, her dad picked her up from the store. He could tell she was feeling worn out and low. "My dad made a point of telling me, 'I don't want you to forget how excited you are to work in the morning, and how lucky you are, and how you've loved it so much that you even changed your school decisions to keep working here. People would kill to go to a job that they love. You're gonna have bad days, but don't forget how important it is, and how lucky you are to have a job that you love.' He was very specific. And I really appreciated it."

Polly was a different kind of validation for Eastbay. Like the rest of us, for years, she never had one clearly defined role. Trying to remember, she rattles off six different titles she used over her time at Eastbay. She took on whatever needed doing, excelled, and in the process learned new parts of the business, to the point that eventually she was our business development department, and great at it, too.

Years later, people would ask her what she did in her time at Eastbay. Given that she did *everything*, it was always difficult to explain, so she coined a term for it. "People always tried to find out what kind of title I had," she says. "I always wanted a business card that just said, 'DOER OF STUFF.' Because I would just throw myself at whatever needed doing. And that's what we all were doing. At one point I had three different business cards, and I would pull out whatever one I needed based on whatever the situation was."

The first extended price list worked well enough that we sent another price list with pictures in '83 for basketball and wrestling. We went toll-free, adding two 800 numbers—not that we were really equipped to handle more calls. Our "call center" was a desk with two phones and a grand total of six separate lines.

Even more precious than the sales these lists generated was the feedback we were getting, from coaches especially. They loved the lists, but they were also asking questions that taught us about the market and what the customers wanted. They wanted more detailed descriptions, or more comparisons. "Hey, can you guys include more pictures? Our kids don't know what an Adidas Arrow looks like."

More pictures was a constant request. Coaches and kids were still hesitant to purchase shoes they had never seen. But we couldn't include pictures for every single item we had for sale. That would have required something four times the size, at least, and the costs would have skyrocketed. Our constraints made this mail-based business grow slowly and steadily through 1984.

In retrospect, the constraints were good for us. We were lucky the price list didn't grow any faster than it did. We couldn't have handled it. We didn't have the phone lines, or the inventory logistics, and we didn't have the money to finance more growth. Already we were pushing all our cash back into inventory. Interest rates were still at 13 percent. We still barely drew a salary—we might've paid ourselves twenty bucks a week by now. We were growing, hiring, and busier than we could have imagined ever being, and yet there were still times we wondered if we would make it. The top line looked so promising; the bottom line was not.

Dr. Molinaro—Art's father-in-law—would often come into the store with Rick's dad, Cliff. Both remained skeptical. Polly was often their first point of contact, and they'd chat her up. "Almost like they were hoping I'd spill the beans on something," she says. She felt like she had no beans to spill. "Even that young, I understood that this was a really cool idea," she says. "I don't want to suggest I had some, you know, immaculate vision or anything. I just knew it was cool. But I had no idea what it was going to become. Nobody did."

As 1984 marched on, we recognized that one thing people really wanted more than anything, always, was the price list mailed directly to them. It represented probably our greatest opportunity. We could send it out more often, to more places. We could add more products. We could make it the thing that made them light up the way they had at the clinics.

So, while what happens next might seem lucky—and damn sure there was some luck involved—it also feels like it was part of this gut feeling that had steered us those first few years.

We took another risk-the-business chance, because we could *feel* it was what people wanted: Color.

14

Prelude to a Rocket Ride

The tremors in the sneaker business in the early '80s had, by 1984, become seismic shifts. Adidas was the world leader, while Nike owned the United States. But Nike wanted it all and launched its initial salvo in its bid for dominance, something the shoe industry had never seen before: team-colored shoes for the Dunk.

It was a major launch coordinated with the start of college basketball's March Madness tournament, with all those teams playing all those games in all those new shoes patterned with the team colors of the colleges Nike had signed to exclusive shoe and clothing contracts. College athletes and their programs were being aggressively recruited to market all this new footwear and apparel. Pro athletes were beginning to get signature shoes.

Cable TV was exploding and with it, ESPN. Kids were seeing more players, more highlights, more games. The league and the media were making legends out of the superstars, Dr. J, Larry Bird, Magic Johnson, and kids, black and white, wanted to be like them. To wear what they wore. We started to see the merging of cultures through sports and through sneakers. The shoe companies saw it too, obviously, and were desperately courting athletes to represent their brands.

And there was MTV, which helped blur the line between sports and fashion. Hip-hop acts like Run-DMC and the Beastie Boys brought footwear-as-fashion from New York into suburban and rural homes across the country. The football player needed cleats, but maybe wanted Adidas Superstars, too, to wear to school.

The new technology, the new designs, and an increased pace of new shoe introductions made kids want to, as Van Halen was singing at the time, "Jump!" Kids wanted the latest, greatest sneaker they were seeing worn by their heroes. To play better, yes, but also—in many cases—to *look* better.

The sneaker wars had begun.

As soon as team-colored shoes arrived, coaches and players flooded us with requests for shoes that matched their schools' colors. Stores were carrying only a narrow set of the most popular colors. Eastbay carried every color. We had been used to every inventory decision feeling fraught, carrying the possibility of leading our company to ruin. Until this. This was different. This time there was no argument over inventory. We never questioned team-colored sneakers, neither one of us.

Nike owned maybe 15 percent of the basketball shoe market at the time, but we understood what it was doing and knew kids would move away from Adidas to get Dunks or Air Force styles in team colors.

At the same time, the apparel companies—allies in the sneaker wars—were ramping up their game. Starter launched team-licensed clothes in team colors. Nike introduced muscle tights in many colors in 1984, in part inspired by Carl Lewis wearing them in his dominant Olympics performance that year. We had already bet on running tights, and with this, they just exploded. We couldn't get enough of them. It felt like the perfect retail market was being created for us.

But we knew that to capitalize, we had to get the price list right. If we were going to go all in on team-colored sneakers and team-colored apparel, we needed color photos. We needed to show as many styles as we could, and apparel, too. We needed to turn the price list into a full-on catalog. That meant we needed a new printer, which we found in a Stevens Point company called Spectraprint. The cost per page skyrocketed, and so did the tediousness of putting the thing together. We'd write out descriptions on legal pads, type them up, proof them, retype. Dozens of descriptions. The design team printed out the final descriptions and took them—along with printed photos we'd selected after shooting and developing those—and tacked them onto a large board, neatly arranged. We stepped back to take it in.

Maybe the Chariot looked out of place where it was or maybe we didn't have the room for both the Elite classic and Pegasus on the same page, or we just wouldn't like the way the design flowed. Move things around, literally cutting and pasting. It was a physical process. We argued over picture sizes and page allotments by sport. Make the basketball shoe section bigger. We sell a lot of racing flats; do they get enough space? Move those ones over there. Put these next to each other.

Finally, once we had everything in place just the way we liked it, someone took a picture of the big board. One page done. We went at it for several days.

We were on edge during this process, as we had sunk all our money into this. But always there was an underlying gut instinct that we were right. We felt it when we stood back and stared at those boards. Even then, we felt a sense of excitement that was hard to contain. *How unbelievably cool,* we thought, *would it have been to have this when we were kids?*

Anyone who laid eyes on all those color choices would react with the same awe that Rick had back when he first saw the color variety at the track championships that started this whole business.

To manage costs, we gang shot the shoes in all their spectral glory, lining all the colors of one model up in a single shot, a regiment of Nike Dunks, shown in orange and white, navy and white, red and white, black and gold, navy and gold, light blue and white, red and silver, and black and white.

We made sure to show shoes in colors we knew weren't easy to find, like the Nike Air Force in green, orange, purple, or maroon, with its colored trim around the heels, the Nike swoosh circling around the heel in a slick thin line, and even matching colored soles. Crucially, we offered sizes 5 to 15—sizes at the edges you couldn't get in stores—because we had noticed from our first clinic that kids with big (or small) feet had a hard time finding shoes.

For the Nikes, we priced individual pairs at $49.95, a third off Nike's suggested retail price of $74.95.

We wrote:

> Finally, a lightweight, flexible air soled shoe. Combines the best cushioning support and flexibility at a good price. The air-sole cushion helps save the legs for late in the game.*

The asterisk connected to a little manifestation language, before we even knew what that was. We declared below the entry, with boldness and naivete and hope: **Limited quantity of special colors, order early.*

Given our well-established connections with teams throughout Wisconsin, our having put out a handful of mailings (now with color photos), and the fact that we already offered team-discount prices, we found ourselves unwittingly at the perfect intersection of trends for offering Nike's—and then other companies'—team colorways to athletes.

And we were right. Team colors changed everything. Sales exploded, as did the amount of work we had to do just to get the inventory of an ever-expanding number of shoe models. We more than doubled, in a year, the number of SKUs we carried of Adidas, Nike, and Converse.

"If Nike hadn't launched team-colored footwear and apparel," Polly says, "then I don't think Eastbay would have become as big as it did. It was very much right place, right time. We had just built the underlying structure we needed when team colors first came out. Art and Rick had the vehicle and the vision to turn that into something."

As fast as it took off, it was only a prelude to Eastbay's rocket ride, and very nearly its crash, a ride that started on November 17, 1984. On that night, a couple hundred miles south of Wausau, basketball icon Dr. J, Julius Erving, and the Philadelphia 76ers came to Chicago for a game against the Bulls. A promising NBA rookie named Michael Jordan stepped onto the court wearing shoes that shocked the world.

PART THREE

Growing Fast

15

Compelling beyond Reason

It was one of those rare events when you know as you witness it that nothing will be the same after. Nixon sweats during the televised debate on TV. The Beatles get off the plane at JFK. Dylan plugs in at Newport.

Jordan walks onto the court in *those*.

Until that moment, Nike was not the dominant player in basketball shoes. For years, the Adidas Top Ten was number one, and the company's Forum basketball shoe had just become the first $100 pair of sneakers. Converse was making noise, too, with the Star Tech high-tops. All the companies made shoes with colors, but mostly they were white shoes accented with colors, and few were as bold as the Nike colorways. None had dared to put one on a pro court. Nike saw an opening.

We still thought of ourselves as a runner's source first, but we sold Nike's Air Ship Pro PE basketball shoes. They were sharp high-tops in white with a solid color swoosh and trim, with all the team colors available. The Bulls would have had the version with a red swoosh. Jordan had worn those.

But in a preseason game in October, he wore a pair that were starkly different than the ones we sold, like nothing anyone had ever worn in the NBA before: Black shoes with red swoosh and trim. NBA commissioner David Stern immediately banned it, as league rules mandated sneakers be at least 51 percent white, and the only white showing on Jordan's Air Ship was the midsole wrapping the shoe.

Nike didn't seem to care. So, on that November night in Chicago, number 23 walked onto the court in a real game in the Air Jordan 1.

The shoe was a masterclass in branding by way of professional and cultural subversion. White leather was subservient to red panels, black laces, and the massive black swooshes on both sides. A red tab on the tongue carried the words *Nike Air* and another swoosh.

The Top Ten had been touted as the shoe the best players wore. Sure, Rick Barry helped them design it, but Adidas said right in its original ad, which highlighted many of the shoe's features, that Rick Barry "tested our Adidas Top Ten . . ."

Air Jordans were touted as the shoe *one* player wore: Jordan, who was not yet a star. His own name, and his own logo—a set of flight wings spreading apart from a basketball—were right there on a red leather strip encircling the ankles.

The TV broadcast announcer called them "the ugliest shoes in the league." Jordan went four for seventeen from the floor and scored sixteen points in a loss. That didn't matter, and nobody remembers that; we only know it because we looked it up out of curiosity. All people remembered, all people were talking about, was the shoe. And with the rising force of ESPN and its nightly highlights show *Sportscenter*, everyone could see the Jordans.

The NBA immediately fined Jordan for violating league policies regarding teammates wearing matching shoes. Nike paid his fines. Jordan continued to wear the shoes, and Nike used the controversy to launch an ad campaign around his shoes being banned, brilliantly implying that they might have been such a cutting-edge design they made Jordan *too* good. "On September 15, Nike created a revolutionary new basketball shoe. On October 18, the NBA threw them out of the game. Fortunately, the NBA can't stop you from wearing them," the commercial said.[1]

Nike and Jordan hadn't invented the concept of a signature shoe. The first seems to have been the Bob Cousy PF Flyers produced in the late 1950s. They looked good—similar to the iconic Chuck Taylors from Converse—and most important at the time, their gum soles created the best contact with the floor you could find, a critical feature before air conditioning.

After that, Clyde Drexler got his Puma Clydes in the 1970s, Converse put out Julius Erving's Dr. J Pro Leathers as a response to Drexler's signature shoe release, and Adidas answered them both with Kareem Abdul-Jabbar's signature Adidas Jabbars in the late '70s.

But the Air Jordan 1 possessed a transcendent aura that was different. We agreed on that. Nike was changing the game and the culture. It shifted the narrative. Team colorways were a huge success, but this wasn't about the team, it was about one player. (Jordan's shoes didn't match his teammates' that night.) The obsession of the shoe companies' marketing to this point had been performance. An Adidas Top Ten magazine ad at the time, for example, ran to hundreds of words, including this spec-heavy copy:

> [Rick Barry] insisted we develop the upper with a special Foreflex™ cut that lets the foot flex easily and in the correct position. And had us add an Ankle Saver™ support system for increased protection

Nike had done similar ads, including one celebrating the importance of the humble shoe last—the block form that shoes are molded around in manufacturing.

With Jordan, the marketing pivoted hard to personality and *style*. One of the original promotions for Air Jordans shows Jordan, alone, fronting a city at dusk, soaring through the air, defying gravity, legs split and stretched, left arm reaching high with the ball palmed and out ahead, above the rim. He's eternally frozen at an outstretched apex, in the pose that would become the silhouette for the brand's iconic "jumpman" logo.

AIR JORDAN HAS LANDED
Nike Air

That's the only text. No specs. No jargon. Six words. Jordan's name is bigger and bolder than Nike's.

Even if Nike wasn't saying it, the shoes appeared to be technically excellent. They seemed durable and, we'd learn, weighed less than just about any other basketball shoe at the time. Still, mostly everyone including us just couldn't stop *looking* at them. They were breathtaking—breathtakingly beautiful, or breathtakingly ugly. People were sharply divided on that. When Jordan made an appearance on *Late Night with David Letterman,* the talk-show host called the shoes ugly, and Jordan even sort of agreed with him.

If you ask Bobbito Garcia, true sneakerheads—he calls them "sneaker fiends"—hated the Air Jordans at first. "The first Air Jordan, in any true connoisseur's view, looked garbage," he writes in his book *Where'd You Get Those?* "The only person who looked jazzy in them was Jordan himself, yet everyone had them and swore they were the shit . . . It was the first sneaker in New York history that gained popularity on the street that it didn't deserve. It was the beginning of a homogenous style for youth and brand loyalty."[2]

Garcia was right, but so were we in our estimation that kids were going to want these. Suddenly the kids at all our clinics began to echo one another in their hunger to become Air Jordan kids, to assert their brand loyalty. Every kid on every team was asking us when we'd have them. Whatever they were—ugly, beautiful, trash, masterpiece—they were compelling beyond reason.

We didn't know yet that as much as the Air Jordan 1 was a pivot in the athletic shoe industry, it was also a moment that would reshape our business model—again. To this point, though we served several sports, we still thought of ourselves as primarily a resource for teams and runners. And like those old-style ads from all the sneaker companies, we were focused on education and fit—on trying to get young athletes into shoes that helped them perform their best. We were running *clinics* after all.

Over time, and this started with the Air Jordan 1, we'd transform from mostly running to running and basketball, to all sports. We'd migrate from team sales to team and individual sales. We'd move from relying only on education and performance to highlighting (even creating) style and attitude, too. How far sports marketing had come—even kids in small towns in the middle of nowhere knew about and pined for Air Jordans. We chalk that up to the rise of ESPN, MTV, and Wieden+Kennedy and its creative director, Jim Riswold, the ad geniuses who started working for Nike around 1982 and, with Phil Knight and the Nike team, transformed the sports marketing game with the iconic early Jordan campaigns.

In some ways, Nike and Air Jordan seemed to embody much of what we had been trying to capture with our entire approach to the business. We wanted shoes to help young athletes, so they could perform better and look better—feel better about themselves and feel *good.* And we wanted our catalog to promise all that, too, in how it presented the shoes and whatever else we put in it.

Nike made the Air Jordans available for retailers to order soon after that. We quickly had to decide how much to buy, but we wouldn't be able to sell anything we ordered for another six months. This half-year float was the trickiest part of the inventory game. You placed your order and then hoped you had read the future well enough that people would want—half a year later—that much of what you had bet on.

Sometimes our friendship slowed down our decisions, and sometimes it sped them up. Rick had always been able to see what new types of track shoes would mean for runners. Now Art, a basketball guy, could foresee what the Air Jordan meant. And as we learned more about that shoe, Art insisted we should grab as much inventory as possible. Rick did not preach caution. We were both all-in on a shoe. We bought as many of them as Nike would let us. Nike was capping orders, hinting at a new scarcity model with shoe releases, used to drive hype and demand—a model that would blossom in the coming decades.

A couple of things broke our way here. One, we could order more than retailers because we could order both as a retailer and as a team-sales business, due to our clinics—retailers didn't have access to team-sales inventory. And two, the retailers didn't scoop up the black-and-red Air Jordan 1s in huge quantities, instead focusing on the more traditional colorways, which were a safer retail bet. Many retailers were probably of the "ugliest shoes in the league" opinion and figured that, although the shoes got people's attention, they probably wouldn't sell. Their model—built around lots of small stores without much storage—didn't lend itself to a big inventory bet on that kind of shoe. We scooped up more of those black-and-red Jordans than we expected we'd get.

It was our largest single product purchase to that point. If those shoes didn't sell, well, we were truly toast, but we weren't feeling too nervous. We were beyond confident, based on the simple fact that neither of us could take our eyes off them.

Even before the first Air Jordans arrived, we put them on the back cover of the spring catalog. We couldn't officially list them for sale, so we pasted the new Air Jordan logo along with two large photos of new Air Jordan apparel: shorts, sweatpants, T-shirts, and tank tops, mostly in black and red. In the middle of all the clothes there was a picture of Michael Jordan himself decked out in Air Jordan apparel, smiling and—most important—with a pair of Air Jordans slung over his shoulder. Nike wouldn't let us *list* them, but we could *display* them, right next to simple but stark all-caps sans serif text in black against a stark white: ***AVAILABLE JUNE.***

The truck with the Jordans arrived in Wausau and took up its spot across the street (we had no loading dock). Washington Street was a two-lane, one-way road with cars zipping down it over 30 mph. We'd dodge traffic to meet the truck, load up a two-wheeler with four cases of Jordans hanging off both sides, and then, like Frogger, attempt to recross while trying to balance the boxes and zigzagging between cars.

We pulled a couple boxes aside and eagerly opened them like Christmas presents. The shoes looked even better in person than we had imagined. They looked fast, and light, and everything about them felt so different from other basketball shoes. Their color was striking even up against other team-colored shoes. They did feel kind of stiff; we wondered if they'd be good from a comfort and performance point of view for all players. Maybe not. But then again, we could tell they were the most "runner-like" shoe for basketball that had ever existed, and the game *was* getting faster. Light weight combined with support was the right formula.

The '85 basketball catalog featured a stylish shot looking up at a basketball hoop, the orange rim stark against a black background and the crisp white net stuffed with eight or nine basketball shoes. Prominently above the rim, the shoe at the top was the Air Jordan 1 in all its red-and-white-and-black glory. The black-on-red-on-black version that many retailers hadn't scooped up was also there.

At the top of the inside cover, we featured a dozen team-colored variations of the Air Jordan 1. The five shoes in the top row were humbly in line with NBA restrictions for mostly white colorways, and although they weren't branded as such back then, their silhouette more closely resembles what you would recognize today as the Air Jordan 1 Mid. The only color on them could be found in the swoosh logo, the Air Jordan logo on the wings, and the trim around the heel. We had them in navy blue, black, maroon, green, and orange. The row below those featured two of the Air Jordan 1 Lo, also all white with gray or navy-blue accents. There were also three all-white Air Jordan 1s in the silhouette you'd now recognize as the AJ1 OG High. This was an *Eastbay* differentiator, born out of our business model. On the inside cover of our catalog, you could access more styles, colors, and sizes of one shoe than you'd ever see in any store. Page after page, brand after brand, it was the same. Endless choice.

Below all those different Jordans was the *pièce de résistance*: First, the iconic banned color combo known today as the "Bred"—all black, with a red toe section, red swoosh, red wings, red heel, red laces, and most audacious of all, the red sole.

Right beside that what's called today the "Lost and Found"—black swoosh, white sections but with red throughout, black laces, black heel trim, and the same vivid red sole.

> **AIR JORDAN.** Sizes 6-15. The hottest shoe on the market. Combines lightness, flexibility, support and comfort. The air sole heel cushion helps save the legs for the fourth quarter. An excellent game shoe. Colors—white, white/black/red, white/blue, black/red. Regular $64.95. **Eastbay $49.95.**

We were still pricing as a team dealer even as more and more individuals were scooping up our inventory, especially the "Breds." Probably should've held onto a few more of them for ourselves, but we sold every pair we had within a week of putting out that first catalog. It was an unprecedented run. Kids called every day; parents came in every day hoping we had more.

For Nike, it was a major battle won in the sneaker wars. Adidas's basketball business never quite recovered from the Air Jordan shock. Adidas is the second-most-worn brand in the NBA today, but at only 10 percent of the market. Nike owns about 75 percent. The Top Ten would fade away as a basketball shoe, though it remains an important sneaker to sneakerheads. It has a special link to Detroit, where the Pistons' Bob Lanier wore them and was an early example of sneakers worn as status symbols in that city. We'd sell plenty of Adidas in the future, but not only to athletes—also to sneakerheads and kids listening to Run-DMC.

Converse needed two years to ramp up as a competitor, and they brought heavy guns in '86: Magic Johnson pitted his purple-and-gold Converse Weapons against archrival Larry Bird's green-and-white ones. Both players were more successful than Jordan on the court that decade, but even they couldn't really dent what the Air Jordan established.

Part of the Air Jordan's appeal was that Jordan was, in some surprising ways, the most relatable basketball star on the planet. Kareem Abdul-Jabbar's signature shoes were perfectly fine, but it's hard for people to relate to a stoic seven-foot-four center. Magic Johnson had an otherworldly quality about him, too, making everything look easy with his smile and his six-foot-eight frame and his effortlessly flashy play. Larry Bird was an absolute assassin, every bit as domineering and ruthless as Michael Jordan, a true wonder to behold on the court with his sniper-like shooting, gaudy assists, and his fearless and sharp cutting and slicing through the lane—but he was also six-foot-nine, and God bless him, we loved to watch him play, but strictly from a marketing perspective, he wasn't Jordan.

Jordan? Crazy as it sounds today, Michael Jordan felt like one of the people. From a visual standpoint, although in real life he was six-foot-six, on television he looked "normal" compared with the other giants on the court. He had a relatable origin story, getting cut from his high school varsity team in Wilmington, North Carolina, when he was a freshman, and then having to work hard to make it the next year. And he combined that with a killer instinct and incredible athletic ability that seemed hard-earned. That's an Eastbay kind of athlete if ever there was one. Work hard. Overcome obstacles. No excuses. Win.

Yet the Air Jordan 1 came out before number 23 had won anything; there was no guarantee then that Michael Jordan was going to become Michael Jordan. Of course he did. And the more he won, the more shoes we sold. The moment he walked onto the court in those beautiful, ugly shoes turned into years of dominance and, for Eastbay, years of turbulence. Jordan seemed almost too good at basketball, and we would find out we were getting too good at selling his signature shoes, too.

But with those first shipments, all we knew was that we were right to get our hands on as many of those shoes as we could. The Air Jordan 1 was so cool, Art nabbed a pair from the truck that delivered that first shipment to Wausau. A week later, though, a coach called and said he needed some for his son and he couldn't find his size anywhere. The kid wore the same size as Art, so Art sent his pair over to the coach.

16

"What the Hell Is Going on Back There?"

Our first full-color catalog went out to our modest mailing list (which mostly spanned fifteen states radiating out from Wisconsin) late in 1985, for basketball season. From a few thousand pairs and $75,000 in sales our first year, we were tracking now to do a million dollars in sales. The color options, cool new apparel, the previous year's Summer Olympics in Los Angeles, and the Jordans were all fueling Eastbay's sudden, absurd growth.

The Fall 1985 catalog was the first that was a stapled book, twelve pages. In addition to the Air Jordans and Jordan apparel, it had all the new colorways shoes, like Nike Dunks, along with apparel to match those colors, like basketball clothes and classic satin team jackets from Starter. We waded into some college- and pro-licensed apparel for the first time, too.

Many kids would see our catalog and call us, asking for, say, purple-trimmed size 15 Air Forces to go with their purple team jerseys, or just because they wanted unique-colored sneakers. They told us the stores said they wouldn't be able to get what they were looking for. But we told the kids, *Yes we have them. And not only do we have them, but we can get them to you in three days.*

"And that," Polly says, "is how Eastbay got customers for life."

We recognized mail order was the future, so that was it. We were going all-in on it. We hired someone to run the Wausau storefront full-time and turned our attention to *Eastbay*, the catalog. We felt like GMs of sports teams, looking for the right talent to build the team that would make the catalog a championship business. We felt lucky we seemed to be finding people who did great work and who were nice to boot. We tried to hire people who had been athletes in high school or college, and people who just seemed happy. Rick's favorite interview question was, "What's your favorite movie?" If they cited a comedy, then they were pretty much in. Rick just wanted to work with people who could laugh.

In a scary move, we deviated from Eastbay norms of hiring family and friends, for the first time hiring four people we didn't already know. All of them started on phones, and then, as usual, moved on to other positions, becoming buyers and supervisors and directing photos of clothing for catalogs. They were so good that it gave us confidence to continue to hire from outside—and we were going to need it. We still weren't above nepotism. We hired Rick's younger brothers Jim and John. Art's brother-in-law Dave Molinaro joined. Polly's two younger brothers, who were around fourteen, chipped in on odd jobs. But although we were a family, when we were at work, we worked.

"Everybody was pretty private at work about their personal lives," Polly says. "But we still developed a very close bond. A lot of us were there until late, until we shut the lights off. And then we'd all go to Wally's and drink together at night."

A handful of employees turned into a few dozen seemingly overnight, and while we're certain we hired people for certain jobs—answering phones, sorting inventory, shipping—most everyone remained, just like Polly, Doers of Stuff.

This first post–Air Jordan growth spurt was chaotic. People were sprinting from the phone desk down to the warehouse and back, and it was getting difficult to keep up with who had put what customer on hold on which line. Two phones on a desk with six lines—this wasn't cutting it. It was stressful, but it was also funny. We laughed through the chaos.

People in Wausau were not privy to our latest strategy pivot to focus on the catalog, and they were starting to whisper. Most of them knew

Eastbay was a store but couldn't figure out why even when the store wasn't busy, Eastbay was. Speculation in town ran rampant.

John Schaefer, an early customer we had outfitted with Adidas New Yorks a few years previously, and someone you'll meet again later, recalls the gossip. He heard wild speculation about massive underground warehouses. "You saw people going in and out of all those back doors, and you'd just be wondering, 'What the hell is going on back there?'" Schaefer says. "The store, it was so small, but it was in this big building, with these odd back doors. It was this big mystery."

Many of the hundreds of calls we fielded every day were from individuals requesting a catalog or making an order. But a few came from coaches, who were exhausted by the legwork of sharing their one copy of *Eastbay* with their athletes and then taking orders from all the kids and relaying the orders to us. They told us how much they appreciated what we did. But at the same time, they reiterated their need for us to figure out a better way for these kids to get their orders to us. They wanted us to send them twenty catalogs so they could just hand them out. Then, when those kids would order, we could add their addresses to our list and just mail a catalog right to them next time.

We weren't sure how this would work without the coaches. Sending fifty catalogs to fifty coaches leading to orders for thousands of kids was keeping everyone busy enough. What they were suggesting meant we'd be sending a *thousand* catalogs to a *thousand* kids, each placing their own order, which meant a *thousand* calls. How much staff would we need for that? And what's it going to cost to print all those color catalogs? How do you figure out how much product to buy?

And what about taking credit-card orders—the pinnacle of tediousness? For every call: Take the card number from the customer. Call the credit-card company to validate the card. Inscribe the buyer's information on a credit-card slip. Slide the slip through the credit-card imprinter to record the order. Over and over. None of us could write legibly, so Rick's dad would write out the credit-card slips, and we'd take our stacks of them to the bank and deposit them along with our checks and cash. We couldn't imagine scaling this up.

As far as we knew, only a few places (Lands' End, J.C. Penney, J.Crew and Sears) were doing mail order, but mostly it was aimed at adults—

particularly women—shopping for clothes and other home goods. Who the hell would be stupid enough to do mail order directly with high-school kids? They didn't have any money. And for shoes? It just wasn't done.

Again, we beg our younger readers to imagine a time when the notion of getting something in the mail, not liking it, and then returning it did not exist. The idea of kids' names and addresses being made available to a company was ludicrous. We understand that today *none* of this is remotely controversial, but we promise you that in those days, these were real obstacles we had to consider before going directly to kids with *Eastbay*.

When kids did want to order from the catalog, we took many calls from skeptical parents. Who were we? Where were we located? Wisconsin? Really?

Location seemed especially important to the inquisitors who wanted to vet us. A coach in New York once called us, and after a brief conversation, told us how excited he was that he felt like he could trust us.

More and more, we began hearing that people trusted us because of our location. People, especially on the coasts, seemed to hold in their hearts a belief in some kind of Midwestern honesty. We also got the sense that they just needed to hear our voices and establish a sense of connection with a real person, and that helped them feel like we weren't going to rip them off. Some coaches would call and ask for a phone rep by name to work with.

And they wanted to trust us, we suspect, because we had good deals. While most companies priced their products as high as they thought a customer would pay, we kept our prices at the team price level, which was usually 10 percent to 20 percent below suggested retail. Sometimes more.

We all learned to be good listeners on those calls, and by listening we were gathering data.

Customers were telling us exactly what they wanted and needed, and what they hoped we had that retail stores didn't. We were getting a flow of information about what customers wanted from the catalog that was like the information we got from athletes and parents at the clinics, only on a much broader scale. Once, we got a call from someone in Montana who couldn't believe we had some shoe they thought they could get only if they were physically in New York City. Many calls showed us how hungry people were to jump on trends. Customers loved the idea of having so much available to them, at their fingertips. We began to envision a catalog overflowing with *everything*. We could tell by the calls that that's what young athletes craved: everything.

The challenge with that, of course, is affording everything. We both loved being able to sell more and different stuff. Rick was a top-line thinker and would say something like, "Look at how the team-licensed apparel is exploding! How can we add more pages and more products? How can we send the catalog to more states?"

Art was as excited as Rick, but also more worried about getting over our skis. "What if we don't have enough product for that? How can we pay for all of that?"

The way the two of us would talk things out, innocent bystanders might have thought that we were fighting, but we were just passionately discussing, trying to balance how much we could offer without starting to disappoint customers by running out of product if we grew too fast.

We would throw our thoughts and ideas and concerns out rapid-fire, with little regard for tone or emotional regulation. It's just how we worked. The bigger the business got, the louder the conversations. Eventually, with sober input from those around us, often on a noon run, we'd find common ground in the middle.

The sneaker wars pushed the shoe companies to introduce more models more often, which created a collector's and fashion-centered market in parallel to the athletes' market we were focused on. The Adidas Americana, for example, with its blue-red-blue stripe pattern and the Adidas logo stamped in stars and stripes on the heel, came and went "in a coach's eyeblink," as Bobbito Garcia wrote in his book *Where'd You Get Those?* "The message was clear . . . if you didn't get them when they came out, you might never see them again."[1] It was the first wave of the new culture of sneakers taking hold—the companies started the wave, and we unwittingly rode it.

The Adidas Top Ten that had redefined the basketball sneaker market in the early part of the '80s was one of our top-selling shoes for several years running. Now, nothing was carried over for more than a year. Sneakers had become like cars, with their annual model rollouts to fanfare, new innovations to brag about, new endorsement deals with athletes. Customers showed a voracious appetite for new models, for rare inventory, for the coolest new thing.

And *Eastbay* was the place they could satisfy their appetite, to find what couldn't be found anywhere else. Our inventory, our ability to ship the same day that orders were made and get these hard-to-get shoes to you in three days, that was our secret weapon. That's what the hell was going on back there.

17

We Need Everyone on the Phones!

Those two years, '85 and '86, were our pivot from coach- and clinic-driven retailer to full-blown mail-order catalog business. We put new employee Tim Strohkirch in charge of the storefront with a handful of employees, but most of the people in the store were taking phone orders and running down to grab shoes from the basement to mail out. We sent others out to do clinics so we could focus on the catalog. That was unnerving. We were so comfortable in the clinic setting—teaching kids directly about fit and what would help them, seeing their excitement at getting their hands on the right shoes. Now we weren't connecting with customers directly.

We were forced to focus on *business* stuff—hiring, logistics, management—that wasn't nearly as joyful as the clinics or looking at what shoes to buy. But we had visions of continuing to grow to something even bigger, even more special, and it demanded that we shift our attention. We were trying figure out where each of us could focus to get the most done in a business moving a million miles an hour.

The Nike team-colored revolution had *just* spurred us to bet on the catalog as the future for our company. Hardly a moment after we laid that bet, the Air Jordan phenomenon showed us it was a good bet. We continued to order as much Air Jordan inventory as we could as quickly as we could, but keeping up with demand was near impossible. Too many people wanted them. Sometimes, we sold all our Air inventory before a catalog was mailed. In one catalog we stamped a *SOLD OUT* graphic over the Air Jordans.

Basketball became our biggest sport, eclipsing track and field. A frenzied pace took over everything in Wausau. But the more we try to remember, and talk with others who remember those years, too, the more impossible it seems to nail down specifics about that time. We all just remember how it felt, the whirlwind of escalating, frenetic activity and energy, and how we worked our asses off. For four years it would be just a hurricane of growth. Our Jordan sale—all our sales—seemed to be limited only by how much we could afford to buy.

We do know we hired dozens more people, mostly part-timers answering phones and people to work in shipping. We know the small phone bank with six lines became a full-time nine-to-five call center. We added phones on our own desks to take calls when the other lines were full. And we know for certain that when those Air Jordans began to sell, the size of our mailing list for the catalog blew up.

Eastbay the catalog still wasn't yet quite what you might remember. Through 1985 we were still sending out just three full-color catalogs per year. A fall sports catalog focused on football, volleyball, and cheerleading. A winter catalog included basketball, wrestling, and cheering. And the spring one focused on track and baseball. The catalog was still just twelve pages of shoes and apparel, descriptions, prices, phone numbers, and an order form. But people wanted it. We can imagine now the affinity people were developing with the catalog, even in that primitive version, in towns all over. Shoe companies were actively encouraging the idea that their sneakers could be so in-demand that they were hard to get. And yet, here they were in *Eastbay*. In more colors and sizes than customers had ever seen. They could order *actual* Air Jordans and get them in a few days.

In 1985, another of Rick's younger brothers, Jim, joined the company after a stint "in the desert," in California working for the Bureau of Land Management. When he came home, "Our dad didn't want me laying around the house," he recalls, "so he talked you into getting me a job." We didn't need to be talked into it. All of Rick's brothers were smart guys who worked hard.

Jim started off like everyone else, a Doer of Stuff, running clinics, taking phone orders, helping with shipments. Eventually he'd home in on our mailing list as the thing he liked to work with the most. He took over managing it, and that immediately paid off.

The mailing list continued to grow, with catalogs going to thirty states. We found many duplicate addresses on the list, which we discovered was because in some families, each kid wanted their own copy. Catalog sales tripled in a year. We sailed right past $1 million in '85 and hit $2.6 million in sales in '86. We were getting savvier with what went in each edition of the catalog based on location and on weather, too. We could put baseball shoes in catalogs bound for Arizona year-round, for example, because kids in Arizona played year-round. We could time delivery to when seasons started in different parts of the country. We had a great advantage over retail in that our inventory was all in one place, not distributed to hundreds or thousands of stores. We didn't have to make the limited bets they did on how many of which shoes to carry in which sizes in which locations. Our "store" could be more flexible about what it advertised and, of course, what was available. On a small scale, in an analog way, we were doing things big online retailers do now.

We made some smart moves, but let us remind you about how we were so lucky with our timing. We jumped on the mail-order business at the outset of the sneaker wars, at a time when media was making it much easier for kids to see their heroes and the shoes they wore. And what a time for legendary athletes. Not just Jordan. Bo Jackson was a two-sport phenomenon, and some say he was the greatest athlete ever. Soon, Deion Sanders, Primetime, would follow in his footsteps and play in NFL and MLB playoff games in the same year. Ken Griffey, Jr., was unlike any hitter before him, putting up monster numbers. The '84 Olympics had created a whole generation of track stars, too, like Carl Lewis, Jackie Joyner-Kersee, and Edwin Moses.

Advertising to the market we were serving exploded, too, and would only grow throughout the rest of the decade. Nike's "Just Do It" campaign in '88, and Jordan's '89 commercial with Spike Lee's Mars Blackmon character—"It's gotta be the shoes!" he tells Jordan—solidified Nike as the coolest kid on the block and the world's number one shoe company. The same year Nike put $5 million into the launch of Air Jordans, Reebok temporarily moved to the number one position in the athletic shoe industry with their launch of aerobic shoes. Adidas was slipping in the United States, but Superstars reenergized them, as the company became a dominant force in the emerging sneakerhead culture on the back of Run-DMC's hit song "My Adidas," an ode to the rappers' favorite sneakers.

These were formative years for shoes as an athletic technology, as a fashion trend, and as cultural artifacts, for all the companies in the business, including ours. While we were working our asses off to keep up with demand, we sort of accidentally found our way into the middle of it all with the right business model at the right time.

We now saw that our business wasn't primarily going to be for teams and coaches only, but also driven by phone orders from individuals who were mostly athletes, along with a growing number of nonathletes who saw the merging worlds of sport, music, and fashion, and they wanted a piece of that too. Orders from clinics started to outnumber the athletes who were there. We'd somehow sell more shoes than there were athletes on a team. Parents were buying shoes for themselves and for friends and family—and other people from town would come to buy sneakers too.

We were getting some concerning signals at the time, too. After we started selling the Jordans, Nike team-sales division leader, Ken Effler, invited Art to Memphis to visit Nike's team-sales headquarters and meet with other team dealers, to talk shop and to talk about ways to drive more team sales. Art was thirty-three, and it was his first plane ride.

In Memphis, Art could tell right off that these sales reps had formed something of a good-ol'-boy network. They knew each other well and seemed to have an unspoken understanding that they wouldn't encroach on each other's territory.

And these guys did not like Eastbay at all. From their perspective, Eastbay was encroaching on *all* their territories, taking sales away from them. Many of the reps pulled Art aside and told him directly. Art felt like we had been breaking rules that we didn't know existed.

He also noticed how much the team-sales division at Nike was focused on going directly to big colleges with sponsorship and sales, a strategy that could crowd out retailers and mail order. Art wasn't sure yet what all this would mean for us, but he sensed it wouldn't be good.

More change was coming; we could feel it. But we focused on keeping up with demand and growing the business as fast as we could while not bankrupting ourselves. We knew our business model was different, and retailers hadn't replicated it yet. We centralized inventory and delivered to customers. Retailers distributed inventory to shops near customers. We had massive variety in style and size and color. They carried only the most popular sizes and styles. We carried far more than that and, especially, large sizes. They hired kids who didn't know feet and how to fit a shoe. We knew the foot. Rick ran "Shoe School" for our employees—"I'm a proud graduate," Polly says—in which he helped everyone understand the intricacies of pronation and arch support, width, weight, comfort, how different materials reacted to different surfaces, and so much more, all to help customers with fit and purpose. We knew if we could continue to build this, if we could get far enough out ahead with our business model, it would take the retailers longer to catch us as the industry shifted.

There were times in those days when we'd run out of people to answer all the ringing phones. We'd yell for anyone who was working, whatever they were doing, to please just answer a call. "We need everyone on the phones!" we'd holler, and people would come scrambling from the basement to help.

By 1986, we added a bold call to action in the catalog: ***DON'T CALL FOR A CATALOG—WRITE IN ONLY.***

Let's take a moment here to pause and observe the brilliance of a mail-order business telling its customers not to call them. Yes, we're being sarcastic. But we didn't see any other choice. We had limited phone lines.

We could use a line either to take an order or to take a catalog request. We'd take an order every time.

When a catalog hit mailboxes, we'd experience an intense rush, suddenly needing to ship thousands of orders per week. This would be followed by returns. Our focus on customer service as a differentiator meant our policy was one that you experience regularly today but that was much rarer back then. We would accept any return for any reason and replace what you returned if you wanted. Once, a guy called and said, "Hey, my shoes are defective. I need you to send me a new pair."

"What's wrong with them?"

"I ripped them jumping a fence running from the police."

We thought for a second, and then Rick said, "Send him a new pair!"

Kid must have been fast. If he was calling us, that meant he got away.

We were lucky to have access to both individual and team-sales inventory, but it came with some risk. Nike had long before instituted a program called "futures," which it used to shift inventory risk. The futures system let us buy products six months in advance at a bigger discount. Nike (and later other vendors) would accumulate all those orders from all their accounts and place one big order at the factory. This was good for Nike, since it could secure bigger production capabilities. And it was beneficial for retailers, and Eastbay, because we could have a steady stream of product coming in during the season. The sooner we ordered futures, the more we could get.

The risk to retailers and to us was that if you ordered too much, or the wrong stuff, you were stuck with it. Taking advantage of the futures system was a mixture of science and art, but as the catalog business grew, we thought we had another advantage over the traditional retailers. Our clinics and catalog sales—*going to* the customer—helped us get better insights faster about what people wanted, insights other retailers didn't have but ones that helped us make better bets.

Ken Effler of Nike team sales helped, too. We got the sense that he felt like we were a breath of fresh air. We had no use for the indulgent flattery that other companies seemed to want. We just wanted shoes quickly, so we could get them in and ship them out. We got the feeling that he thought we were doing right by Nike and that, as a former athlete himself, he thought we were doing right by the athletes and coaches. Plus, we took positions on large sizes, wide versions, and colors that others wouldn't.

We were selling to so many teams that Nike started rushing our orders—if we got them in before 2 p.m., he'd ship the same day, and that inventory would arrive from Nike's Memphis warehouse just three days later. We could guess how many pairs we would sell for a couple of days of clinics, then order replacement pairs from Effler almost daily. This gave us the opportunity to have pairs on hand as the catalog started eating up more of the inventory we'd previously earmarked for retail and clinic sales.

When the color options proliferated, though, the sheer variety made futures ordering trickier. In '86, for example, we went from twenty-seven options for Nike basketball shoes to sixty. But since we worked directly with schools, we could sort of predict color needs based on what school we'd be at. And we tracked sales daily to see what sold when and where and to whom. Our technology for this was legal pads, sharp pencils, and *big* erasers. Sales analysis was done by hand for thousands of orders across multiple sports.

The team-sales departments of all the shoe vendors were what allowed Eastbay, this capital-challenged company, to grow one of its most important advantages: well-managed inventory. Without that we couldn't have grown so fast or kept the doors open. It was a strategy that wouldn't have worked before, or after. Inventory has never flowed like that at any other moment in the sneaker business.

And we capitalized. One day, upon learning about our mail-order operation, the owner of the local Athlete's Foot franchise down the street told us, "You guys can't do this!" He came into the store and gawked at a huge rack of Air Jordans stacked against the wall, in all colors and sizes. He couldn't believe what he was looking at.

He told us we had more size 12s than he had Air Jordans, in all sizes and all colors, in his entire inventory.

18

Thank You for Your Patience

The excitement of sending shoes and apparel to thousands of customers a week gave us confidence and a profound sense of satisfaction and joy. We can see that now, anyway, in hindsight. But we're not sure that during that period we fully appreciated just what we were beginning to accomplish. We simply didn't have the time. We were constantly thinking, "If we're going to keep growing, then what else do we need to do?"

We knew that if we didn't figure out how to better handle the growth, then no amount of Air Jordan orders could save us—we were going to drown in the operational inefficiencies that our growth had exposed.

Our biggest operational issue was our *state-of-the-art* inventory tracking system, which worked like this: Someone would call in: "Do you have the Converse Fast Break with red trim in a men's 14?"

"Please hold."

Run to the basement with the flashlight. It was dark and dusty down there.

Locate the Fast Break in red, size 14.

Take them upstairs. "Yes, we have it. What is your address? ZIP code?"

"No, that's your area code, we need your ZIP code."

"Can I get your credit-card number? Thank you, please hold."

Pick up a second phone to call the credit-card company for authorization.

Receive authorization, complete the order form.

Take the shoes to the shipping area—a space in the back of the store.

That's a best-case scenario for an individual. Imagine when a coach called with 60 orders for football cleats.

Sometimes we wouldn't have a Converse Fast Break in red, size 14. So then:

"Sorry, we don't have that now. Are there other models you might like? Yes, a New Balance Worthy 740 would be a good alternative. Please hold."

Back down to the basement, and back up. And so on.

Some employees spent their entire days just making this run over and over. Luckily we had a lot of athletes on our team. One minute, on the phone speaking in inviting, warm, confident tones. "I'm sure we have that. Just give us a moment while we check our inventory." A minute later, back at the phone, sucking wind, gasping out "Sorry (pant) not (pant) in red. (Pant). We do have blue though. Or, yes (pant), I can check on the New Balance (pant). One moment please . . ."

One phrase was uttered more than any other on those calls: "Thank you for your patience."

By the end of the day, climbing back up from the basement felt like climbing a mountain.

The thing in that description about the area codes and ZIP codes was a real problem. Buying things over the phone was so new at the time that as much as we had to learn how to sell by phone, the people calling had to learn how to buy that way. They simply had never had to give out their address or credit-card number like that. One time, Art's brother-in-law Dave Molinaro was working phones for us over the summer. A young man called and ordered Jordans. Dave asked where to send the order to, meaning what town. The kid didn't really know what Dave meant, so he mumbled, "I dunno, deliver it to Michigan." Dave, assuming the kid was giving him an address heard, "Liver, Michigan." That's not a place, but that's where we sent the order.

The upshot of all this was that the system wasn't sustainable, wasn't scalable. "We were hand writing all of the orders," Jim Gering recalls. "Hell, we were hand writing everything." All our shipping manifest sheets, phone orders, customer database, inventory records, receipts, anything else you can think of—all of it was written down and stored in filing cabinets. "It was—not a complete mess, exactly, but, well, an organized mess."

We couldn't hire people fast enough to deal with the spikes in calls after a catalog landed in mailboxes. We couldn't keep up with the catalog requests or the phone orders or the returns. We couldn't handle it. We had to ramp up every aspect of the business any way we could. We needed more hours; nine to five became eight to six became seven to nine. We needed more catalogs with more pages, so we started planning an overhaul of the catalog.

We'd reached thousands of SKUs and were still using the basement and the store to hold it all. We needed more space, so we rented out two more buildings as warehouses. We needed people to staff all those warehouses and figure out, on the fly, a way to negotiate that complex network so that we could ship orders by 6 p.m. on the day they were placed, which would ensure our promised three-day delivery.

Don—Trebs, who by this time had become heavily involved in managing the shipping processes and order intake—decided to fix this, which we desperately needed. And he did not rest until he did fix it, with a gigantic, expensive, new-fangled piece of technology called a computer. It was a monster made by Sun Microsystems. Eight grand and the size of a refrigerator. Probably had less power than your watch. We hooked it up with some new software called MOME, for Mail Order Management Enterprises. Pronounced "mommy."

Mommy didn't do much more than create a name database but that was crucial as the business model evolved away from clinics and toward catalogs. It became a strategic priority to have names and addresses of customers and people who wanted our catalog all in one place.

Within a year Trebs came to the rescue again as we upgraded to custom software, built specifically for Eastbay by Al Langsenkamp's company Sigma Micro, automating a lot of what we had been doing by hand and hypercharging our capabilities, not the least of which was its ability to automatically verify credit-card information. Its inventory tracking was practically witchcraft compared with what we had been doing. No more running to the basement. No more calls on hold. Just tap a few keys and, "Yes, the Adidas Arrows size 9 are in stock." Maybe the athletes we hired weren't getting their workout in running back and forth between phone and basement, but it became the backbone of the business for the rest of the time we were there and beyond. Rick's brother

John joined to run our IT, and we kept updating the software to adapt to the business. Jim Gering would eventually use the computing power to develop his own system for tracking response rates on catalogs we sent out. We used his data to decide which people on the list should receive which season's catalog. Target marketing and list segmentation. For Eastbay it was brilliant; it cut costs without denting sales. Neat trick.

All of this sped up processing and improved customer service in ways we didn't think were possible before. We added more sports to each catalog. It sent us into another tornado of growth. Before the Air Jordans, we were under $500,000 in revenue. Three years later, after the Air Jordans, with the software in place, we passed $5 million.

We had completely outgrown the little Washington Street shop, and in the spring of 1987, we got to talking with Larry Niederhofer, who was part of a group that owned a gigantic three-story building on the corner of Third Street, at least three times the size of the Washington Street store. It had been a J.C. Penney until a few months prior. He was looking for new tenants. We wanted in.

Niederhofer didn't understand. He, like most of Wausau, harbored a healthy suspicion about our business, which was still the subject of rampant speculation. "He was just dismissive of the whole idea that these two guys could fill a building that big," says John Schaefer, a Neiderhofer employee at the time, and a friend of Tom and Jim Gering.

Niederhofer thought we were in over our heads, and he didn't want to do the lease. We pressed him, but he wasn't budging.

Art's father-in-law, Dr. Molinaro, happened to be a friend of the building owners. Doc Molinaro, you may recall, once tried to talk Art and Barb out of investing in Eastbay, telling Art he was foolish to give up his teaching and coaching career. He and Rick's dad would skulk around the storefront, pumping Polly for information on just how bad business was.

Doc Molinaro told Niederhofer and his partners to believe in us.

We got the lease.

19

Hitting Our Stride

The new headquarters relieved pressure, literally and figuratively.

It was big, filled with the electric sound of phones ringing one after another and people taking orders and hustling boxes of shoes from storage to shipping. There was a palpable sense of vitality and energy. The retail space was an open area in the middle that made a great humming sound when it was filled with families looking for shoes at the start of a season. Rick remembers the sound being like music good enough to back the Temptations. It also finally allowed us to set up dedicated spaces for all our departments. Buyers had a space, and so did customer service, sitting alongside a space for the creative and graphics team. We had taken design of the catalog in-house, perhaps emboldened by Apple's desktop publishing software. We'd seen what computers could do for operations, and we thought that they might be able to cut our costs and improve the catalog, too.

We put ourselves on the other end of this huge building. This limited our micromanagement, as we couldn't possibly run back and forth across the building and up and down stairs all day.

Doc Molinaro and Rick's dad, Cliff, kept coming into the store, but they weren't there to look for signs of imminent collapse anymore. Rick's dad knew they weren't toast. "They'd come in and just want to feel the buzz of it all," Polly says. "Things really got moving and grooving. By then, they knew—it was going to be special. The buzz was unbelievable."

We kept growing. The landlord had been worried the space was too big for us, but it wasn't long before we needed a bigger call center, so we rented one of the empty shops next-door, busted a hole in the wall, and put the call center over there. Problem solved, for now.

We got Maddie Opal to join us in that new call center. She was a local track and basketball star now in her early twenties whom we knew as a flower delivery woman who came by in a converted mail truck painted pink. Her friendliness was fantastic and contagious, and we loved how, even on the phone, you could hear a smile in her voice. We offered her a job working the phones, and we're lucky and grateful she said yes.

We gave her an accidentally unpleasant welcome, though. On her first day, she returned from lunch and sat down at her desk and gagged. "What *is* that *smell*?" she asked.

Rick's future sister-in-law Shelley was working the phones and pointed to a corner cubicle full of sweat-drenched T-shirts and shorts from the noon run, which by this time included a dozen or more people. "That's what happens," Shelley told her. "You'll get used to it."

It wasn't enough to knock the smile out of Maddie's voice, who was brilliant at customer service. "It's really about just being who you are, just being happy and being there for the customer," Maddie says. "Sometimes, you can be there but not really be *there,* be in tune with that customer. I would share that in training constantly—be in tune—because you can *hear* but not *listen.* That, and never, ever overpromise and then underdeliver. That's where we had challenges with Eastbay." She laughs. She means we were too good at *overdelivering.* "We would give away the store. And the thing is, that's not always what the customer actually wants when they call you with a problem. They want us to resolve their problem, right there on that call. I'd call it first-call resolution. That's what it's all about—that's what they want. 'Resolve my issue. And do it in a way that I don't have to keep calling back.'"

By '89 she was running the entire call center.

Everything felt slightly less chaotic than it had at the old store, but people were working as hard as ever. Trebs recalls Rick's brother Jim "working until ten-thirty at night sometimes taking phone calls. Art and I talked to him once. 'Jimmy, do you want to work this late?' And he said, 'What else I got to do?'"

People like Shelley and Jim, doing what they *wanted* to be doing, they were part of the reason that Eastbay continued growing so well. Another longtime employee, Don Baptist, recalls, "It was about recognizing what people were great at and letting them do it."

For example, it was around this time that Rick's brother Tom and another longtime Eastbayer, Tim Strohkirch, replaced us as buyers. Tom would buy for track and football and Tim for basketball and wrestling. The options for buying were exploding. The Olympics were coming, so we knew the track business was going to spike, and the team colors for basketball were a massive job to manage. We had become excellent inventory bettors, so it was a big deal for us to give that over, to let go even that little bit. Of course, they turned out to be excellent buyers.

When you like what you're doing, you have fun doing it. We all certainly had fun. In the warehouse, batched orders for shipping came in with such frequency that to save a few minutes, staffers wouldn't bother with finding ladders. They'd just climb the metal shelving units and toss the boxes down, OSHA regulations be damned. You'd see someone digging through Nike boxes hanging off the top of a rack twelve feet up, and they'd look over and wave at someone else doing the same on the New Balance rack.

And while you were climbing or doing anything else in the warehouse for that matter, everyone had to be on guard for spontaneous squirt-gun battles. We got into it, scrambling for cover, diving behind desks and shelves, sourcing hidden weapons stashes. We, the company owners, would walk in to discover our entire warehouse staff engaged in epic squirt-gun warfare. And we did the responsible thing, grabbing the nearest squirt gun we could find—there was an alarming ease of access to squirt guns in that warehouse, now that we think about it—and leaping into the fray.

"That was probably the single biggest, most important thing about Eastbay, especially at that time," Polly says. "So many lifelong friendships came out of that time of the company. We just had *fun,* man. We were always working. We knew how to get stuff done. And we did. But we loved to play, too."

We even found a way to make otherwise mind-numbing work such as quarterly inventory checks fun, by supplementing them with endless deliveries of pizzas and beers right to the people in the shelves doing all that tedious counting. Sometime later, you might climb a rack for some Adidas Forums and find the odd slice left behind.

When you're living this, you take it for granted. Especially if you've never really worked in another setting for a long time. We just thought this is what work *was*. We recognize in retrospect as we recount these fond memories that this was a lightning-in-a-bottle experience that not everyone gets—when good timing, good business, and good people come together and make something special. As fondly as many look back on the catalog today, that's how we think about being there in the office making it.

Things couldn't have been going better, and we were starting to feel like nothing could stop us. We had our ongoing stresses about catalog development and inventory flow and staffing, but in general, we felt great. We felt like you do on a run when you catch your second wind and are carried along with an effortlessness that makes you feel like you could run a thousand miles.

One afternoon in late 1988, we were back at the old Washington Street store cleaning out the last of what was left over there. Three men walked in. We'd never seen them before, but we knew they were deeply serious by the look on their faces and by their slick, combed-back haircuts, and most of all because they were wearing suits.

One was a Nike Vice President of Who Even Remembers. The other two were lawyers from a large firm representing Nike.

How can we help you?

The conversation was brief and cordial, but tense: Nike was removing its entire line of Air products from all companies selling through the mail. That included us. Well, that was *mostly* us. This visit was our official notice that Nike would stop sending us Nike Air products and we were to stop selling all Nike Air products, including Air Jordans by mail.

We had just moved from this humble little grease-stained storefront we were standing in to a massive new headquarters and operations center and retail store, with its commensurately massive rent. We had blown out walls to expand the space. We had pulled catalog creative in-house and expanded the catalog's size and the number we printed so we could send it to all fifty states. The mailing list was growing massively in part due to the insatiable demand for Nike Airs. Nike Air was a regular on the cover, and it often took up the first pages of product listings. We had hit our stride, feeling carried along. And now . . .

Even today, we can easily recall the intense panic, and sadness, and anger we felt, but we forced ourselves to keep that under control in the moment. *Don't burn a bridge with Nike.*

Still, we were confused and, truthfully, terrified. Why was Nike doing this, and without any warning or attempt to negotiate? What were we going to do? What if other shoe companies did the same thing?

We knew our customers and our staff would be confused, and that felt devastating, too. Our business was about to take an enormous blow.

Nike Air made up about 40 percent of our revenue.

20

Taking the Air Out of the Building

Art immediately remembered Memphis, and the good ol'-boy network he encountered there. He thought about trade shows in Chicago and Atlanta, where we began feeling like the black sheep of the shoe business. We'd hear chatter about how retailers and vendors didn't like what we were capable of doing. Years later, we'd find out that what felt like idle gossip to us was deep frustration, even hatred of Eastbay among retailers and vendors.

The unrest seemed to have started, ironically, not with the catalog. It started with ads that we ran in *Runner's World* magazine—something we did for years to get names and addresses and goose sales in between sports seasons. Fairly simple lists on top models and discount prices.

The ads touched a nerve, though we weren't sure why. At the time, we sensed that Nike and the retailers just saw a successful, fast-growing operation that they didn't yet understand. They didn't understand our model of going directly to coaches and athletes, or its potential for future growth. (Again, we must ask you to scrub your minds of what you've come to assume over the past thirty years about how we all buy things like sneakers. In 1988, you mostly sold stuff in retail stores. Any other business model was unusual; in sneakers, any other model was unheard of.) And what executives don't understand or control, they tend to fear.

We suspect now, too, that the vendors and retailers were lumping us in with a few shady renegades in the mail-order world who had emerged using dubious business practices. They'd buy Nike Airs on the black market and then resell them at a discount, through small ads in the back of magazines—the same place we ran our ads.

We hope that by now you know that we were *not that.* But we suppose that back then, to Nike, we were all just *mail order* that made Nike look bad. The company was cultivating a premium public image. Even by controlling inventory using the scarcity model, it wanted to convey how special its shoes were, hard to get, top of the line. Mail order diluted its brand. When the Nike delegation came to Wausau they said as much, telling us we made their Nike Air shoes look ordinary.

We puzzled together what we thought was the reason they made this rash dictate. Cutting us off would let Nike hit pause, take a step back, and figure out just what the hell we were up to, what this business model was all about. Then the company could decide whether it wanted to partner with us, maybe buy us. That was our optimistic view. In darker moments, our pessimistic view was that it was a siege to put us out of business.

Today, as we reflect on everything, we can see the company's perspective. For one thing, Nike was navigating its first slip-up in a while. Here's how *Fortune* magazine described it in August 1987:

> Nike . . . has been dethroned by Reebok, which took over the No. 1 spot in domestic athletic shoe sales last year. Nike almost completely misread the evolving aerobics craze. Sneaker buyers became more interested in style and comfort, characteristics they identified with Reebok, not Nike. Only the spectacular success of Nike's Air Jordan shoe has kept the company from losing even more ground.[1]

Michael Jordan was on his way to legend status, and his Nike team had crafted the perfect shoe and marketing plan around the burgeoning star. They had a deep sense for what they wanted their Air brand to become, what it needed to become to stave off Reebok's insurgence and challenge Adidas for top shoe brand in the world. The Jordans were *crucial* to Nike not losing even more ground than it had, so it makes sense that the company would want to protect that at all costs. The Nike team was as convinced about what they were doing as we were about what we were doing. Only, those two things were out of alignment.

It made sense to us that retailers might loathe us. We were their direct competition, and we were much better at getting kids the shoes they wanted in the sizes and styles they wanted at a better price. It made less sense, however, that a shoe company might loathe us. Even though we were small relative to some of those retailers, we felt like Nike could appreciate what we had to offer its Nike Air line: Steady business. Big inventory bets. If the company had wanted us to do something differently, we could have had those conversations, but it didn't go that way. The company's first move was to destroy our bottom line to start that discussion. We heard later that some inside Nike were against the move.

Even today, we think Nike could have handled it differently. At the time we felt bullied, and we still feel that it could have treated us with more respect and consideration. It was devastating. But we weren't entirely without fault either. We were naive. We didn't play the game. We'd show up at trade shows the way we showed up to work: in shorts and T-shirts. We were happy and confident about the fact that we were the only ones doing what we did, and about the fact that it was *working.* It seemed *easy* to us, and we didn't understand how no one else got it. We thought at the time we had to build the catalog, and the industry veterans might see us and think, *Those guys aren't serious. Those are the mail-order guys that advertise discounts in the back of magazines.*

The irony was striking: Nike had built a nearly billion-dollar business based on this premium product that kids couldn't wait to get their hands on. We were experiencing massive and explosive growth, albeit on a smaller scale than that of Nike, helping kids get their hands on those premium products, kids like we had once been, who *couldn't* get them before *Eastbay* made it easier. Nike seemed to us to value perception of its brand in *Eastbay* over sales of its product in *Eastbay.* It was easy for a company Nike's size to forgo a few million in Air Jordan sales to protect itself; it was an existential threat to us.

We didn't really know what Nike's issue truly was. Maybe it was their perception of mail order. Maybe it was team discounts, but we were at a loss. We obviously couldn't stop mail order. We could offer the Air line at suggested retail price—if Nike would even let us do that, we didn't know—

but that felt like a betrayal of the reason we started Eastbay. Rick felt particularly strong about maintaining team pricing. If we sold at suggested retail price, he'd say, then we lost part of what we were as a company, and perhaps even sacrificed a part of our souls. And he meant it. We'd always based our pricing on team-sales discounts, but we'd grown so fast we never stopped to think about the growing chunk of customers who were buying as individuals. We didn't have time to stop and think about it.

All we knew was Nike was holding firm: No mail-order company would be able to sell Nike Air, period. We could sell them in our retail location, and we could keep selling Nike's non-Air products in the catalog, like track spikes, football cleats, and other shoes. Nike wasn't completely cutting us off. It was just cutting off the mail-order business model from Nike's top products—the ones it needed in its fight against Reebok and Adidas. We felt totally lost.

We'd need another new business plan. We hoped to figure out a way to get Nike Air products back, but we knew that was going to be a long road with no guaranteed success. We began loading up our Nike Air inventory to ship back to Beaverton, and we began laying the groundwork to do whatever we could to absorb the blow.

The annual tent sale, which had become a happening in Wausau, momentarily put smiles back on our faces. It was our biggest tent sale yet. A line wrapped all throughout downtown Wausau, more than a mile long, hours before we opened. Ten thousand people came, some from Chicago and Milwaukee, and Iowa and Ohio. Opening was like the running of the bulls, with people crashing into tables, shoving each other, and tossing boxes to find the size and style they wanted. There was an electric joy in the air, palpable and invigorating.

Rick got so caught up in it that he brought out boxes and boxes of just-arrived Adidas Adilettes, iconic slide sandals, one of the products we'd argued about how many we should order back when every inventory decision was make-or-break.

"Rick!" Art yelled. "Those aren't supposed to be at the tent sale!"

"But look how happy they're making people!"

Discount chaos reigned—it was beautiful free-for-all for four days. We messed up traffic in Wausau, too. The chief of police, the fire chief, *and* the mayor came by and told us we'd have to find somewhere else to do this next time. Then they started rifling through the shoes to buy some for themselves and their families.

Art's other brother-in-law Tom believed that Nike couldn't just pull Air Jordans from *Eastbay*. This would be an unremarkable note were it not for the fact that Tom was also a lawyer, and Tom knew the Wisconsin Fair Dealership Law, the WFDL. According to the State Bar of Wisconsin's website: "The WFDL greatly circumscribes the ability of a *grantor* to alter its relationship with a dealer, even in difficult economic times. A grantor must have good cause to make any substantial change in the competitive circumstances of the relationship, and the change must be essential, reasonable, and nondiscriminatory."[2]

Here was hope. From our side, everything about what Nike was doing appeared nonessential, unreasonable, and discriminatory. Tom believed that we might have a case to sue Nike for the right to continue selling its Air products.

The last thing we wanted to do was sue Nike. Lawsuits are expensive and time consuming, we had little spare cash on hand, and what we did have needed to be poured into inventory to replace the Nike Airs. But we thought that if we properly invoked the WFDL, we had a strong and pretty straightforward case, and we should give it a shot. Even if we somehow lost, it would feel good to be doing something about the situation. We'd fight. This would be like when we were kids, scrounging through the trash for wheels to put on our go-karts, taking on the older, bigger kids in the neighborhood. Only now, it wasn't just the two of us. Now, we had a whole team of people working with us that we wanted to, needed to, take care of.

There was one other immediate and major benefit from filing the lawsuit: an injunction. Nike could not stop us from selling Nike Airs, or loading up on inventory, until a judge ruled in Nike's favor. That would likely take six months or more.

We filed our lawsuit and then ordered all the Airs we could afford. Someone from Nike called. "You realize," they said, "that if you lose this case, then you'll be left with all this product and nothing to do with it?"

Well, we said, good thing we don't plan on losing.

21

Just Delusional Enough

The next six months were a dark and anxious time. Often, Art would wake up in the middle of the night covered in sweat, with his heart pounding and mind racing, wondering what would happen if we lost.

To deal with the constant stress, we did all we knew how to do, which was to keep working. Keep moving forward. We maintained our routines. We still went on our runs every day at noon, though they'd gotten a bit more tense, with a turbulent undercurrent of existential crisis. The runs often would ebb and flow. Art ran slower than Rick, so when we were talking about business sometimes, we'd have a runner pull up to get some message from Rick to Art, drop back to convey that message, and then speed back up to relay what Art's reply was, or vice versa. If we really needed to talk, everyone would slow down to Art's pace.

At this time those runs focused on how to square the loss of nearly half our revenue with all the investments we'd made. We had a big new headquarters and warehouse, and with that some new and larger bills. We had young families, and young children now—Rick had a daughter, Elizabeth, and a newborn son, Tommy. Art had Jessica and James, and another, Jenna, on the way. And we had all the people who worked with us to think about.

We tried to focus on other positives that maybe wouldn't have registered as much if we could still lean on the Nike Air. For example, we were noticing how many good products were coming from all the other vendors that we thought we could sell.

We flew to Beaverton, Oregon, Nike's turf, to give depositions, which themselves were uneventful, just a few hours of answering questions about our business practices, our relationship with Nike over the years, how we had developed the catalog, what our plans were moving forward. And that was mostly it. All we could do then was wait for the case to be heard by the judge. We didn't even have to be in court for that. The legal process was on one level unsettling, almost offensive given the stakes for us. We were standing up for ourselves on a matter that could change the entire course of our business and our lives. But on another level the entire process was banal, and we were hardly present for it. There would be no cinematic courtroom testimony, no cross-examining of Goliath, who was trying to take half of David's business; no thunderous and self-righteous proclamations of truth, justice, and the American way. There were depositions and there was paperwork, and then there was waiting.

Thankfully, our next annual tent sale again provided a bright spot and a much needed sense of creative novelty. Having been kicked out of downtown the year before, we moved it to Marathon Park, a two-hundred-acre expanse that turned out to be perfectly situated near a highway that brought in out-of-towners and made the event bigger than ever. We filled a hockey rink with tables piled with tens of thousands of pairs of shoes, excellent shoes, most priced between $5 and $25. The point of the sale was always to clear out inventory and prepare for new models coming in, a way to deal with the downsides of mail order: returns and excess inventory. For the tent sale, coaches who lived hundreds of miles apart coordinated their arrival times so they could meet while they were in Wausau. We gave employees and coaches early access, and they'd load up. Sneakerheads, if they were there, would have been torn. On the one hand, they could *find stuff* here—cool shoes, old models, rare colors—and they could grab that stuff for a tiny fraction of what they were used to paying in the collector's market. On the other hand, there were no boxes, and throngs of people were pawing the shoes and tossing them around. They weren't necessarily mint condition.

Some people stopped at the tent sale as part of their summer vacation. Others used it to buy all the running shoes they'd need for the year. The mayor, police chief, and fire chief paid us a visit, and thanked us for sparing downtown.

We noticed kids, ten years old, eleven years old, searching feverishly for a cheap pair of Adidas Rivalries or Converse Weapons and so many others. When they found them, they'd light up as if one of Santa's elves had personally handed them something plucked straight from their dreams. And then we'd see the kids' moms and dads light up in the same way when they looked at the price tag in rapturous disbelief. We'd notice their shoulders relax, a weight lifted, tears because they could get their kid the Air Jordans after all. For us, the joy that made us feel never got old. Every time it happened it felt kind of like we were the ones getting those shoes when we were kids; that it was our Christmas in July.

For a few days in Marathon Park, all the Nike Air stress faded away, and it again reinforced why we needed to fight for what we believed in.

We've learned that what makes a good entrepreneur succeed is that they're just clueless enough and just delusional enough to believe that any idea they have can and should work. If they just throw all that they have at it, everything will work out. In some ways, good entrepreneurs are naive, at least in the beginning.

But that mindset can work against you when it's coupled with inexperience. And in this case, taking on a behemoth like Nike, well, we received an enormous dose of . . . *experience.*

We assumed—and here was the naive part—that because we were, by all accounts and through all manner of logic and reason, on the right side of the law, we should have little issue proving our case.

Nike, meanwhile, found and retained one of the top law firms in Wisconsin. Its lead attorney was a Wisconsin native who also happened to be one of the lawyers who, years prior, wrote a book about the Wisconsin Fair Dealership Law. The law we were citing.

We were told that the judge assigned to the case had a reputation for being big-business friendly. We knew he would be hard-pressed to rule against a quintessentially American success story like Nike, one that we admired ourselves. Phil Knight had gone from selling shoes out of the back of his car to building an empire. Nike's aura was that of conquering, of winning, through hard work. From the perspective of an old-school conservative judge, we could easily be seen as a freewheeling and immature operation that was glomming onto Nike's success.

Sometime near the start of the summer of 1988, the judge made his decision. Art's brother-in-law Tom came to the office. He didn't have to say anything. We knew it as soon as he walked in, slumped in his suit. He apologized for failing us, but we weren't having it. None of us knew what we were getting into when the legal business began and sitting here second-guessing wouldn't change anything.

To give ourselves a few more months, we appealed the case, this time retaining a large firm from Milwaukee. We made it to the fall of 1988 and squeaked out a thirty-two-page back-to-school catalog that year that included the Air line, including the Air Revolution and the Air Jordan 3. But the Milwaukee firm fared no better. In another wild coincidence, the lawyer we were assigned was also the attorney who'd edited the book that Nike's attorney had written about the WFDL. We were forced to accept the terrible truth that we'd lost the Air line for good.

And we still had so much of it: The Air Jordan 1, the AJ2 and AJ3. New, in-demand Air Max Air Assaults popularized by ascending rapper and actor Will Smith. There were Air Windrunners and Air Trainer 1s and the Air Walker Maxes.

We had so many Nike Air shoes in our unheated warehouses where, on a frigid Wisconsin winter day after the verdict, some Nike guys in suits walked through the racks, counting the inventory. We felt the shock and grief crash hard on us. We could see where the market was going and to this day, Rick gets upset thinking about how we were put in a position to miss out on the exciting things happening in the shoe business. There were new styles, there was new tech, and there was new, cool marketing coming for shoes like the Air Max 1, one of the most exciting shoes we had seen. But we were caught in a pickle. We wanted to get Nike back, but we were committed to the business model that drove Nike away.

We also felt another immediate, hot fear: Precedent was set. Asics could do this. Or Reebok. Or New Balance. Or Adidas. Any of them. Or all of them.

22

Rollerblades and Jogbras

In our 1988 basketball-season catalog, we wrote:

> Dear Valued Customer:
>
> Over the past few months, there may have been confusion over the availability of Nike Air products from Eastbay.
>
> At this time, Nike Inc. will not allow us to make their Air product available to you through the mail. Although we are disappointed with Nike's decision, we can offer you the non-Air Nike products along with the Aerospike and Stamina, as well as a wide range of highly technical products from other companies that meet our high standards for performing athletes.
>
> Be assured that Eastbay will offer you the same quality service and product knowledge and our famous Eastbay guarantee on all the products we continue to sell.
>
> If you would like Nike to reconsider its policy, please feel free to write us here at Eastbay and we will forward your letter to Nike.
>
> Sincerely,
>
> THE STAFF AT EASTBAY

People always talk about how the worst things that happened to them helped them become the best version of themselves—and that would be true for Eastbay—but they never mention how terrifying it is in between those two end points. Fear is a hell of a fuel. Devastated and uncertain, with no clear vision for how to move forward from this, we couldn't turn our work brains off after we left the office for the day. We were stressed, minds never at rest. Rick remembers that we were spending less time together in the odd hours we weren't working, sometimes going home to deal with the stress ourselves, just relieved not to have to talk about the Nike problem for a while. It would have been even worse if our wives, Barb and Sue, weren't so supportive and so good at knowing when to ask questions and when to give us space. They kept life feeling normal on the outside even if we were complete wrecks on the inside.

The office became a war room to strategize on how to recover. Maybe we'd lost Nike Air, and maybe we now had to live forever in fear of other companies doing the same thing to us, but what we could do, what we could control, was to hold true to our vision and get better at mail order.

Karla Turzinski, who helped manage the call center operation, recalls that, "It seemed like every other call was about Air Jordans." So, we had people answering the phone keep a dedicated notepad for tracking every time someone called asking about any Nike Air products. We wanted that data.

Our first maneuver: Make new bets on new products. This seemed to go directly against the intelligent businessperson's playbook, which told us to just circle the wagons and pull back, save every penny possible.

We didn't. We expanded inventory and depleted our remaining cash flow to do it.

The catalog shifted focus to Reebok, Adidas, Converse, Puma, Asics, Saucony, and more—we doubled and tripled down on them. We filled our warehouses with more aerobic shoes. Those had helped push Nike out of the number one position, after all. More trainers, more apparel, and anything else that helped us fill the catalog, which we had expanded to thirty-two pages or more, depending on the season.

The new strategy wasn't pure lunacy. We were aware, even as we went through the lawsuit process, that the ongoing sneaker wars meant other shoe companies had seen what Reebok had exploited. It had gone on the offensive against Nike, tapping into the NBA's growing popularity. Many of these efforts looked like cousins of the Air Jordan 1, such as Reebok's Commitment, a boot-like design endorsed by Danny Manning, who'd won the NCAA championship with Kansas and then joined the Los Angeles Clippers as the first overall pick in the 1988 NBA draft.

Converse had released a similar shoe in 1988 called the ERX-400. It was a high-tech design with an array of vents and a big belt-like strap around a high leather upper. Stitched across that was the word that would become its identity: *CONS*. It was an outlandish design, and a lot of NBA players began to wear it, though none of the superstars did. Magic Johnson did modify his Converse Weapon Player Exclusives to resemble the Cons, adding a strap at the top and some less gaudy vents throughout.

Adidas got back in it with the Rivalry, which was connected with superstar power forward Patrick Ewing of the New York Knicks, archrivals to Michael Jordan and his Chicago Bulls. More black shoes and team-colored shoes followed.

Okay, what else can we sell? we kept asking. We turned to other sports. We added more baseball cleats and bats and gloves, over time going from carrying a couple of each to a couple dozen of each. We added more training gear, volleyball gear, anything that we thought might appeal to young athletes. We loved shoes, and shoes were why we had gotten into this business, and we would be shoe guys forever, but all this other inventory was necessary to keep us afloat. If we couldn't help you run to first base with Nike Air cleats, at least we could help you crush the ball with one of several aluminum Easton bats.

And here the people we hired, our team, were heroes. We had feared at the time that many employees would leave Eastbay. Any time a company is cut in half overnight, surely people will worry about their job security, or simply walk away, believing their employer's luck had run out.

But the Eastbay team didn't bail, and we wouldn't bail on them. We've always thought one of the best moves we ever made was hiring a bunch of athletes to work for us, because they understand teamwork and they like to hustle, and they know how to get things done, even when the score is dire. But here they offered more than we ever imagined they could.

We believe to this day that hiring athletes was crucial to our success. Sports and business aren't so different, and that goes beyond the simple idea that you either succeed or fail. For both, you need to build a great team. You need people who can work as a team, and who can perform under stress. People who've learned to deal with losing and who can come back better after. The mindset of the athlete is precisely what we needed as we emerged without Nike Air.

We had hired former stars in track, basketball, football, soccer, baseball, shot put, javelin, even cross-country skiing. We gave them a simple task: Figure out where we can buy all the stuff *you* would want. Buy the inventory. Fill the warehouses.

We had only the roughest of market research. Again, savvier businessmen would've made different choices. But we had our gut instincts, and those instincts were telling us what we knew from our experience: People *loved* the catalog. And we made the conscious effort to always include new products in every catalog. Most catalogers, if they're sending catalogs every month or six weeks, would just flip sections of the catalog around to make it look like new. Even in later years when we were producing a catalog every month, we'd always find something new to put in there. It was a huge credit to our buyers that they could continually find new things that kids wanted, and our graphics department would find ways to constantly redesign pages for the new products.

We printed *more* catalogs and expanded as planned to all fifty states. We found names and addresses for coaches across the country and sent as many catalogs to as many of them as we could afford. Coaches would leave the catalogs out for kids, who would call to place an order and then sign up for the catalog themselves. We removed that "Don't Call for Catalog" line, finally. The list grew.

The Christmas '88 catalog was a turning point, our most ambitious edition to date. With it, we shifted to a more connected and personal tone, trying to come off as more than just a place to shop an endless array of options. This was one of our earliest swings at creating personality, an attitude with the catalog.

The cover featured a couple of young women who worked for us sitting in our store with a wall of shoes behind them, surrounded by boxes and apparel strewn about. They're holding shoes and talking to Santa, who sits in a chair holding a massive list. For some reason, Santa's wearing black Rollerblades with red wheels, matching his suit.

It was forty pages. We opened with a full-page spread of pictures: people working the phones, with catalogs spread across a table behind them, more employees passing massive stacks of shoeboxes, a shot of the retail store, and a nice shot of the old Washington Street storefront. Text weaving throughout the pictures told our story:

> The business began . . . out of a basement. Using an old car as a delivery truck, we traveled with our shoes to many schools, clinics and races.
>
> Having been in your shoes (pardon the pun), we know you need it fast, so we stock and ship accordingly.
>
> We stock over 100,000 pairs of shoes. We offer all team colors, A through EEEE widths, in all sizes including Men's from 6–18 and Women's from 4–12. We've got the shoe you're looking for.
>
> The basement has become a computerized customer service and distribution center; the old car has been replaced by Eastbay vans and hundreds of UPS trucks; yet our goals remain the same. We want you to get the right shoes, to get them quickly, and to be satisfied with your purchase.

As we proofed that edition of the catalog, we felt like it could still spark that joy, that loyalty and sense of possibility for kids even without Nike Air. We opened with Adidas:

> **ADIDAS FORUM**
>
> Sz: 6–13, 14, 15. 18 oz. Soft full-grain leather for comfort and strength. Extra toe rubber for those who drag their feet. Unique figure eight ankle strap for super support. Foam midsole wrapped by the patented Dellinger Web for great cushioning. Reg $110. **Eastbay $94.95.**

We had Avia 880, Avia 840, Avia 822. Converse Cons. Converse Fast Break (men's and women's). Converse Weapons. Reebok Commitment and Reebok Integrity and Reebok Breakaway. New Balance NB 800 and

NB 700. Brooks Highlight. Etonic Evolution I and Etonic Dream. Pony Specialist. Kaepa Jam Series and Kaepa Vertical Series.

And gear. Adidas duffel bags, Nike Gore-Tex beanies and mittens, Tru-Fit knee sleeves and ankle braces, brands that supported Eastbay throughout this time. There was the Jogbra. And spandex running shorts.

We added a Leisure section with Rollerblades (*that* explains Santa's footwear) and walking shoes and hiking boots from Nike and Reebok. There were Eastbay private label T-shirts.

Variety wasn't going to be a problem without Nike Air. We just weren't sure if variety could make up for lost Nike Air sales. We thought it could. We were finding out if it could. In many ways, this period, this next business strategy, could be summed up in one word: Testing. We were testing inventory bets, testing catalog ideas, testing which equipment to carry. Test, succeed, push the envelope. Over and over, until we had a massive breadth of products.

Do not mistake this newfound energy for some kind of peace. As we said, fear is a hell of a fuel, and we were afraid every day, not knowing if we were buying the right stuff. Not knowing if what people really loved about *Eastbay* was just Nike Air. Not knowing if a couple more lawyers would walk through the door and take another 20 percent of our business away.

Many days, we would find ourselves double- and triple-guessing inventory bets on this order of Mizuno baseball gloves or that order of running tights. Should we add more Rollerblades? Will anyone buy the training shoes with the funny soles?

We had each other, and that helped us with the stress. If you're going to deal with the level of anxiety we'd had at several times with the business, whether it was when we had no customers and drew $5 a week in the early '80s or trying to recover from Nike's blow in the late '80s, having someone right there who knows what it feels like, then turning that fear into problem-solving together, helped so much. That's also why we'd run every day—to hold moving meetings.

And every time, every single time, pulling on the running shoes and hitting the road, feeling the steady thud-thud-thud of rubber on pavement beneath our feet, feeling the burn in our legs and our lungs like a warming fire, feeling the sun and the sweat and the crisp Wisconsin air pumping in and out of our lungs—every time, putting some miles under our feet eased the stress, released the anxiety, cleared the fog, even if only a little, even if only briefly.

We leaned on our noon runs. They didn't solve our problems, but they cleared our minds enough for us to work with our team to dream up solutions.

And you know, when we reflect long enough on that time, we know there were some days, too, when it didn't feel so awful. Reps for other companies came through Wausau with cool new shoes. The team remained so impressive through this hardest time.

Many of them would go to a bar downtown for drinks together on Friday nights. Now and again, we'd go along. And quite often, even in those dark days after Nike did what it did, one of us would look at the other and say something like, "Boy, even if we're not making any money, we're still having fun." We meant it, but maybe also we were trying to convince ourselves.

23

A Year without Air

You trust your instincts. You make bets. You work. Sometimes you hold your breath. Then all you can do is wait for results.

And our first year without Nike Air, 1989, turned out to be nowhere near as bad as we had feared. The gut-instinct strategy—more inventory, plenty of testing, better catalog, a team that just wouldn't quit on the game—managed to get us to about $18 million in revenue that year, making up *almost* everything that Nike had taken out.

Our worst fears had been alleviated. We saw a steady uptick in sales across the new inventory we'd ordered, and we saw the black-and-white Adidas Rivalry, Patrick Ewing's shoe, become our bestselling basketball shoe.

The Christmas '88 catalog experiment emboldened us. Starting in '89 we would push the catalog even further.

We also began experimenting with Eastbay private-label apparel. Although we'd slipped some products with our logo on them into a previous catalog, our 1989 Fast Break Back-to-School catalog felt like the true debut of Eastbay clothes, as we also debuted a new logo: a weathered circle with *EASTBAY* curving over the top and *ATHLETICS* the bottom, with a weathered star in between. We sold T-shirts, team-colored basketball apparel, tearaway pants, duffel bags, and more.

EASTBAY SHOOTING SHIRT

100% polyester. Our *Eastbay* Shooting Shirt has all the features you've been asking for! Deep armholes and loose sleeves

> make for tremendous freedom to move—the open bottom means it won't ride up! You'll not only look great but be comfortable too! Match the shirt with pants or wear separately—either way you'll love both pieces! Made in the USA. **Eastbay $29.95**

They'd be consistently reliable sellers well into the late nineties, as would Eastbay T-shirts with various slogans on them that we started selling in the nineties. A longtime Eastbayer, Susan Peloquin, remembers the team going for drinks at a close-by bar and brainstorming ideas for slogans on T-shirts, which always sold well:

> If you want to play, practice (front), If you want to win, practice harder (back)
>
> When a dunk is worth 3, I'll start doing it
>
> Pain is temporary, Pride is forever
>
> Softball Math: 6 + 4 + 3 = 2
>
> No Whining

We got more creative with the catalog covers, creating a kind of *Eastbay* sensibility that would develop over the years into a unique voice and become part of what made kids love the catalog so much. One of our favorite Christmas designs was white, showing just tracks in the snow. The tracks weren't from boots. They were from basketball shoes and baseball cleats. It was our White Album.

Giving the catalog more of a voice seemed to be working. Demand surged, and we noticed that our response rates from rural and remote areas were extremely high. It wasn't just Nike Air, after all, that made kids want *Eastbay*. It was access to this *world*, and the more kids saw it, the more they wanted it. Even today we hear stories from fans of the feeling they got running to the mailbox to see if *Eastbay* had arrived. The giddy pleasure of getting mail with your own name on it. What would the cover be this time? The lost hours spent flipping through it, drooling over the new models. Circling the shoes you wanted, dog-earing pages with the colors you couldn't believe were there. Showing it off at the lunch table. Once a kid had *Eastbay* in their hands, it opened a world to them that they'd dreamed about and created a bond that we didn't think the shoe companies or retailers, smart as they were, really understood.

We had evidence, too. By the end of 1989, despite no Nike Air listings, we'd received *one million* new catalog requests.

Reebok, Asics, Adidas, and New Balance became our largest vendors. Reebok had a cool line of casual shoes called Classics, along with a technical high-top called the Freestyle that looked best in near-all-black with a white sole. Reebok was also making more moves back into basketball with its Royal Highs, and it would soon release a brand-new line of Reebok Pumps, the shoes you could inflate with a round rubber pump on the tongue until it felt snug. New Balance started breaking new ground, too, with the debut of the all-white P550 Basketball Oxford, a low-top alternative amid a sea of high-tops. The more our buyers looked around, the more we realized there was so much more than Nike Air to offer young athletes. We found a pair of all-white Varsity brand cheerleading shoes that sold well. We were surprised by how well hiking boots and casual shoes moved, and the licensed team clothing was hot, too.

No single product or product line could replace what we'd lost, but every Varsity cheering shoe, every New Balance P550, every Starter jacket that did well, helped to fill the gaping hole left by Nike Air.

The orders started pouring in again. First slowly, and then much, much faster. As we entered the '90s, we'd fully absorbed Nike's body blow and yet again found ourselves growing faster than ever before—30 percent!

This unexpected growth spurt pushed us, again, to our operational limits. We needed to ramp up, again, on hiring, training, logistics, everything. We needed ample cash reserves, or at least larger lines of credit from bigger banks than we were used to dealing with. We didn't know how to acquire that kind of credit, let alone manage it.

Being an entrepreneur is one thing, a businessman another, and we were beginning to suspect that we might need some help with the latter.

Art and the buyers took a class in inventory control and merchandising. Then we hired our professor from that class. Then we found out that professors are in academia for a reason. Rick's brother Tom Gering took it over and did much better.

The growth was just astonishing, even without the most popular line of shoes on the planet in the catalog. We had reached—really, we had gone beyond—the point where we thought we could get. But that only emboldened us. Our vision for the business continued to grow to a point far past our capacity to make it a reality. If we were going to stay on the rocket ride, we needed more help. We needed to help Eastbay grow up.

PART FOUR

Growing Up

24

SWOT

Ask our wives: Our maturity levels, and our management capabilities, had a ceiling, and we were fairly certain we'd reached it. You could see it in our work attire. Rick was a T-shirt and flip-flops guy. Art usually wore shorts to work, and only freezing-cold weather or meetings with shoe company executives got him to begrudgingly put on dress pants. He would at least wear a golf shirt from time to time.

But the growing up we had to do wasn't about dressing the part. It was about protecting Eastbay from our limitations, one of which was that we didn't much like some of the aspects of business that were becoming necessary. We loved shoes. We knew what our customers would want and what shoes would be hot. We were good at inventory. We knew mail order inside and out. But we didn't love managing, or HR, or finance, or logistics. We weren't great with trade shows and schmoozing. Eastbay was too big now, our vision was too big, to operate on our gut instincts, trial and error, and squirt-gun fights. We saw so much opportunity for Eastbay that no one else in the shoe business seemed to see, but we were reaching our personal capacity for managing it. After stagnating with the loss of Air, our sales were going up fast again. By '91 they'd doubled, but costs were going up faster, so we were seeing less and less money that we could put back into the business. We were in deep trouble, and as entrepreneurs, we knew it was our names that were on the loans. The cash-flow crunch made paying the bills tight, and sometimes we had to call vendors and ask for more time to pay them. For the first time in a long time, it felt like we might be toast again. And without Nike Air, our margin for error had narrowed such that the way we'd made strategic bets and pivoted business models in the past (we'd had, what, four or five of them) seemed a bit reckless now. We had endured a year-plus of existential stress and didn't want another sudden, market-shifting shock to put us through that again. And we saw some potential shocks out there, including Nike going directly to customers, dabbling in retail with its premium Niketown stores, and New Balance opening its own stores.

We also had a *lot* of people counting on us to make the right moves at this point. Our own families and our Eastbay family were still growing in 1990. We wanted to take care of them. We also wanted to take care of our friendship—which we felt could be in jeopardy if something like the Nike problem happened again.

We needed help. We needed a more sophisticated strategy than "throw all our money at inventory and catalogs and cross our fingers." We needed experienced people who loved to do the things we didn't.

We mentioned all this to our landlord, Larry Niederhofer, who ran a holding company called Apogee. He suggested we talk with Apogee's group president, who oversaw ten medium-sized manufacturing companies. His name was Harry Colcord.

We knew Harry. Everyone around Wausau knew Harry. Flashy guy, very successful. He'd gone to high school with Art. In fact, he was voted Newman High School's Least Likely to Succeed his senior year, right before Art received the same honor. In the '80s, Harry became part of Running Wild, our Eastbay running club. He agreed to give us some feedback on our operation, and as we got to know him, we found ourselves genuinely impressed by Harry, who like Art had overcome that high-school "honor."

He began working for Apogee when he was sixteen in the Wausau Metals shop. He worked his way up from shop floor to sales. When Harry was twenty-six, Niederhofer respected and trusted him enough to name Harry the president of an entire division, and that eventually turned into the ten companies he ran now.

Conversations with Harry eventually led to weekly strategy meetings in his basement in the summer of 1991. Last time, when Nike ditched us, we just threw every spaghetti noodle of an idea we had at a whiteboard in the office, seeing what might stick. This time we were doing the grown-up version of that, a SWOT Analysis. SWOT, we learned, stood for Strengths, Weaknesses, Opportunities, and Threats, which we'd map out for various parts of our business on two-by-two grids.

Come September, Harry summarized the sessions in a twenty-plus-page memo. We still have it in a binder, all typed up with notes in the margins, scratch-outs, and additions. On one page Harry scribbled in a note to us explaining something about meeting minutes—we really had no clue when it came to professional processes.

"You truly were terrific operators, in the entrepreneurial sense," Harry says now. "You always trusted your gut instincts, and you were usually right, but gut instincts, at a certain level, become inadequate."

Harry helped us put into words what we always felt and knew about what our company was, and what it could become. He emphasized that we were growing so fast that we needed better discipline with delegation and control—or any discipline at all. Ultimately the memo listed eleven threats, and we added five more in our notes while discussing the memo. The top two were the ones we lost sleep over:

- Suppliers cutting us off or setting limits
- Suppliers issuing their own catalogs

On the other hand, perhaps owing to our optimism, but also probably because we lucked out with our timing building the business, the memo listed forty-three opportunities, and we wrote in eight more. Some of these seemed like business blocking and tackling, like:

- Promotion to suppliers
- Hiring key players to improve performance
- Selling to women (currently 75% male)

Others were more ambitious:

- Athlete endorsements
- Video catalogs

Others were, well . . .

- Buy a sports team/become sports agents
- Sell Eastbay, start new

On Harry's do-well list:

- Quick shipping
- Creating an environment people liked working in
- Being fair to employees and customers
- Being willing to change

That last one especially mattered as soon as we read Harry's do-poorly list:

- Balancing inventory
- Financial planning
- Organizational structure (we had none)
- Training, evaluating
- Disciplining employees
- Putting out fires
- Having a chaotic office space and an even more chaotic and messy warehouse

Our goals were to "be respected at what we do," and "acquire quality people so that planning can be done by Art and Rick."

Harry said he thought we could bring in HR and finance talent that could help get us more organized.

We knew this was true, even if we didn't talk about it. We'd tried to work with consultants to help with some of the management tasks we didn't love, but we were outgrowing that model. We needed the kind of expertise they brought on staff permanently. We also kept thinking about how Nike seemed to view us, or at least how it convinced a judge to view us: as just another cheap discount catalog company not run by *real* businesspeople.

But we didn't quite get exactly what Harry was saying at first. We thought he meant we needed some managers to help bridge the gap between frontline operations and us. No, Harry said. You need leaders at the top. Not to replace us, but to free us up to do what we did best and let them run operations. On Harry's advice, we decided that we'd bring on a vice president of business operations, or something like that, and create HR and finance departments.

Entrepreneurs early on need freedom, flexibility, and passionate people who put in the extra work to learn as they go, and that's what our team did. They built the business from nothing, and they did such a good job that we grew massively. But we knew at this point Eastbay needed structure in the form of an HR department, and a finance group, to add to the incredible team that to this point had built Eastbay.

As we took in Harry's report, we experienced a surprising array of emotions. On one hand, how exciting. We now had a detailed breakdown on exactly what our company needed to grow to the levels that we thought and hoped it could. But on the other hand, to do what Harry recommended would mean that sometimes, those jacks and jills of all trades who were so crucial to Eastbay were going to feel pushed aside. A few people left, but many grew into more specialized roles as more management structure took hold. "Some people survived the process," Polly says, "and they grew into it, and they were able to specialize and learn as they went. But when I returned I noticed that some other people sort of jumped off the bus, although they might argue they were pushed more than they jumped. But you're going to have those people, and those sorts of moments and decisions are going to come with some hard feelings." We had to learn to be grateful for what they'd provided, while focusing on moving forward to build a better company and doing more for our customers. But maybe that person who didn't survive the process was on your squirt-gun team, or maybe you had tossed them up a slice of pizza during inventory counts. It wasn't easy.

There was one more thing in the memo, something that we had discussed at length in our meetings with him, and something that we knew would be as important as a VP of Ops. It was in the strategies section. Harry wrote:

- Better Catalog

25

Soul of a Catalog

Let's wind it back for a second to 1990, before Harry's SWOT. The catalog was good. It continued to grow—we mailed nearly five million total copies over six editions that year, and we were proud of how they were put together. Rick served as creative director, his brain producing about a million concepts per minute, many of them spilling onto those densely packed pages. We both were heavily involved in its design and production, but we'd also hired a de facto art director to oversee much of the work of putting our ideas into print.

It'd come a long way from its modest beginnings as a one-page price list for a dozen sneakers. We typically ran forty to forty-eight pages of vivid colors and eye-catching photography. But what pulled people in and kept them there, we believe, were the jam-packed pages of product. The depth of our descriptions. Size, color, weight, shoe components, what the shoe was good at, price. If you remember the catalog, you'll remember how much we stuffed into those pages.

This was one of the advantages of mail order that people didn't seem to get. People who got sneakers in *Eastbay* were getting more and better information than they got at a store, and they were having more fun with it. If we could get what they saw in the catalog to them in three days, well, that was worth the wait.

So even before Harry said "Better Catalog" in his report, it was already finding a voice. We had started moving away from stock photography on the covers. On the All Sports '87 cover, for example, there was a stock picture of a pile of sports equipment—mitts, golf clubs, a football, a basketball, jump rope, running tank top. Our logo (in blue) was above that, and above *that* was a strip of five pictures of top-selling sneakers. This was typical mail-order stuff.

By the time of the back-to-school 1990 edition, you could see personality emerging. That cover featured a Macintosh computer, with some books stacked on it, one was called "*Eastbay 101,* by Rick and Art." A pair of feet decked out in the hot Reebok Pump high-tops were kicked up on the desk, where you could also spot an *Eastbay* catalog, the same one you were holding. Another cover in late 1990 showed a basketball going through a hoop in an explosion of sparks, buffered by the all-caps exclamatory: *GOODNESS! GRACIOUS! GREAT BALLS OF FIRE!* The Christmas 1990 catalog cover featured the Third Street Eastbay storefront with a Santa-red UFO emblazoned USS *CLAUS* beaming up an endless stream of shoes through the store's roof.

Much of it was amateurish, in the best way, that kids could relate to—it had the same scattershot energy they did. Somehow, it all hung together, loosely. The sense of our attitude—positive, imaginative, boundary-pushing, kid-like, and most important, beyond excited about sneakers—came through on those early covers. It was a sign of *Eastbay*'s soul emerging.

We let the readers get to know us, sharing funny anecdotes, always signed with just, "Art + Rick." We scattered Easter eggs throughout the pages. We'd wish a coach well on their upcoming season or create characters who seemed to live in the magazine. In a summer 1990 catalog, a nameless, square-jawed cartoon hunk would show up on various pages giving random sports tips:

> TO AVOID BEING CAUGHT IN INCLEMENT WEATHER, USE NATURE TO HELP YOU PREDICT FUTURE CONDITIONS. FOR EXAMPLE, IF HAWKS INCREASE THEIR CIRCLING IN THE SKY, A STORM IS COMING.

Random, yes, but in a way that kids seemed to get. And we had evidence it was working. In 1987, 170,000 customers ordered from the catalog. By 1990 it was a million.

Even if you added up all the athletes at all the high schools and colleges in the United States, you wouldn't reach the business we were

Above: Despite going to different high schools, we hung out and played sports together all the time. *All photos by the authors unless otherwise specified.*

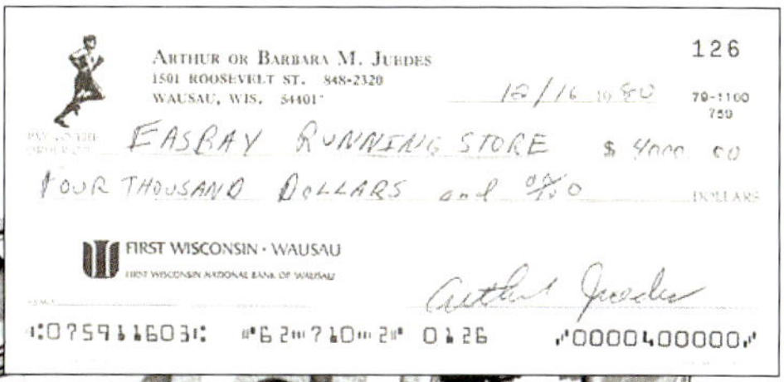

126
ARTHUR OR BARBARA M. JUEDES
1501 ROOSEVELT ST. 848-2320
WAUSAU, WIS. 54401
10/16 19 80
79-1100
759
EASBAY RUNNING STORE $ 4000.00
FOUR THOUSAND DOLLARS and 00/100 DOLLARS
FIRST WISCONSIN · WAUSAU
FIRST WISCONSIN NATIONAL BANK OF WAUSAU
Arthur Juedes

mirman's

Above, middle: Having spent all our money, we left Milwaukee with hundreds of pairs of shoes to sell, stuffed in Trebs's AMC Gremlin, like the one seen here. *Source: Bob DuHamel via Creative Commons. Above, bottom:* "Nobody would have a clue you were doing any business out of here," our retail neighbor Ralph Mirman said of our first storefront (to the far left) on Washington Street. *Source: Bob Becker, Marathon County Historical Society/Geisel Collection*

Above: We opened our store on April Fool's Day. When Rick's dad looked around the dingy place, he said to us, "I think you guys are toast."

Right: Wally's was one of our watering holes during those slow times between clinics when the store was doing nearly zero business. *Source: Marathon County Historical Society*

Left: Early on, when business was slow, we started running every day at noon. Those runs became a time and space to talk through and solve problems, and we'd carry on the tradition for two decades.

Above: Much of our success is due to our wives Barb and Susie, who supported us even when we were drawing $5 a week in salary—and even when we had mustaches.

Right: When we outgrew the Washington Street storefront, we took over the J.C. Penney building on Third Street. Eventually we'd take up the whole block. *Source: Marathon County Historical Society*

Below: Explosive growth forced us to find whatever warehouse space we could in town. One of those spaces was the massive old Murray machinery foundry, which always smelled like oil and had a layer of soot on everything. *Source: Marathon County Historical Society*

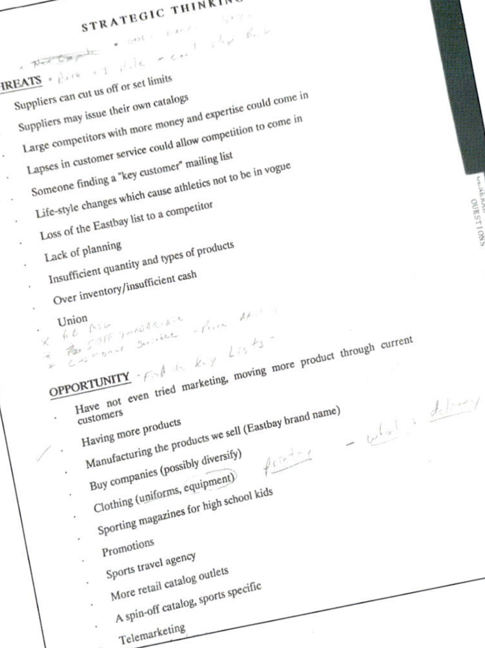

STRATEGIC THINKING

THREATS

- Suppliers can cut us off or set limits
- Suppliers may issue their own catalogs
- Large competitors with more money and expertise could come in
- Lapses in customer service could allow competition to come in
- Someone finding a "key customer" mailing list
- Life-style changes which cause athletics not to be in vogue
- Loss of the Eastbay list to a competitor
- Lack of planning
- Insufficient quantity and types of products
- Over inventory/insufficient cash
- Union

OPPORTUNITY

- Have not even tried marketing, moving more product through current customers
- Having more products
- Manufacturing the products we sell (Eastbay brand name)
- Buy companies (possibly diversify)
- Clothing (uniforms, equipment)
- Sporting magazines for high school kids
- Promotions
- Sports travel agency
- More retail catalog outlets
- A spin-off catalog, sports specific
- Telemarketing

Left: The detailed SWOT analysis we produced with Harry Colcord helped us grow up and led to him joining Eastbay.

Money

Eastbay

Friendship gives birth to thriving Wausau business

By Melissa Lake

Operators are busy:

Right: Harry joining brought a new level of attention to Eastbay, and the business took off again.

Below: When Harry (front middle), John Schaefer (back, second from right), and Dick Johnson (back right) came on, Eastbay began to shift from scrappy startup to a more mature business. Here we are signing a new deal with our printer. *Source: Dick Johnson*

Left: At one of our charity carnivals, executives were told "bring your suits" for a dunk tank. Dick Johnson brought his suit, all right, and gleeful employees made sure he got dunked. *Source: Dick Johnson*

Above: We tried to never miss a noon run, even on this day in 1994, when it hit 20 below zero.

Above: After we went public, it seemed like everyone knew who we were and wanted to talk to "the Eastbay guys." It was a dream to meet so many greats who we admired, like Shaq and Ken Griffey, Jr., pictured here.

Above: We outgrew the old J.C. Penney building, and after our successful IPO, we moved into a massive new facility along the Wisconsin River, still home to Foot Locker today. *Source: Bob Becker*

Above: A familiar pose from our lifelong friendship.

Left: We always called ourselves "business typhoons." After the IPO, we dubbed ourselves "Corporate Stooges," complete with our own vintage.

Below: After we sold to Foot Locker, John Schaefer and Dick Johnson had Eastbay championship rings made to celebrate our extraordinary years together. *Source: John Schaefer*

Above and left: Eastbay closed down, but the memories remain. *Source: Brandon Sneed*

Right: Our favorite pose. Staying friends for 70+ years, through all the highs and lows, is our proudest accomplishment.

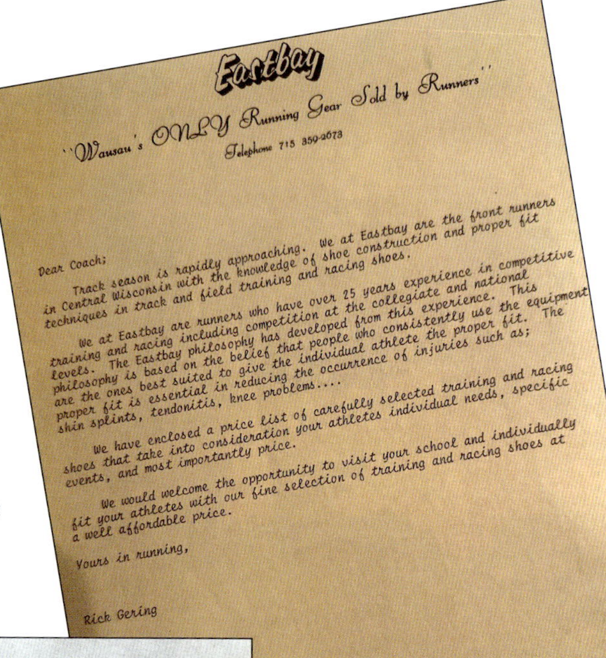

Eastbay

"Wausau's ONLY Running Gear Sold by Runners"

Telephone 715 359-2673

Dear Coach;

Track season is rapidly approaching. We at Eastbay are the front runners in Central Wisconsin with the knowledge of shoe construction and proper fit techniques in track and field training and racing shoes.

We at Eastbay are runners who have over 25 years experience in competitive training and racing including competition at the collegiate and national levels. The Eastbay philosophy has developed from this experience. This philosophy is based on the belief that people who consistently use the equipment are the ones best suited to give the individual athlete the proper fit. The proper fit is essential in reducing the occurrence of injuries such as; shin splints, tendonitis, knee problems....

We have enclosed a price list of carefully selected training and racing shoes that take into consideration your athletes individual needs, specific events, and most importantly price.

We would welcome the opportunity to visit your school and individually fit your athletes with our fine selection of training and racing shoes at a well affordable price.

Yours in running,

Rick Gering

Right and below: The first letter we sent to 35 coaches asking if we could come to their schools to run a clinic. It worked so well we'd soon add price lists for wrestling, football, and basketball shoes.

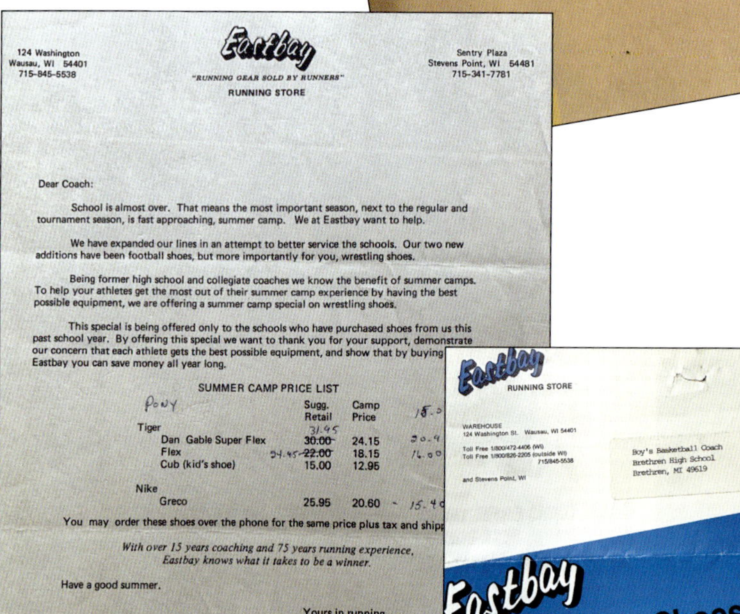

124 Washington
Wausau, WI 54401
715-845-5538

Eastbay

"RUNNING GEAR SOLD BY RUNNERS"
RUNNING STORE

Sentry Plaza
Stevens Point, WI 54481
715-341-7781

Dear Coach:

School is almost over. That means the most important season, next to the regular and tournament season, is fast approaching, summer camp. We at Eastbay want to help.

We have expanded our lines in an attempt to better service the schools. Our two new additions have been football shoes, but more importantly for you, wrestling shoes.

Being former high school and collegiate coaches we know the benefit of summer camps. To help your athletes get the most out of their summer camp experience by having the best possible equipment, we are offering a summer camp special on wrestling shoes.

This special is being offered only to the schools who have purchased shoes from us this past school year. By offering this special we want to thank you for your support, demonstrate our concern that each athlete gets the best possible equipment, and show that by buying ... Eastbay you can save money all year long.

SUMMER CAMP PRICE LIST

	Sugg. Retail	Camp Price
Tiger		
Dan Gable Super Flex	~~30.00~~	24.15
Flex	~~22.00~~	18.15
Cub (kid's shoe)	15.00	12.95
Nike		
Greco	25.95	20.60

You may order these shoes over the phone for the same price plus tax and shipp...

With over 15 years coaching and 75 years running experience, Eastbay knows what it takes to be a winner.

Have a good summer.

Yours in running,

Art Juedes

Rick Gering

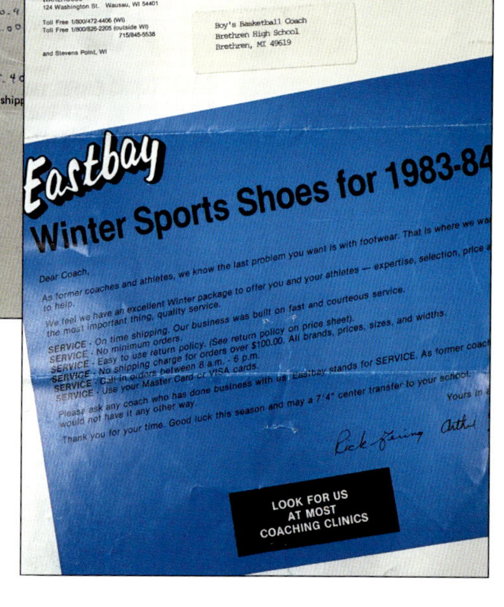

Eastbay
RUNNING STORE

WAREHOUSE
124 Washington St. Wausau, WI 54401

Toll Free 1/800/472-4406 (WI)
Toll Free 1/800/826-2205 (outside WI)
715/845-5538

and Stevens Point, WI

PAID
PERMIT N...
WAUSAU, W...

Boy's Basketball Coach
Brethren High School
Brethren, MI 49619

Eastbay

Winter Sports Shoes for 1983-84

Dear Coach,

As former coaches and athletes, we know the last problem you want is with footwear. That is where we wa... to help.

We feel we have an excellent Winter package to offer you and your athletes — expertise, selection, price a... the most important thing, quality service.

SERVICE - On time shipping. Our business was built on fast and courteous service.
SERVICE - No minimum orders.
SERVICE - Easy to use return policy. (See return policy on price sheet).
SERVICE - No shipping charge for orders over $100.00. All brands, prices, sizes, and widths.
SERVICE - Call in orders between 8 a.m. - 6 p.m.
SERVICE - Use your Master Card or VISA cards.

Please ask any coach who has done business with us. Eastbay stands for SERVICE. As former coac... would not have it any other way.

Thank you for your time. Good luck this season and may a 7'4" center transfer to your school.

Yours in ...

LOOK FOR US AT MOST COACHING CLINICS

Right: The trifold price list was our first move toward a catalog. It even included some humor, like where we say, "May a 7′4″ center transfer to your school."

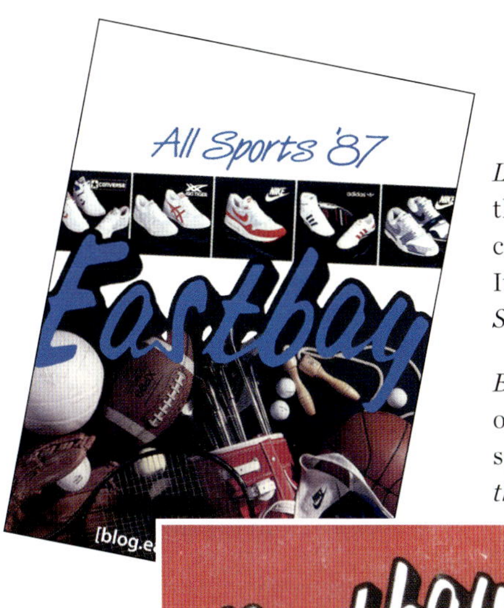

Left: The All Sports '87 catalog was the first that went to young athletes as well as to coaches and wasn't dedicated to a single sport. It marked our transition to a catalog business. *Source: blog.eastbay.com*

Below: Early catalogs felt like traditional mail order and hadn't yet taken on Eastbay's unique spirit, but they were effective. *Source: Marathon County Historical Society*

Left: Team-colored shoes changed everything, for the sneaker business and for Eastbay.

AIR JORDAN

A. MULTI SHORTS - Sizes: S-XL, Youth S-XL. Red, black, grey. **Eastbay $9.95, $8.95 (youth).**

B. A.J. MUSCLE SHORT - Sizes: S-XL, Youth S-XL. Red/black, black/red. **Eastbay $15.95, $14.95 (youth).**

C. A.J. GUSSET PANT - Sizes: S-XL, Youth M-XL. Nylon taffeta, black/red. **Eastbay $29.95, $24.95 (youth).**

D. A.J. MUSCLE PANT - Sizes: S-XL, Youth M-XL. Nylon taffeta, black/red. **Eastbay $32.95, $28.95 (youth).**

E. REVERSIBLE TEE - Sizes: S-XL. Red/black, grey/white. **Eastbay $17.95.**

F. AUTHENTIC REVERSIBLE TANK - Sizes: S-XL. Poly/cotton jersey. NBA cut — fits large. Red/grey, red/black, grey/white. **Eastbay $17.95.**

NIKE

AVAILABLE JUNE

A. CAP SLEEVE OVERLAY - Sizes: S-XL. Poly cotton/mesh. Black/red, grey/red. **Eastbay $15.95.**

B. TEE SHIRT OVERLAY - Sizes: S-XL, Youth M-XL. Poly/cotton/mesh. Black/red, grey/red. **Eastbay $15.95, $14.95 (youth).**

C. COMBO TANK - Sizes: S-XL. Black/red, grey/red. **Eastbay $11.95.**

D. WRAP JUMPER TEE - Sizes: S-XL. Poly/cotton. Black, red, grey. **Eastbay $11.95.**

E. TANK TOP - Sizes: S-XL, Youth S-XL. Poly/cotton. Red, black, grey. **Eastbay $8.95, $6.95 (youth)**

F. LOGO TEE SHIRT - Sizes: S-XL, Youth S-XL. Red, black, grey, white. **Eastbay $8.95, $7.95 (youth).**

Eastbay

RUNNING STORE INC.

WAREHOUSE
124 Washington St. Wausau, WI 54401
Toll Free 1/800/472-4406 (WI)
Toll Free 1/800/826-2205 (outside WI)
Customer Service 715/845-5538

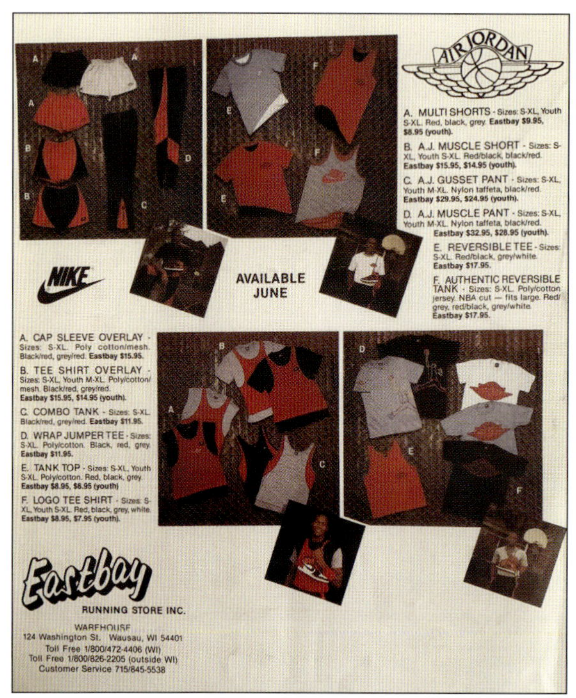

Left: Even before we were allowed to sell Air Jordans, we snuck in a picture of MJ himself with the revolutionary sneakers slung over his shoulder. Demand was immediate and unstoppable.

Below: In the late '80s the covers took on more personality, often with an inspiring tone, and you could spot bits of humor in the interiors too, like Santa pumping iron.

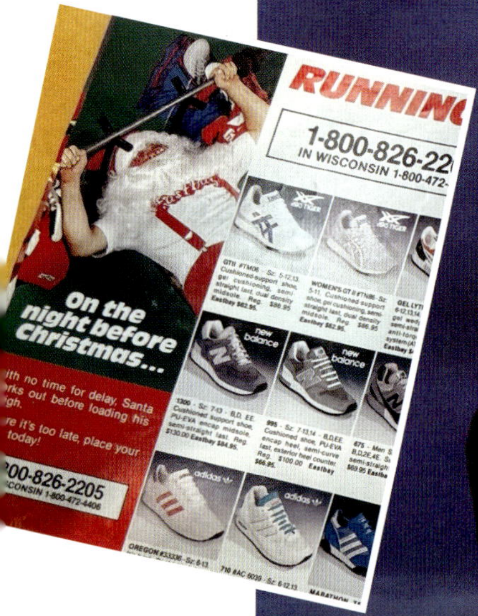

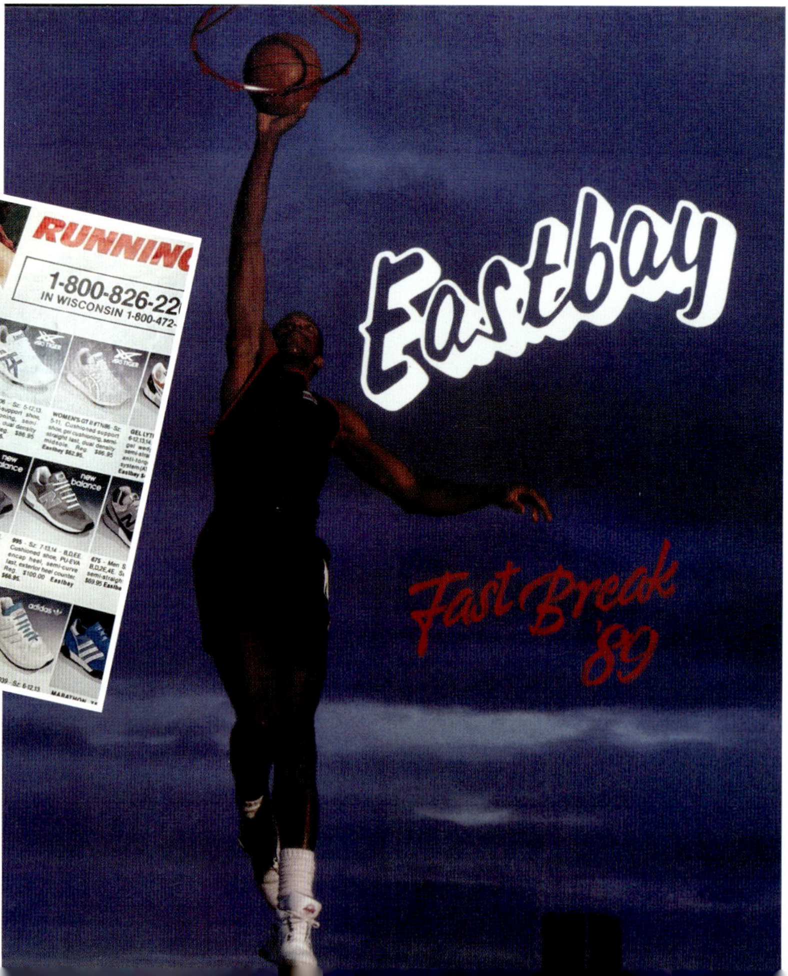

Source, right: Marathon County Historical Society

The late '80s and early '90s defined the Eastbay voice and aesthetic—sometimes humorous, sometimes inspiring, always energetic—that athletes and kids coveted.

Source, above and right: Marathon County Historical Society

Source, top right and bottom: Marathon County Historical Society

Page after page. Brand after brand. Seemingly endless choices. The overstuffed aesthetic became part of the *Eastbay* brand and had kids poring over the pages for hours. *Source, top left: blog.eastbay.com; all others: Drew Hammell/@eastbay.archive*

We were amazed at the superstars who began to grace the covers of Eastbay in the Foot Locker years, inspiring a whole new generation of young athletes and sneakerheads.

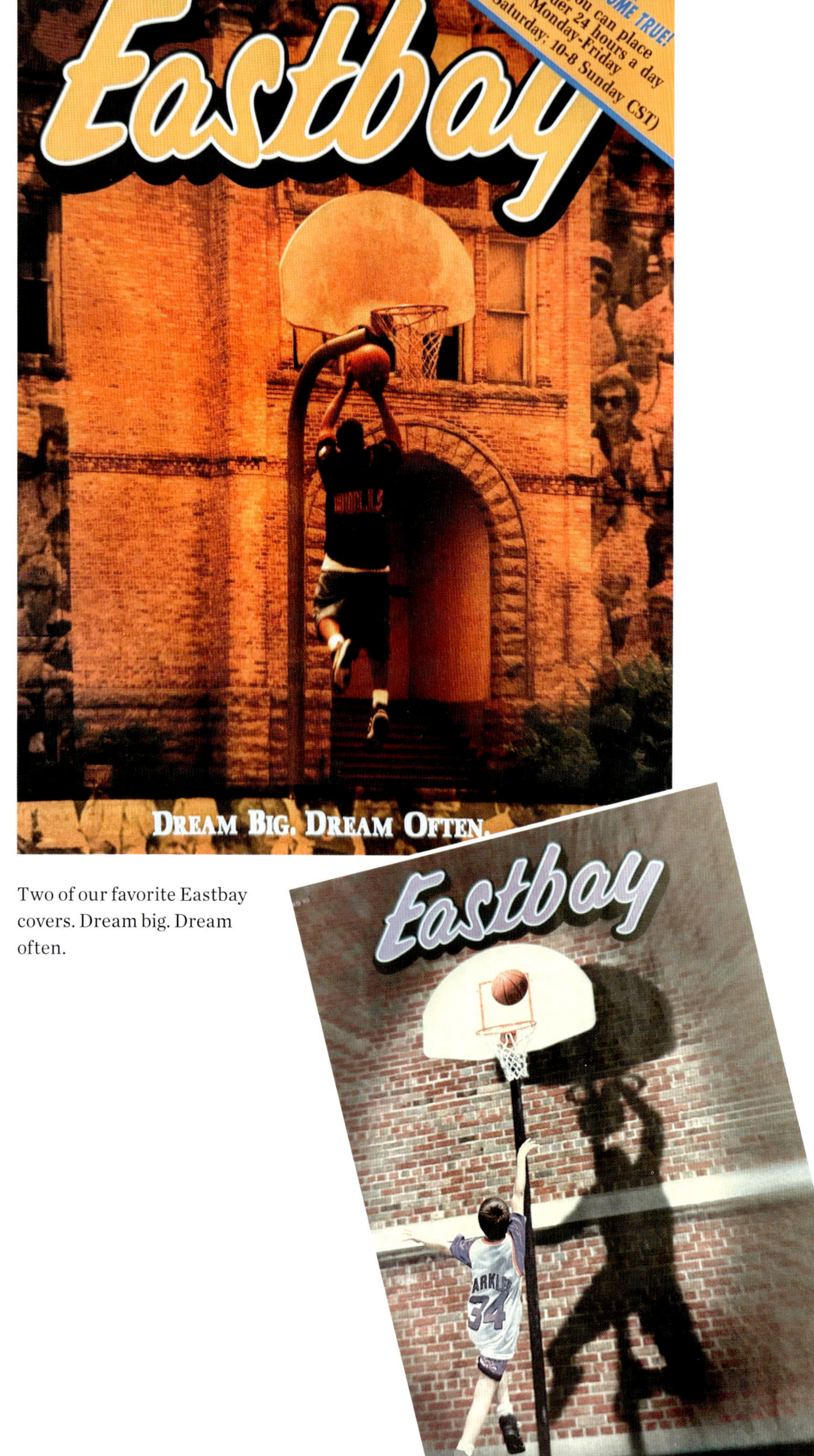

Two of our favorite Eastbay covers. Dream big. Dream often.

doing. Something was going on. Sometimes we wouldn't have someone's size, and they'd take whatever size we had—*okay, no 10s, I'll take the 7s.* That struck us as odd, but now we see that that was part of the growing contingent of people who were collecting shoes. We thought of these extra sales as "the casual market," but we weren't focused on it. We didn't yet see what it was.

We didn't see what Bobbito Garcia saw from the other side, as he recalls the lengths to which those early sneaker fiends would go to find the cool shoes and how *Eastbay* transformed that. "At the time," Garcia told us, "there was no precedent. As consumers, we would go to the shops, or go to flea markets, and gaze, basically, right? We would look through store windows even if we weren't going inside." It was so hard for these kids to know precisely the sneakers they were looking for, Garcia recalls, that "if a player got injured, you were happy—not that he got injured, but because that's the only time you got a closeup of the sneakers. He's wearing light blue Dr. J's! That's crazy!" Then suddenly, all these kids so hungry for a glimpse of the shoes that the heroes on their posters were wearing got to see *all* of them in *Eastbay.* "In that era, you might have had a *Playboy* magazine right next to an *Eastbay* catalog underneath your bed. Because literally, it was insane to see."

But our assessment was right. The catalog still needed to be better.

He noted in his report to us that beyond the cover and some playful and thoughtful design touches within, the catalog's "user experience" was still more utilitarian than entertaining. We still used some stock photography inside, and it still felt somewhat restrained in there. Overall, the catalog needed to be more, in Harry's words, "consumer friendly." It needed "better . . . timing and content" and, in general, a "better image."

We agreed. We wanted to create a mail-order catalog that felt less, well, mail order. In fact, we really didn't want to be like a mail-order catalog. At all. Maybe part of that, subconsciously, was a reaction to Nike's lumping us in with less savory versions of the business, but mostly it was our desire to express our passion for the athletes and shoes. We didn't want to just be *consumer friendly.* We wanted to make people *feel something.* Feel surprised. We wanted to create a kind of mash-up of catalog and *Sports Illustrated,* with hints of *Wide World of Sports* and a dash of *Mad* magazine.

But getting there felt difficult, and that was a function of the tedious and rigid production process. Creating a full catalog took weeks, sometimes months. We were still forced to endure the arduous process of combing through film negatives and laying everything out on big boards by hand. Everything was still analog. The best we could do was make six in a year without doing much different from catalog to catalog on the inside. Just managing the growth in size and getting it out, never mind making it *better*, was wearing us down.

So, we made some investments. We hired a professional copywriter, someone who knew and loved words as much as we loved shoes. Someone that was like Ed Wodalski, a sportswriter we poached from the local paper. Nice guy we'd known since grade school. We also hired a photographer and several graphic artists to bring more of the catalog production in house.

Within a year of that, we made two of our biggest and smartest investments. First, we hired Fritz Menzel as director of catalog production. Second, we let Fritz immediately begin digitizing the entire catalog process, starting with the purchase of a striking new technology called *the digital camera*. We're not entirely sure, but odds are good that it was the Kodak DCS-100, the world's first fully digital commercial SLR camera. It cost north of $20,000, but with the hard drive and cables and everything else, we spent much more than that. And for that investment you got a 1.3-megapixel camera and 200 megabytes of storage.

Worth every penny. Suddenly, photographers could take virtually unlimited pictures and then proof them right there in the office, using new graphic design software. All together, we went in for north of fifty grand, but it meant we could take the whole catalog production in-house. We knew it would pay for itself quickly, and it did.

The technology brought a new level of efficiency. By 1991 we published seven catalogs that ranged from forty-eight to eighty-eight pages, plus three sales catalogs and a summer test mailing.

But it also brought a new kind of untethered creativity that would let us create the magazine-like mail-order catalog we had imagined. In some ways, it was as if the tech had just caught up with Rick's imagination and the team could use the tools to channel it.

Sometimes, in disruptive moments when you have a million ideas and as many options, it takes some time to get the creative right. You need a few hacks at it to see what's an out, what's a double. What's a home run.

Not this time.

As soon as we had those tools, the voice of *Eastbay* blossomed. The creative dabbling from before became a design ethos, a *voice* throughout the early and mid-1990s.

It's the style you remember if you were a fan. That sense that we somehow seemed to smash so many pictures of sneakers in so many colors on a page (usually with at least one turned over so you could see the sole). The Fall '92 catalog's Converse basketball page, for example, showed *thirty-two* different Cons. Other pages would display row upon row of baseball bats, or scatterings of team hats, or fanned-out team jackets in all their iconic colors. But then there'd also be a picture of an athlete and a small story about them. And brand logos and dot-whacks shouting *NEW* or *LARGE SIZES!* and boxes with trivia—"Did you know that in February 1895 the Minnesota State School of Agriculture beat Hamline in an early college basketball game? MSSA crushed Hamline, 9-3."

And then, of course, all those descriptions of the sneakers that kids would pore over.

CONVERSE ACCELERATOR RS1 MID

Basketball isn't just a big man's game anymore. It's a game of speed. Watch Kevin Johnson play and you'll know what we mean. In the **Accelerator RS1 Mid** you can drive the lane faster than ever because your feet are so light and so well-cushioned. **REACT** technology under your heel gives you amazing cushioning. The synthetic upper gives you maximum strength, minimum weight and high breathability. Molded upper package for lightweight support. Size 7-16.

Reg. $90.00
Eastbay $79.95
Wt. 14.0 oz.

Somehow, we got this description, plus a list of ten colors, plus three other descriptions, plus the thirty-two images of shoes, all on one page.

We started injecting editorial throughout the catalog. Inspirational quotes and pictures and stories about athletes. Sometimes it was like a baseball card come alive—for example, the image of Ken Griffey, Jr., amid a page stuffed with Nike baseball cleats.

> **KEN GRIFFEY, JR.**
>
> The former MVP missed half of 1995 due to a broken wrist but made a remarkable comeback. Junior returned to the lineup with a vengeance, finishing the season with 17 homers in only 72 games. By playoff time he was the Ken Griffey, Jr. of old. The Gold Glove center fielder slugged five home runs in the five-game first round series versus the Yankees. Only 26, this second-generation star has career numbers of 1,039 hits, 585 RBI, 189 homers, and a .302 average.

By adding these editorial elements, we were amplifying the dreaming you could do with *Eastbay.* It was one thing to see the vast array of stuff to buy, but then to know that Ken Griffey, Jr., was wearing the same cleats or that you could look like Kevin Johnson on the court—that tightened our bond with customers.

More than anything, though, the transition from catalog to dream book happened with the covers. Energized by the digitization, Rick insisted on going much, much further with the covers, which would shed all mail-order sensibility.

It culminated in the definitive cover for *Eastbay*'s new era, the cover we think represents *Eastbay*'s soul and essence.

A young man is alone outside playing basketball. You see him from behind in a Chicago Bulls warm-up jersey and long, baggy shorts. He's pulling up and hanging in the air, forever at the apex of his jump shot, just about to release the ball toward an old hoop against an old brownstone. You start to build the story in your head. He's been practicing there by himself for hours. He's taken this shot ten thousand times. He's trying to get better. And then, it catches your eye. You peer at the brownstone's brick walls more closely. You notice something you hadn't seen at first, but now you can't unsee it. The shadows against the brownstone are not just shadows. They're people, sitting in the stands. Many are looking right at the kid taking the shot. This young man isn't alone at all. He's here with his imagination, playing in front of an arena full of fans, rooting for him, ready to go wild when he drains the shot.

He sees the countless faces watching him from the stands.

He sees what his future can be.

Beneath the image, four words we came up with together: *Dream Big. Dream Often.*

26

Harry

After six months of interviews, we still needed a vice president of operations, or finance, or whatever we'd call it, but nobody we met with seemed right. We had floated the idea to two of our best friends, Jere Trudeau and Bill Roth, who had finance backgrounds, but neither showed any interest. We kept coming back to Harry. "We like working with Harry, right?" Rick said. "Why don't we just ask him?"

We still doubted he would consider it, but one day we just mentioned it to him offhand and our timing, yet again, couldn't have been better. Harry had grown restless at Apogee managing so many companies. His bosses had told him that he was in over his head, and pulled him from managing one of the companies, a company that Harry himself had helped create. At the time, it hurt him, but later he conceded it was getting to be too much.

Harry knew us well by now. He recognized our passion, and our vision, and understood that we were going to pursue this at all costs. He knew we'd go back to running Eastbay without a salary again if that's what it took to keep it going. And the three of us had had fun working together on the SWOT.

He also liked that we worked with giants in our industry that he revered, like Adidas and Reebok and Nike. He welcomed the prospect of fighting to get Nike's Air products back.

On the other hand, he worried about leaving all he'd done—gaining a national reputation for leadership in his industry, and the salary to go with it—to join a mail-order shoe company and possibly fall on his ass.

He talked it over with his wife at the time, who observed to him how much fun he seemed to have had working with us on the SWOT, and who said it was worth a shot. "So," Harry says, "I said, 'Screw it. I like the guys. They lost Nike, but they're truly focused on the market in a genuinely concerned way for young athletes.'"

Harry took a big pay cut to join Eastbay, but in exchange we offered him a good, incentivized profit-sharing deal. Harry liked the challenge in that.

Harry also asked us not to give him an official title for the first six months, and not to give him his own office yet. He wanted our people to see his involvement as something that felt good, not threatening, because he understood how much of their loyalty had been built on a foundation of working closely together and knowing each other for years. He wanted all of them to see him as someone working closely *with* the two of us, and by extension, *with* everyone else, instead of as a guy being brought in as some new corporate overlord.

Made sense to us. We agreed to those terms.

And another thing, Harry said. If he was going to come in and help us run a company, then we were going to run this company as if we might, at some point in the future, go public. We were going to operate by the rules of rigid documentation and transparency as though we had already sold stock to the public and gained shareholders. We'd have a—gulp—budget, and quarterly goals, and meetings to see how we were performing against them.

Real grown-up stuff. It would certainly be a learning curve for us, but if he was the one running that side of the show, then we trusted him.

Oh, one last thing, Harry told us: We had to give ourselves a raise of at least $30,000. "I demanded it," he recalls. "I wasn't going to take a job where I was getting paid more than my bosses, and they simply were not paying themselves enough."

Fine. We'll do it. The deal was done.

In May 1992, Harry Colcord resigned from Apogee to join us (we didn't apologize to Larry Niederhoffer for poaching him until thirty years later). When he left, one of his employees gave him some friendly hell for it: John Schaefer, the guy who had gone to high school with Tom and Jim Gering, and who'd come in for shoe fittings in the early days. He'd become an accountant, and then president of an Apogee division, where he'd worked with Harry for seven years. He said, "You better take me along."

"I'm going to need you," Harry told him. "I'll give it a try."

"One of the things you gotta give yourselves credit for," John Schaefer says now, "is you never let your egos, or your desire to be known, get in the way of what was best for Eastbay. For a bunch of years, no one knew who the hell Eastbay was."

But people knew who Harry Colcord was. "He was well known in the community," Schaefer says. "Involved in local politics. And always kind of out there. He was a big personality."

This proved as beneficial to Eastbay as his business acumen. We needed his promotional instincts. We just wanted to sell shoes, and we didn't see why we had to bring our own names into it, let alone our faces. But Harry understood the value of people—partners, salespeople—connecting with leaders at a company.

Local newspapers picked up on the story of Harry's move. If people in Wausau didn't know about Eastbay before, they sure did now. It wasn't just a confusingly large shoe store downtown, they learned. It was a company doing millions of dollars in mail-order business.

Bringing Harry onboard was the most significant move yet in our process of growing Eastbay.

We'd need him right away. A month after Harry joined, Asics came calling. It had a successful line of Asics Gel running shoes, another 10 percent of our business. And Asics, like Nike, was thinking of pulling them from *Eastbay*.

27

Cheat Code

In June 1992, we held a soiree for Asics executives at the fanciest place in town, the Wausau Country Club. Since one of the company's executives was from Japan, we included an authentic Japanese feast, or at least the best Japanese cuisine that we could muster. We thought it looked great, but after the exec took a big bite of fried rice and hibachi steak, we saw in his face that it looked better than it tasted. He chewed and swallowed and took a big sip of sake. Then he smiled and said, "This sake is really good."

This was our chance to convince Asics not to pull its Gels from *Eastbay*. Although its execs couched everything in careful language, we could read the room well enough to sense that their issues were effectively the same as Nike's: guilt by association with mail order, and our approach undercutting their desire to appear premium.

We pointed out the good work we had done since 1988 to elevate the catalog above the mail-order crowd. We had stopped running ads in the backs of magazines where some charlatans operated. We had added "call for price" in connection with some premium shoes like Asics Gels. We reminded them of our excellent and growing subscription numbers despite the absence of Nike Air.

We introduced them to Harry, who assured them we were becoming a well-structured corporation. We were targeting customer segments more effectively. We were digitizing, which would make for easier expansion and new creative possibilities for the catalog. *Eastbay* was becoming a cultural touchstone, we told them, full of content not just about the shoes athletes wore, but about the athletes themselves. It was a dream book for kids.

This was the tension brought on by professionalizing the operation, a tension we'd feel often in the coming years. Growing up meant doing things in a way that aligned with the needs of major companies, *partners*, like Asics. We had to show them that we had grown into a serious company that they could feel comfortable partnering with. We knew that we could reach athletes and customers in ways that companies like Asics could not. The companies may even have believed that, but our model was still not aligning with theirs.

It wasn't the hibachi, but the soiree didn't work. They were polite about it. They told us that they would continue to keep an eye on us, and that they wished us all the best—but they weren't letting us sell Gel running shoes anymore, though we could still sell Gel for basketball, baseball, and volleyball. There, they needed us.

We felt foolish, and we felt like failures, and we felt guilty, because Harry had just left his job to come work for us, and as soon as he'd joined us, we once again lost a flagship product from one of our largest vendors.

We also felt frustrated by this sharp persistent disconnect between who we knew we were and who these companies thought we were. We knew that we were implementing challenging but invaluable changes to the operation, working toward becoming the premier athletic footwear and apparel mail-order dealer, a one-stop shop for people anywhere in the country. And if all went well, the world was in play.

But companies couldn't see it yet. Nike and Asics still held mail order, and us, in such low regard that they'd forgo revenue to stay away from it. These massively growing international brands based on the coasts and overseas still looked at us like those kids in the Midwest—we're sure they called it "the middle of nowhere"—with that annoying little catalog.

In retrospect, it's ironic, because kids getting the catalog, our customers, took the opposite view of us, whether they were in L.A. or Maine, New York or West Texas, Detroit or Baton Rouge. They didn't care where we were, because we were where they were. We were the ones who *got it*. Who got *them*. We put their buying decisions for something important to them literally in their hands. We were the best source for athletes—and growing masses of sneakerheads—who couldn't find in their own towns what we offered. Kids understood the scarcity model the shoe companies were using, but they also knew, no matter what their local retailer told them, that they *could* get the Asics Lyteflex wrestling shoe in the Flash Orange / Grape Fusion / Grape color combination. Collectors knew we'd have the latest models and in rare colors and sizes. *Eastbay* was like a cheat code for the scarcity model. And we respected the kids. We had the same passion for sneakers they did, and it came through in the increasingly unique voice of the catalog editorial. It made the catalog feel like what it was, something just for them.

And we knew it was working. Organically, the customer list was growing by more than half a million names a year.

We had anecdotal evidence, too, that *Eastbay* was more deeply entrenched than Nike or Asics understood. For example, a day or two before the Major League Baseball All-Star Game in July 1992, somebody called who said that they represented Roger Clemens—the Boston Red Sox pitching legend. Somehow, he had arrived in San Diego without the specific pair of cleats that he liked to wear in the color he wanted—Pumas, size 13, with a specialized support for his ailing toe.

Local stores rarely carried pitching shoes in team colors and in sizes above 12. Clemens's people couldn't find a pair with the pitching toes anywhere, and Puma couldn't overnight a pair. But they knew about us and asked if we could help him out.

Yes, our inventory system told us, we had exactly that pair of Puma spikes in that size and color in stock, and we would have someone immediately arrange for UPS to overnight them. As Clemens pitched in the fourth inning to help the American League maintain its 4-0 lead over the National League, the camera zoomed in on the shoes that had been in our warehouse the day before, as the television announcer described this "special shoe" with "a reinforced toe area."

A month later, American sprinter Gwen Torrence was in Barcelona to compete in the Summer Olympics. After a training session one morning, she returned to her equipment bag to discover the track spikes for the 100-meter finals had been stolen. She had no shoes to race in, and Mizuno was out of stock. Someone from Team Torrence called us, desperate for help.

We had what she needed, but we didn't have much time. Overnighting a pair of baseball cleats to San Diego was one thing. Getting track spikes 4,300 miles across the Atlantic Ocean, in and out of customs, into Barcelona, quickly enough for Torrence to run the final in them was another.

But if we got someone on a plane immediately to get them to the president of Mizuno, he could fly them to Barcelona. Some hero at Eastbay—we don't even remember who, tragically—grabbed the Mizuno spikes from the warehouse and dashed to the airport. The spikes arrived just in time for Torrence, who finished the 1992 Olympics with a gold medal in the 200-meter race, a gold medal as part of the 400-meter relay team, and a silver medal with the 1600-meter relay team. And she came within 0.2 seconds of medaling in the 100-meter finals, too.

All while wearing track spikes that had been in a warehouse in Wausau a couple of days before the competition. In one summer, we pulled off two miracles.

The customer service here is part of the story, but so is this: Someone who represented Roger Clemens knew what *Eastbay* was and what we could do. Someone from one of the big international footwear companies, most of which looked down on us, had an emergency and turned to us to save them. We were onto a business model that *worked.* And we knew it. Today we all know this business model, this kind of customer service, and we take it for granted. Back then it sometimes felt like we were the only ones who got it.

It was maddening. Despite our location and our lack of business chops and whatever other criticisms those companies would lay on us, we were ahead of them in understanding the customer and the market. We lived by the idea of taking care of customers and doing *whatever* it took to get them what they wanted, no matter how carefully the shoe companies were controlling the inventory. We knew the role of inventory and how it was *our* cheat code to making the catalog work. If we show it, we have it. (Or had it; now and again we had to stamp *Sold Out* over a shoe that sold too fast.) We put our money where our pictures were. We were doing things in the '80s that Amazon and Zappos would be celebrated for doing many years later.

We're there saying, *This is big, guys! This is an amazing way to sell shoes.* And it just wasn't something that they cared about.

We were starting to dream again. We had a sense that as our bigger, bolder, more magazine-like version of the catalog became established—now bulging to ninety-six pages—it could help us help the vendors see what was so plain to us. But that would take time. We didn't know how much time, either. And until that happened, we felt very much at risk of losing more of the most popular products as more shoe companies pulled their shoes from our pages.

Eastbay, the catalog, was the plan. We needed people to see us for what we wanted to be—really, for what we were becoming.

For what Shaquille O'Neal knew *Eastbay* already was.

28

The Shaq Effect

The Orlando Magic used the first pick in the 1992 NBA draft to select Shaquille O'Neal, a seven-foot-one-inch center with astonishing power and athleticism for a man his size, an unstoppable big man with an unstoppably big personality.

Nike and Reebok both wanted Shaq for an endorsement deal—probably the biggest such deal since Jordan.

We don't know if it's true, but we had heard that as Shaq went through the process, he was cool to a potential deal with Nike, in part because Nike Airs weren't in *Eastbay*. We had also heard that at Reebok, Shaq was greeted with an image of the embossed leather jacket they'd designed for him, and some other products. We were told that Shaq noticed one of Reebok's "Above the Rim" T-shirts and pointed at it excitedly and told the Reebok execs that he had just ordered that shirt from *Eastbay*. Rumor was, he even went to Nike after visiting Reebok, donning all Reebok gear.

We knew the catalog was special. We knew it lit kids up and that they coveted it. Now we were getting signals of *Eastbay*'s cultural reach and significance even at the pro level. Roger Clemens, Gwen Torrence, Shaq. It turns out that when you send a catalog to millions of kids with dreams, some of those kids make it to the big leagues. When they start name-dropping *Eastbay* to shoe company executives, those shoe company executives start getting the signals, too. Maybe there was more to that catalog company in the middle of nowhere. Shaq being that excited about *Eastbay* told those execs in no uncertain terms that we were not only a legitimate and valuable part of the sports retail marketplace, but we were also relevant to sports culture in a way that not many entities, especially retailers, are. To put it bluntly, we felt like we got Shaq better than Nike did.

We decided to go on the offensive and hold on to all the vendors we could while we also executed an aggressive plan to get Nike and Asics back. We didn't want to wait anymore for them to come around or rely on serendipitous name-dropping by number one draft picks. We would hear what they needed from us and show what we could do to help them fulfill those needs. We got on the road.

With Harry, we went to Peabody, Massachusetts, for meetings with executive Pat Hambrick and her team at Saucony. We shot up to Bangor, Maine, for a tour of one of its factories. We gave Saucony what we'd given Asics over hibachi and sake—the numbers, the demographic profile of our list (vendors couldn't believe how good our list was), the grown-up business we were putting in place. We showed Saucony mockups of new catalog spreads featuring its products and raved about how much we loved what the company was doing with its new shoe line with Grid technology. At the factory, each of us crafted a custom pair of Saucony Jazz shoes for ourselves. We felt good about this trip, and we could tell that the Saucony execs did, too. Before we left, they told us they were happy to keep their products in our catalog for years to come.

Meetings with Puma, and Mizuno, and a few others went well enough for us to leave with the same good feelings. Jim Davis, the New Balance CEO, did everything he could to set our minds at ease. New Balance was a natural fit with Eastbay. Like us, it was known for reaching underserved markets, with its innovative products and wide-width shoes and a larger variety of models for women—and they were made in the USA.

On these trips, Harry brought strengths we didn't have—the external influence, the relationship building, that were crucial. Harry made us look better to these big companies, and he had a feel for making our new, grown-up image known in ways that were subtle and authentic. In a lot of ways, Harry was our George Martin, the legendary producer for the

Beatles. The Beatles were brilliant, for sure, but the classically trained Martin could see what they wanted to do and somehow channeled their creative energy into masterful, *professional* compositions.

Harry could handle the media, something we never liked doing. We would do interviews occasionally, and of course, we understood in a hazy sense that publicity was a good thing for a business, but we hated it with a deep and abiding passion, and as such, never developed any sort of feel for how to leverage such things to help the business.

Harry had no such aversion; he understood the publicity game intuitively. He told one newspaper, "These guys really target their market on a grassroots level, and that's the athletes. They know what the athletes need and go out and help them get it."

We just never knew how to *say* things like that in public. It felt uncomfortable and self-aggrandizing, even if we believed it. Harry did it naturally. He carried himself with a demeanor that was calm and warm and engaging but that also conveyed a graceful sense of authority and healthy ambition.

There were countless moments in the years that followed during which one or both of us would be in Harry's office (he finally took one) going on about one issue or another, and Harry—a passionate man unafraid of expressing himself—would sternly tell us to let him do his damn job, and feel free to stay out of his responsibilities. Rick's wife Susie remembers days walking up to the office and being intercepted by our assistant Lisa, who would tell her, "You don't want to go up there right now." Still, Harry took a lot of stress off us so we could concentrate on our vision for the company and for the catalog and products.

And maybe even above all of that, one of Harry's most valuable contributions to the company in his early days there was how he managed disagreements between us, a job that used to fall to Trebs, who hated that job. As the business got bigger, so did the stakes of the arguments. Trebs later told Harry how much calmer things became around the office once Harry got there. Harry's secret was that he never cast a deciding vote when we were at odds. He would listen, offer his opinion, and let us arrive at our own consensus.

Many employees still wondered what Harry's arrival meant for them, and what to make of the half-dozen consultants skulking around the office that we'd hired to help with our growth plan. The consultants questioned Harry's plans—all of them—and even wondered aloud if we needed him there at all. When Harry told us we needed a new controller—John Schaefer, who'd asked to be taken along from Apogee—every one of our consultants took a firm stance against the move. A couple of them got angry. "You're spending all this money on Harry," one of them ranted, "and then he needs to bring in someone to help him? I thought Harry was supposed to be your salvation?"

John didn't know anything about our business beyond buying some shoes from us on Washington Street back in the day. But we thought it might be a fit. The consultants didn't. We were listening to all sides.

"I'm telling you right now," one of the consultants said, "that if you hire John Schaefer, that is going to mean the end of Eastbay."

Schaefer started that August. Harry swore that he was one of the best numbers guys he'd ever seen. The man could turn two plus two into six, and he would.

Fully aware of what some of the consultants had said about him, Schaefer took a particular satisfaction in letting them go. He recalls that "they were collecting $100,000 a year and coming in once a month and basically telling us, 'Mail everything.' [Harry] told me to just kind of deal with it," Schaefer says. "Which didn't surprise me at all. But what did surprise me was he didn't give me a place to sit."

We were away on business on John's first day, and we seem to have forgotten to set up an office for him. An executive assistant improvised: "There's an empty cubicle up on the second floor where creative is."

Our new controller took himself there and sat down next to the photographers and graphic designers, and he started in on a book about cataloging that Harry had given him. He knew nothing about how our business worked, not Eastbay, not shoes and apparel, not retail in general, not mail order. "I came from manufacturing," he says. "I didn't even know what a SKU was. So, I'm reading the book, and Fritz comes over—" Fritz, the director of catalog production who got us our first digital camera.

"So," Fritz said, "I hear you're the new controller."

"Yeah," Schaefer replied. "I guess so."

"Well," Fritz said, "let me tell you about all the problems I've got."

Fritz unloaded a list of grievances about the price of paper, a marketing guy he didn't like, the cost of prepress production, and whatever else was preventing him from fulfilling his true vision for the catalog.

The two never really got along, truthfully, but to his credit, Schaefer listened. And as he investigated Fritz's complaints, he realized they weren't meaningless. "He was giving me items that I could put in a budget and then save us a boatload of money."

Schaefer ended up spending most of his first week up there hanging out with the creative people, completely out of his comfort zone. "The first thing you realize," he says, "is, creative people are wackadoodles. I'm an accountant, right? So I'm, like, how does this work? If you gotta do A first, then you do A first, then it's B, then C—you don't do A first by first doing F-G-Z, and going, 'Oh, I forgot about B.' They're zoning in. They're zoning out. But I learned in that week, leave these guys alone, because somehow, they know what they're doing." Schaefer is right. They knew what they were doing, all right, and they managed an impossible task—building a process to sift through a mountain of ideas to create, eventually, sixteen to twenty unique catalogs per year. They marched to their own drummer, sure, but worked so hard to set the catalog apart from anything else out there and give *Eastbay* its distinct voice.

As John acquainted himself with the business, we still had other growing up to do. One day in the fall of 1992, Harry said to us, "we're not putting 'trademark' on the catalog name."

We looked at him, in his word, "bewildered."

"Where's your intellectual property file?" he asked.

"Yeah," we said. "We don't have one."

"You did twenty-seven million dollars last year," Harry said. "And you don't have a trademark on the business name?"

We looked at each other and then back at Harry. "No. We don't have anything."

Once Harry recovered from shock, he made acquiring trademark rights his next mission, enlisting his wife at the time, a business attorney, who discovered that a guy named Tom Rodiez owned the Eastbay trademark and was doing business at the old Eastbay store in Milwaukee.

Tom Rodiez was the father and business partner of the man who ran the business, Tony. Dave Hill had sold it to them so that he could go work with Brooks, one of the major running-shoe brands. "Every time the damn phone rings now," Schaefer remembers Rodiez saying, "it's somebody who wants the *Eastbay* catalog, and we don't have the *Eastbay* catalog, but they call us, and it's driving us nuts."

Well, Harry had the perfection solution: "Let us buy the trademark. You could change your name, and everyone's lives will get better."

"Sure thing," Rodiez said.

"Great," Harry said. "How much would you like?"

"One million dollars."

Negotiations would continue for a few more weeks, Harry making multiple diplomatic missions to Milwaukee. At one point, Harry remembers Tom Rodiez proposing they hold a boxing match for the rights to the trademark and the name. Harry believed he was serious.

Now, Harry was in good shape, a runner who could cover a healthy number of miles. But Rodiez, although probably ten years or more Harry's senior and only five-seven or so, was a keg of a man, well-built, muscular, clearly with many years of sparring under his belt.

Harry declined. Eventually, Tom and Tony agreed to accept $150,000 for the trademark—and we'd stay out of the Milwaukee area.

In his early days with Eastbay, John Schaefer started to notice something peculiar around town that we'd noticed, too. At his morning swim group, for example, conversations with the people in the group, whom he'd known for years, took a noticeably negative turn. Other conversations were similarly caustic. "I got a sense that there were people that were surprised at how well Eastbay was doing," Schaefer says. "They were a bit shocked that Harry was hired. They wondered why. And there was this underlying tone to everything they were saying that *really* said, 'How can these two guys running a shoe store be doing so well that Harry would actually leave a great job to join them?'"

Schaefer says he sometimes sensed that people in town wanted Eastbay, or Harry, to fail. "It wasn't like, 'I hope it blows up in their face,'" he says. "But it was like, 'Boy, it will feel good to say *I told you so* if it doesn't work.'"

There was still that chance. Harry and Schaefer had gotten us on solid corporate footing, and we were starting to operate like a real grown-up business. But the specter of losing more chunks of business, even as we got commitments from vendors that they'd stick with us, was real.

Reebok won the Shaq sweepstakes, and was set to launch O'Neal's first signature shoe, the Shaq Attaq. The company was considering cutting us off from the new shoe, which we were sure would be a smash hit, and cutting us off from the company's superhyped Reebok Pumps.

Reebok didn't send lawyers to just cut us off, like Nike had four-plus years before, fortunately. Instead, Reebok invited us to its headquarters in Boston. One more time we had to sell a company on why it should let us carry its shoes in *Eastbay.*

Our answers were all the same as the ones we'd given the other companies about how we'd matured and had all the great data and the vision for the catalog.

But also, our answer was that we knew Reebok had ceded its number one spot in the business to Nike, and we could help make the Shaq Attaq the next Air Jordan.

29

Launching the Attaq

Heading to Boston, we had already heard the rumors of Shaq's icy position toward Nike. We had also heard that Reebok had included a mock-up of an *Eastbay* spread featuring some of his apparel. We felt that was a good sign, but we also knew that we *needed* Reebok to stick with us.

In our presentation, we highlighted our expansive mailing list. Reebok president, Bob Mears, jumped on that, telling us he wanted access to that list and said he'd pay $1 million for it. This was common practice. We'd rented mailing lists from *Sports Illustrated* ourselves. At the time, reaching people was much more difficult than it is now, especially twelve-to-twenty-four-year-olds, a demographic in which we had gained ground that no one else had.

But we didn't really need to consider the offer, because we already knew we'd say no. Our relationship with our customers was sacred, particularly because so many of them were young kids whose parents had entrusted us with that little bit of access to their worlds. If those kids suddenly started getting Reebok mailers that they and their parents had never asked for, we imagined the families quickly connecting the dots back to us, thinking we had violated their trust just to make a few bucks. That didn't feel right to us, which was hypocritical in the sense that we would rent other lists—though they never performed like ours—but we protected our own fiercely. And that was that.

Let's talk more about the shoes, though, we said.

Reebok execs said early reviews of the shoes had them concerned; they worried that people thought the shoes were ugly. In the sneaker world, we'd heard people call them "dogs." And honestly, some people within Eastbay found the Attaqs to be aesthetically challenged. But the company was asking what we might be able to do with them.

We told them we thought they were asking the wrong question. This wasn't about the aesthetic appeal of the shoe, and how to increase it, it was about accessibility to the dream. *I wanna be like Mike!* wasn't just a catchy slogan, It was something a kid could, even for a dreamy second, imagine to be possible simply by stepping into a pair of his shoes, which, let's remember, were considered ugly once, too.

But as charismatic a person (and salesman) as Shaq was, and as dominant a ballplayer as he was, when you looked at Shaq as a kid—hell, even as a grown man—you saw something unattainable. Many didn't dream of becoming Shaq the way they did Jordan, because it was beyond their control, regardless of whether they wore his shoes. Leather on your feet couldn't make you a foot taller with sixty more pounds of muscle.

We thought that maybe that was an unconscious bias that customers carried, because deep down, they struggled to find a natural connection to a signature shoe endorsed by a man who wore size 22s and was seven-feet-one, chiseled like a Greek god, and agile like a, well, a rhebok—the African antelope Reebok was named after.

The Shaq dream was not quite as accessible as the Jordan dream, because Jordan, while tall and obviously elite athletically, wasn't mythologically large.

The kids who *did* want to "be like Shaq" were the smaller percentage of young athletes who also were relative giants and who grew up dreaming of becoming powerful and dominant NBA centers and post players, a very specialized group. Reebok would have a hard time targeting those specific post-up dreamers to hit the retail sales figures it hoped for from the Attaq.

But Eastbay could. We told them that we could put the shoes right in front of the kids that do have that dream of being a dominant big man.

All right, Reebok said. *Let's see what you can do.*

The company sent a shipment of Attaqs to Wausau for testing. The first catalog that carried them hit mailboxes on a Friday. By Monday, we were sold out and we reordered that morning.

Reebok was fully sold on us.

Moving into 1993, while we still had a long way to go, we felt like we were in a good spot. We'd settled into our roles: Harry on business, Art on merchandising and inventory, and Rick on creative and marketing. All of us on vision.

John Schaefer was working, too. "One of the smartest numbers guys you'd ever meet," Trebs says of Schaefer. He was finding money everywhere. He discovered that our printer, RR Donnelley, was charging us a premium because it thought we couldn't find anyone else to print our catalogs. Schaefer gathered a handful of bids to show Donnelley otherwise, and its reps cut their prices immediately. It must have really scared them, because they got really helpful really fast. They called Schaefer one day to let him know that we used a lot of yellow ink in our catalogs, and that that was the most expensive ink to print with. So, we stopped using so much yellow and saved a few more bucks.

Our catalog circulation swelled to fifteen million, and the company generated $53 million in revenue and $5 million in profit, up from $32 million and $2 million the year before, the kind of growth any company dreams of.

And that was without Nike Air and Asics running Gels. "And Harry wasn't shy about letting people know how well we were doing," Schaefer says. At their morning swims, the tenor of the conversation had changed from skepticism to wonder. "All of a sudden," Schaefer says, "it's like, 'Wow. These dudes are for real.'"

In February 1993, Reebok, newly smitten with us after the Shaq Attaq catalog drop, invited us and Harry to be the company's guests at the NBA All-Star Weekend in Salt Lake City. It was an unforgettable weekend of skiing and watching the best basketball players on earth. We went to dinner one night with Reebok executives, who brought along special guests including the Hawks' superstar Dominique Wilkins, and Shaquille O'Neal himself.

What a surreal moment that was for us, watching him approach our table and sit down with us. For two kids who grew up idolizing even the high school and college athletes around town, let alone pros we read about in the paper and sometimes saw on TV, this was like dinner with a god. We remember first, as most people do, Shaq's imposing size. You think you get it from seeing him on TV, but you don't. It takes a minute to get used to.

What didn't take a minute was to recognize how friendly he was. After we introduced ourselves as the *Eastbay* guys, Shaq made us feel like he was genuinely as excited to meet us as we were to meet him. He was, he said—in every way—a huge fan. He was validating that gut feeling we'd had, that sense that regardless of what vendors and retailers thought about us, the kids we'd built *Eastbay* for, the athletes who mattered so much to us, felt the same about us in return. The catalog meant something to them. They connected with it in a special way the retailers were only starting to understand.

"I've been buying from you guys since I was a kid," Shaq excitedly told us. "You were the only guys who carried size 22."

30

Trust

Growing up as a business helped us grow the business, for sure. But so did the ongoing sneaker wars and the sports landscape of the '90s. Companies continued to vie for the attention of kids who lusted after their sneakers—basically our mailing list. A new era of NBA superstars fueled interest. The '92 Olympics brought fresh heroes, and the apparel and shoes from those games filled our catalogs in '93, and most of those items sold out.

The catalog became everything *we* thought it could be, especially the covers. A genuine, fully realized voice had emerged. Sometimes we went for inspiring covers, a stunning photo of kids playing a pickup game in a golden-hour haze. Or there was the track catalog with nothing on it but our name and a runner crouched over on a track looking down. He's wearing an Eastbay-brand tank top. The picture is stylized, almost smudged, which makes you feel his exhaustion from training. In small type underneath: *You've got to want it.*

Sometimes we went playful. One Christmas cover was a Norman Rockwell–like send-up of Santa asleep in a rocker as little elves go about outfitting him with a baseball mitt, a hat, a basketball. One elf is tying the laces of Converse Cons on Santa's feet. Sometimes there was a chaotic energy of comic-book-style superheroes popping off the page. On the '93 spring sports catalog, a baseball player hurls a pitch right at you, with a sprinter in front of him, fist forward holding a relay baton.

> "COMMANDER K AND SPEED DEMON COMIN' AT YOU WITH 52 WAYS TO IMPROVE YOUR GAME!"

Don't think about the logic too much. The story doesn't need to make sense as much as the energy of it does. The vibe. Kids got it. That issue also featured the debut of our new tagline: *Eastbay: The Athletic Sportsource.* It was a sign of the times, as we had fully shifted away from being primarily the source for runners and for teams, to becoming the source for anything athletic. And we mean anything. Some catalogs ran to 104 pages now. We added a women's catalog. We started carrying hiking boots and "brown shoes"—industry lingo for casual, nonathletic shoes like boat shoes. We heard from one executive who sold casual shoes that he had been complaining about us, asking what the heck his company was doing in *that* catalog, until one day he came home and his son ran up to him excited and said, "Hey Dad, you made the *Eastbay* catalog!" Athletes need brown shoes, too.

We had plenty of evidence that whatever affinity people had for the catalog, it was growing in numbers and intensity. Revenue was on a steady climb, and our office was becoming a well-oiled machine, or, okay, somewhat better-oiled. We were a dramatically different, dramatically bigger operation than we had been in 1987, when Nike first sent the suits of doom into the Washington Street store. We did all this without the Nike Airs. We knew we could go on without them and we would be okay. We knew there was plenty of growth to be found in other places. But we didn't want to go on without them. We love shoes, and we loved Nike Airs, and we knew our customers did, too. We still had customer-service reps keeping a tally of calls we got about them, even all these years later. So, we were going to put another full-court press on Nike.

We'd reached out several times during the past few years but never got a response, so we decided that this time we'd reach out through the catalog.

We designed a School's Out issue, with a cover of a playground and hundreds of people playing on it, like *Where's Waldo* (we're on there; you'll have to find us). Inside, we featured the Shaq Attaq across a massive spread in the first pages of the catalog, the best real estate after the cover. The page was overloaded with an array of Shaq-branded Reebok shorts, hats, jerseys, and more Reeboks, sneakers like the Central Park Mid, South Side Low, Intimidator, and the Pump.

On the next page, we featured an enormous photo of one of Shaq's size 22 shoes alongside more common sizes, just for fun. The page across from that showed tiny images of some of the non-Air Nikes we *were* allowed to carry. The Nikes were dwarfed by Shaq's Reebok, looking like they'd be crushed by the Attaq. It wasn't exactly a subtle message.

We sent twenty copies of the catalog to every single building on Nike's campus.

We're not sure if it was a coincidence, but it took only a couple of days for a Nike exec named Mark Duggan to call, and within two weeks, he had made the toilsome multileg trek from Beaverton to Wausau and was sitting in our conference room.

In some ways, Duggan felt like one of us. He'd been a top runner in college. He even joined us on our noon runs during his visit to Wausau. He playfully complained about the trip, which required two connecting flights. *Such a pain in the ass,* he said chuckling. But we got the sense that other execs wouldn't have cared and didn't care to subject themselves to the trip to Eastbay.

The catalog drop had the intended effect on everyone out in Beaverton. Mark conveyed the general sentiment at Nike regarding the Shaq shoe in *Eastbay*: *What the hell are you doing with* that *shoe in such a prominent position in the catalog?* The implication was obvious: Nike wanted *its* shoe in that position.

Just a few years earlier, we'd sued Nike for the right to put its shoes in that very position in our catalog. Maybe, we told him, if we still had the Air line of shoes, *they* would be there. And hey, no hard feelings—we'd still be happy to reopen that discussion.

At this moment we were glad that we never burned a bridge with Nike. We had heard rumors—far-fetched, perhaps, but prevalent enough to make us wonder—that other direct marketers who had Nike Air shoes pulled by Nike had sent their excess inventory directly to Phil Knight's house in protest. We never retaliated or bad-mouthed Nike. And we knew that we had plenty of advocates within the company. That made this suggestion that we reopen the discussion plausible.

"Well," we remember Mark saying, finally, "I think they'd like it if you guys could come out for a visit."

So, we went to Oregon with Harry. Nike's campus was always an amazing place to visit. Its main buildings were surrounded by a berm with a running trail on it, usually full of people running (no one walked at Nike). Every building seemed to have gyms, also usually full of people working out. Smoothie shops and health-food cafes, day care, and everything you could think of, really, no matter what your sports might be, was all there. We could see Phil Knight's hand in everything. It was an athlete's paradise.

The way this place made us feel created a striking juxtaposition between our admiration for Nike as a company and the way that company had treated us, the undeniable existential stress it had subjected us to.

But our goal here wasn't retribution or closure or anything like that. Our goal was for Harry to pitch the execs on why they could trust us with Nike Airs.

The meetings felt tense but not combative. Gary DeStefano, a longtime Nike executive, spearheaded the first meeting. Phil Knight wasn't at that one, though we remember him dropping by to introduce himself and exchange handshakes and small talk. It was also likely a way to make it known to us that he was paying attention.

Some on the Nike side of the table seemed to like us just fine. Others weren't sold on us. But even the anti-*Eastbay* cadre seemed to recognize now that we had *something* to offer. Nike had regained its position as the number one shoe company, but the sneaker wars were ongoing, with more factions now and a growing market to grab. Once anathema, direct mail was now a potential ally in the war as more consumers became more comfortable with the model. Retail alone couldn't help the vendors scale the way they wanted to (it may have even held them back). They'd lost ground to Reebok before, and the Shaq Attaq spread clearly woke them up. We made sure they knew that we also knew of that certain gigantic NBA player's feelings about Nike not featuring Air products in *Eastbay.* We humbly suggested, as we had to Duggan in Wausau, that if they gave us something that they felt was better than the Shaq Attaq, then they may well get a full and proper spread, too. Give us Air, give us the Jordans again, and we'll do right by them.

The brand dilution remained an issue, but we thought Harry handled that one easily over several meetings by showing them how much we'd grown up since '87. We showed them our growth, our new structure, and all the ways that we had matured as a business in the years since Nike Air was pulled from the catalog. We showed them how their products would be presented with the highest levels of taste and respect. They were impressed by how fast we shipped. We showed them we were smart and serious about the business in a way they wouldn't have detected in 1987. We could segment our mailing list by who the customer was, what they bought, when they bought, where they were. Our forecasting was sophisticated; we knew exactly what weeks to mail what season's catalogs to different regions based on the weather and how to manage inventory against that. We showed them our breadth of inventory. Knight didn't know we had sold seventy thousand track spikes, that we were in fact their top seller of track-and-field shoes, and that track was our original heritage, same as he didn't know the numbers we were doing for their team sales and other track products, something we think resonated with the former college track star.

We sensed they were softening. But a key issue remained, and it seemed to come down to one word: trust. We remember part of the conversation going something like this, from their end: *We want this product to be seen as something of value, and we're suggesting a retail price, and your opening price point is below what we suggest, and that means you don't agree with us. Why would we want to work with you when you don't agree with us?*

We told them we never intended to cheapen Nike—we didn't start discounting to make cheap, fast sales. We'd simply started our company as a team-discount dealer and maintained that same business strategy as we evolved into offering individual sales. "We never thought of it as cost cutting because we wanted to sell more," we told them. "We just wanted to get the best shoes possible to more athletes." We knew, we said, that if they got better shoes, they'd keep buying better shoes. They got used to how much better they felt and how much better they performed in them. We weren't just selling a discounted pair of shoes; we were gaining a customer that would trust us and buy those shoes for years. And we had the data to prove it.

Nike execs countered that they spent millions of dollars developing these shoes, building relationships with those athletes, and then developing graphics, slogans, and other marketing materials around these shoes, and they did all of that with not only revenue targets in mind but also a specific level of respect they wanted the public to have for the final product. They wanted people to see their shoes as the most premium brand in an industry of companies at war to gain that distinction. Nike needed to *trust* that anyone selling those shoes would value the shoes the same as Nike itself did.

That philosophy differed from ours. No getting around it. But Knight and Nike had a clear vision and purpose behind why the image of Air as *the* premium sneaker was so important to them, and we felt grateful for his clarifying that to us.

We reminded Nike that we did things that no other retail store did or could, especially around inventory. Foot Locker couldn't sell size 15s (never mind Shaq's 22), because it didn't have room to carry sizes that only a few people need. But those who do need 15s, *need 15s*. We carried them all, in every color. We told Knight and his execs that we sold two hundred thousand pairs of shoes from size 12 to 20. To whom? Probably a tall kid, playing basketball (and we realize now, years later, also to collectors). You want that tall kid to see your products. Shaq came to us because we had his size. No one else did. The profiles of our sales by size, when you put them on a curve, were unlike any in the industry.

And Roger Clemens came to us. And Gwen Torrence. And we shipped fast.

In addition, we told Nike, we knew the foot. We loaded our catalogs' pages with data about the shoes, weight and material, and what kind of feet they'd be good for. One of our original running-club members, Jim Sisko, led a group that tried out *every shoe* we brought in, and entered notes into the computer system about fit and purpose, so customer-service reps had good information when people called in.

We ran spreads of famous athletes along with short articles telling their stories and describing how they became stars—connecting their greatness with their shoes. We put emotion into the product list. We got kids to spend time with our catalog. They formed a bond with *Eastbay*, and they were loyal to us.

We were not a ding on Nike's reputation, we told them. We were a conduit; a spotlight, a projector, a megaphone—pick your amplifying metaphor. Like us or not, we clearly had a foothold in the industry, we had cultural currency, and we were in many ways more relevant and more effective than major retailers. You want people to believe you have the best products? You believe your products *are* the best? Then let people *see* them, side-by-side, with everything else out there. That's what we did. We cut through the hype and gave customers all options and some information so they could be informed, then put the decision power in their hands. And they loved us for that.

Maybe, compared with Nike, we were still just a little operation in a little town in the Midwest, but we knew we could do things with products now that not even Nike could do. We knew we made it so much easier and more fun for the customer, and we knew customers loved us for that. Nike had scale and muscle we couldn't fathom, sure, but we had agility and customer connections Nike couldn't create.

We'd come a long way from hauling shoes to clinics in the Beast.

We should note here how great the Nike execs were during this process. We were in awe of Phil Knight, who was nice to us, even though we had sued to keep Nike Air at Eastbay. It never seemed nasty between us. It was just a difference of point of view. Nike execs even had a question for us. They'd started experimenting with their own catalog—a threat to Eastbay that the three of us—Art, Rick, and Harry—had identified. But putting the catalog together and getting it printed and shipped took them a long time. They were able to produce only one, maybe two a year. *How,* Knight asked us, *can you guys put a whole catalogue together and get it out all in just two months? It takes six months for us just to get a picture approved.*

Perhaps this scene has you thinking that Nike rushed back into our arms, that we went for a nice long run around the Beaverton campus together to hammer out the details, and that we all lived happily ever after.

Nope. The meetings ended amicably, probably more amicably than how they started, but also without a resolution. Nike said it'd be in touch. And that was another thing about Nike, same as most companies that size: nothing moved quickly.

But we felt good. We'd left the impression we needed to. We couldn't help but laugh about the six-month turnaround on one catalog photo. We were shooting and approving photos within an hour some days. *Six months? For one photo?* We felt a certain pride after hearing that. As we laid out all our capabilities to Nike execs—in buying, shipping, customer segmentation, customer service, the catalog—and saw how they continually were surprised by our operation, we couldn't help but feel good about what we'd built.

That night at the hotel, Harry got his own room, but since we were trying to save every penny that we could, the two of us shared a room with two queen beds.

At breakfast the next morning, Harry asked how we'd slept.

"I'm about to die," Art said. "Rick was up 'til two a.m. watching *F Troop* on TV. Next trip, you're bunking with him."

"If I have to try to sleep with him watching that all night," Harry replied, "I'll resign."

"I'm just paying him back," Rick said, recalling one of Art's childhood pranks. "Whenever I would sleep over at his house when I had my morning paper route, he would set the alarm for three in the morning. And I thought it was time for me to get up."

Payback.

31

Family

John Schaefer, who like Art had loathed running before Eastbay, wanted to get in on our noon runs, especially after a doctor recommended that he lose fifty pounds. We promised him a $20,000 bonus when he reached that. He got there in six months.

As his waistline shrunk, his job grew unwieldy. Even without Nike, we'd grown 30 percent to 40 percent a year for a few years now, a testament to bringing in experienced managers and to the vendors who'd stuck with us. Sales were tracking to increase another 30 percent, to almost $69 million by the start of '94. We had moved our shipping center out of the J.C. Penney building we'd been sure we'd never outgrow. Our new shipping center was at the edge of downtown, and we still had inventory strewn across five different warehouses.

Schaefer was worried the entire organization was starting to get overwhelmed and needed more structure. Harry told Schaefer to find a director of merchandising , and if he did, Schaefer would become CFO. At the time, Schaefer was interviewing for an assistant controller position, and one candidate showed up for an interview who appeared to be completely overqualified. For starters, he was wearing a suit.

They shook hands and the man introduced himself as Dick Johnson. Dick was thirty-five and he already had more than a decade of experience in corporate finance, most recently as a director at Graebel Van Lines, located just a couple blocks from Eastbay's HQ. He'd been a runner all his life, and his wife, Mary, was a runner, too. Having spent years coaching high-school cross country and track in southern Wisconsin, he'd regularly ordered his team shoes and gear from *Eastbay,* and he always found our business fascinating. When he saw the job opening, curiosity took hold.

We knew of Dick, who knows how, probably through track connections. Wausau's not that big. A couple years before this, Rick had a notion to talk to him about Eastbay. Rick walked over to Graebel, but Dick wasn't around and nothing came of it. We wonder what those couple of years could have been if we'd got to him back then.

Schaefer told Dick, "You're pretty overqualified for an assistant controller job," but he was also excited by the interview. After they finished, Schaefer raced up to find us in our offices to tell us to look out the window. He pointed at Dick crossing the street on the way back to Graebel. "You see that guy?" Schaefer said. "That's going to be our new vice president of merchandising."

A couple of days later, Dick returned for a follow-up interview. From here, we would like to allow Dick to tell the story, because he tells it so well:

> And here I am, coming from a company that's very much a suit-and-tie environment, early July, hot, summer day, and I'm all suited up. Harry's in jeans and a sportscoat with a T-shirt underneath. Art's wearing a golf shirt and shorts. And Rick's just wearing a T-shirt and shorts. And they're all wearing running shoes.
>
> We introduce ourselves. And right away Art opens up the Milwaukee *Journal* to read the sports section. Harry's asking me questions about business and leadership and all that, and Rick's asking me these esoteric questions about life in general and why runners are so good at what they do. You know, things that are not necessarily pertinent to the business, but after you get to know Rick, you understand where he's coming from, and you see how this matters to him.
>
> Near the end, it's got to be seventy-five minutes later, Harry asks if I had questions. I ask a couple, and the whole time, I'm thinking, *This guy across from me, Art, hasn't asked a question, hasn't even made eye contact since we shook hands. Does he even realize I'm in the room? Have I just wasted this hour?*

> And then I look closer, and it's yesterday's sports section. That made it even worse in my head. *Are these guys just pretending they want to hire somebody?*
>
> Art puts the paper down and says, "Well, I've got a question for you." Oh, okay, now that I'm about to stand up and walk out, now you've got a question. He says, "Do you think you can come to work in shorts?"
>
> Of all the questions I prepared for, that is not one that made my list.
>
> I pause for a second, and say, "Well, I've never worked in shorts, but if that's the dress code, then I guess that's the dress code, so I sure could."

The truth was, Dick struck us as quite possibly the calmest and most thoughtful man we had ever met, and we could always do with more of that.

Later, we learned that Dick didn't expect to get any job. But when he had seen the opening, he told his wife, Mary, "I'd really like to meet the guys at Eastbay. They did such a great job taking care of our cross-country teams, and I've never had the chance to meet them." So, he applied for fun. "I had no interest in being an assistant controller," he says. "But I thought I could at least learn some more about the business, and learn more about the operation, and, hopefully, get a chance to meet our rep."

Harry offered Dick vice president of merchandising. Dick told Harry he didn't need a fancy title. "I just wanted to get to work in that kind of environment," he says now. "I felt like I belonged there, and I could be successful, and the culture seemed right." Harry gave him the title anyway.

We also learned another remarkable thing about Dick Johnson: He was the guy who'd interrupted one of our games of catch in, what was it, 1983, around Valentine's Day. The guy who pulled up to the empty shop, in a real hurry to buy some racing flats for his girlfriend because he was going to put an engagement ring in one of them.

"I tried to walk in through the retail store," Dick says of his first day, "but it was closed, so I ducked in through the phone banks. It was crazy. They must have had a hundred phone stations. The first thing I notice is this palpable buzz. And I was like, *What the hell is going on?*

What the hell was going on, he learned, was we were in the middle of back-to-school season, fielding endless calls from customers needing cross-country spikes, volleyball shoes, football cleats, training gear, clothes, and shoes, shoes, shoes.

Within weeks of starting, he'd learn about the Eastbay family. On an August night, the wife of John Braasch called Art. Braasch was Art's first running and former high school coach—the one who helped him train for his first marathon. They loved running together.

Braasch had gone for a run that afternoon, his wife told Art, and he had never come home.

Art knew all his routes, so we jumped in Art's car and immediately went tracing their favorite routes. We drove through a cemetery we used to run through, a scenic place with acres and acres of gorgeous evergreens and fountains and picturesque monuments, beautiful and reverent. But there were also six miles of hills between the cemetery and his house. Brights on, flashlights out the window, we called out for him. We spent all night searching, but we couldn't find him. None of us spoke our fears aloud. We only wondered why John would've gone for a run on an oppressively humid August afternoon.

Next morning, Dick Johnson was in his office when Rick's three younger brothers barged into the store anxious, sweating, and in a hurry. They were yelling to people to leave their work for later and come help find John Braasch. Swaths of Eastbay workers flowed out the doors to join a citywide search for a dear friend.

Our worst fears were confirmed when John's son found his body in the cemetery under a tree. We had to have been no more than ten feet away from him in the dark of the night before. Medical examiners later confirmed that he'd suffered a heart attack. Art never ran another marathon.

Dick had started his Eastbay experience with the controlled chaos and buzz of the call center at the height of the fall-sports catalog season, and within weeks, found himself out on this search, a terrible but poignant moment. Dick never forgot what it felt like to see how the Eastbay people responded. An entire business stopped, dozens of people from every part of the organization abandoned their posts in one of the busiest seasons of the year to look for a lost friend. "Right away I get this experience with just how much this culture really was about family," Dick says. "Everyone says that now. 'We're like a family.' But they're most often not. It's just words. At Eastbay, people never really said that, though. They just did it."

PART FIVE

Getting Huge

32

Carefully Orchestrated Chaos

As 1993 rolled into 1994, the deadline arrived for us to pay Harry his bonus. Our plan was working. Harry loved working at Eastbay, and we did not want to lose him, so we figured a way to keep the party going. We converted what we owed Harry from the bonus arrangement into a stake in the company that would eventually become about 12.5 percent. Our first and only junior partner, and we were thrilled to do it. It was, as Harry used to say, a "good win-win."

We continued to find more astonishing examples of how *Eastbay* was making a larger mark in the world, too. Polly, who by now was doing corporate relationship management, went to Super Bowl XXVIII in January 1994 in Atlanta. The NFL invited us, as we were working with the league on NFL Shop catalogs. At one of the schmoozing events for Super Bowl advertisers, Polly grabbed a cocktail and sat down. Joe Namath sat down across from her. "We never thought that anybody had a clue who Eastbay was, so I introduced myself the way I always did. 'I'm Polly, and I'm with Eastbay. We're a small sporting goods catalog out of northern Wisconsin.' And that's all I got out of my mouth."

Namath jumped in, excited. "All he wanted to talk about was *Eastbay*." His daughter was a track athlete. "And he was talking about all the things they bought and how she loved the catalog," Polly says, "and how he'd grown to love the catalog, too. And it was one of those moments when you realize that if he's saying all this, we're kind of a big deal. And we really had no idea. I started to get a whiff of it in moments like those, or when people would steal my *Eastbay* catalogs on a plane when I'd use the restroom and left a copy on my seat. Things like that."

Nike moved slowly. Shuttle diplomacy continued and would stretch out over eighteen months, with semiregular trips to Beaverton for meetings, and even the occasional visit from a Nike exec in Wausau, during which they'd inevitably complain about the travel. Or their hotels. Or the food. (Who doesn't like deep-fried cheese curds?)

When Dick gave them tours of our operation, they seemed both impressed and unimpressed—they could see some method to the madness, but mostly they could see the madness. They probably wondered how we were running such a successful company with the order intake, inventory storage, and shipping processes that we had. As our new vice president of merchandising, Dick Johnson had to explain all of this. In fairness to Nike, Dick says that at first, even to him, "It just felt like chaos."

Our call center, now operating twenty-four hours and with about four hundred employees, was a raucous symphony of ringing phones and constant chatter, noisy and echoing throughout all three floors of our Third Street headquarters. (All call-center reps still had their designated Nike Air tally notepads and still logged every request every day, even after six years.) "The call center didn't *seem* very professional," Dick says. "But they were very effective."

Our entire operation was like that. Chaotic but effective. We had leased basically a whole block of downtown Wausau. From the outside you'd see what looked like vacant storefronts with their windows papered over. You'd have no idea that a $60 million operation was in there. None of it was air conditioned. When executives from big companies visited, we'd rent giant barn fans to run air through and hopefully cool it down just a bit.

We had inventory stashed all over town in warehouses with names that evoked their heritage. There was the Hoofer Glass Warehouse, the

Morley Murphy Wholesale Hardware Building, the Callon Street Warehouse, the Murray Machinery at the edge of downtown, a too-massive old foundry with thirty-foot ceilings. That one might have been the worst. It always smelled like oil, and a layer of soot made its way onto everything.

Warehouses were staffed 24-7. We shipped all orders placed before 3 p.m. on the same day, which meant we had trucks running around Wausau all night as workers moved from one warehouse to the next based on what inventory the computer said needed to be replenished where. It may not have made sense to visiting executives from Beaverton, but it made sense to us, and we were proud of the people who built and managed this carefully orchestrated chaos. We'd gotten so good at same-day shipping due to the systems built by John Schaefer, Maddie Opal, Keith Wolfgram, and Trebs that allowed us to do what no one else doing mail order could back then—get you your shoes in three days. In all our years in business, through winter storms and warehouse moves and software updates and whatever, we never missed a day of shipping.

Our lack of automation combined with the explosive growth meant we even sometimes enlisted UPS drivers to haul stuff out of warehouses into their trucks. Winters were challenging, too. Sometimes it was so cold, cars wouldn't start, or they'd be snowed in. But we didn't want to miss the same-day shipping, so we would send an army of SUVs and 4X4s to help our people get to work.

Nike's tour of all this was planned during warmer months, but not the warmest. We met the company's reservations about our operation with assurances that we were working to streamline everything—which we were. "It wasn't a sexy tour by any stretch of the imagination," Dick says.

The tenor of our trips to Beaverton grew warmer. We'd still see Phil Knight occasionally, but usually we were meeting with other legendary Nike executives like Tom Clark, Gary DeStefano, Mark Duggan, and head of team sales, Bink Smith. By now we knew how to have a good time on Nike's campus too. We went for runs. We ate great dinners.

Still, meetings always ended with us being told that the execs would have to confer with their bosses, so it seemed like whatever decision needed to be made, the decision-maker was never in the room with us. Maybe they were off trying to approve photos for their catalog.

33

The Intersection of Athletes, Music, Fashion, and Pop Culture

We had to wonder, why was Nike was being so slow and deliberate? We gave the company all the data it needed. And every month while Nike dithered, the catalog grew—in circulation, in size, in *awesomeness,* and we'd learn, in cultural significance.

The catalog now ran up to 120 pages, every one packed with shoes and data and inspiring pictures and anecdotes about the athletes. Look at Christmas '94, and a page full of Converse basketball sneakers. The Destroyer ("sleekly styled for back lot games"), the Backjam ("a unique rear strapping system"), the Merit Mid, and the Sky Rider ("stability from the React Juice under your heels"). Twelve shoes shown, also "Free Poster with Every Purchase"—the poster was of J.R. Rider. Also, some comic-book lettering of phrases stuffed in (following the issue's theme): ***DOUBLE DOWN!*** and ***ROAR!*** And there's star hoops player Larry Johnson, looking fierce, his quote in a classic comic talking bubble right next to his picture: "You don't put a hurt on guys just by throwing around a few elbows. You do it by taking it to them for 48 straight minutes."

Right under that, more comic-book lettering: ***THUMP!***

We had more products than ever. There was surging demand for "brown shoes"—boat shoes, hiking boots, work boots, and the like. Even the sneaker companies got in on it. We started selling Timberland's wheat work boots, which became a phenomenon all their own. We'd sell thousands over the years. *Eastbay* fans always remember the Strength training shoes we carried, too, which just looked wild, like a sneaker with a big flat extension under the front of the sole, like some pedestal holding the sneaker above the ground.

- Add 5 to 10 inches to your vertical leap
- Cut your 40 time by 2/10 of a second
- Medically documented to be safe and effective

We think the Strength trainer was a kind of symbol to *Eastbay* fans—though we sold quite a few—a symbol of that idea that we just had *everything.* Years later, when Eastbay shuttered, one fan posted to a discussion group just a picture of those strength trainers. No words. Someone else replied, "Came for this."

The covers had taken on a life of their own. They seemed to be graphic manifestations of Rick's sprawling and untethered imagination, harnessed by our amazing creative team into a cohesive sensibility—images and words working together in a way that spoke to our customers. There was the cover made to look like a tabloid newspaper, with news of aliens placing orders and operators delivering packages second-day-air on the space shuttle. There was the one with a seven-year-old hitting a six-hundred-foot home run after buying training products from *Eastbay.* We put Bigfoot on the cover, finally finding a shoe that fit him and making Eastbay his exclusive supplier. Another featured a werewolf, which was in fact a Photoshopped Rick with the caption that he "couldn't decide between lined or unlined Eastbay jackets." Some of Rick's ideas were impossible—*Let's make it look like the cover is literally on fire!*—but by starting with the impossible, we'd land on something incredible, like a hoop exploding in electric sparks as a jump shot hits nothing but net. One of our most inspired cover designs was a riff on Leonardo da Vinci's Vitruvian Man, clad in spandex shorts orbited by Charlotte Hornets team Starter jackets, Eastbay private label wind suits and duffel bags, Carolina Panthers hoodies, Above the Rim sweatshirts, tan Nike Mega Force shoes, and more. Across the top: *Some things never change.*

June 1993 was another iconic cover, and another of our favorites. A child shoots at a net in front of a brick wall; it recalled the cover with the young man shooting in front of the brownstone. This kid is smaller, unable to even fill out his Barkley number 34 Phoenix Suns jersey. His form is loose, arms flailing like it's taken all his effort to get the ball to where it is, just above the rim. It's hard to tell if it'll go in. The light casts his shadow against the wall.

His shadow, though, is a grown man dunking. Across the bottom: ***DREAM BIG.***

"It's the kid playing now *and* seeing who he's going to *become*!" Rick would rave like a zealous preacher, as excited as that kid himself. It was this energy that came through on every page of the magazine that kids connected with. It was hard to land on a page in *Eastbay* if you were a young athlete and not feel inspired by the picture of Michael Johnson sprinting out of the blocks surrounded by a page full of his signature shoes. Or energized by the essay on Charles Barkley, "One Dribble," and how he could do it all on both ends of the court. Or bemused by the factoid next to the picture of Barry Sanders ". . . Barry Sanders was a defensive back in high school. The coaches didn't like his running style. They said he was too small. Last season Sanders ran for 1,500 yards and a touchdown . . ."

It was a feeling that whoever was making this catalog totally got you. And we spoke directly to them. Here's our letter from the kid-shooting/shadow-dunking issue:

PLAYERS ARE MADE IN THE SUMMER . . .

You know what it means to become a player. It means that now is the time to make the commitment. If you're going to be part of the team this fall, you've got to work on your skills this summer. After all, you've got to have the skills before you can play the game. Work on your talents—the individual moves and plays that you'll bring to a winning season this fall. Or work on the mental aspect of the sport—the determination, the drive, and the killer instinct. Set a goal. And reach it. Read the tips inside that tell you what it took today's pros to make it. And never give up the dream . . . because if you make yourself a player this summer, the team could be yours this fall.

Art + Rick

We tried to make every page drip with inspiration. Those humorous Easter eggs we'd started planting now built inspirational connections between the kids and the athletes they worshipped:

> Marquette recruit **Anthony Pieper** really started to improve when he pledged to shoot 10,000 baskets one summer—and did it! He still has the records his mother kept to prove it, too.
>
> **Larry Johnson** played one-on-one basketball with a friend eight to ten hours a day—outside, in 90-degree-plus, 100% humidity when he was growing up in Houston.
>
> **Bob Cousy** was cut from his high school squad his first two years and only made the team by playing summers in a tough community league in South Boston.
>
> **Scottie Pippen** left his high school team—and almost left school—in 10th grade but returned for his senior year. At the end of his senior year, Pippen was 6′1″ and weighed 145 pounds. His scholarship to the University of Central Arkansas was as manager of the basketball team. But by his junior year, he was 6′5″ and an All-American.

New entrants to the athletic shoe and apparel business harbored fewer suspicions of us than the big vendors. They were seeking us out. The folks from And1 came to us when they started their brand. We sold thousands of their T-shirts and their great baggy shorts and helped them launch shoes. Starter launched a breakaway jacket with a design for every team in every league, and we bought virtually all of them, and showed virtually all of them in the catalog. *Starter's* sales reps used *our* catalog to show off their product line. Those jackets got so hot we were ordering containers of them. Kevin Plank came to us when he was ready to introduce the world to Under Armour—which wanted to bring tech and function to sports apparel that still looked cool. Under Armour always sold well for us and got plenty of cover placement.

Given the way we'd started, we took great pride in working with these companies. It was satisfying and rewarding to help underdogs, people like us, just crazy enough to build something against the odds, and so many of them succeeded.

It's easy to see how focused on athletes we were; we always had been. We are not sneakerheads. Of all the things we stumbled into in our lives, sneaker culture beyond athletics was one of the biggest and most unexpected. But it makes sense in retrospect. *Eastbay* created *access* to unique styles that were becoming collectibles.

Sure, we knew that sneakers were showing up more outside the lines. We saw Will Smith wearing Jordans in *The Fresh Prince of Bel-Air.* "I wanted them before they were out," Smith said in 2020, reinforcing the collector's mindset that drove that part of our business. "I wanted people to see them on *Fresh Prince*."[1] In *Jumanji,* Robin Williams's character, Alan, is the son of a shoe factory owner who makes custom shoes for a basketball star, shoes that deeply resemble Charles Barkley's signature Nike Air Max 2s. Brendan Fraser, playing the title character in *George of the Jungle,* becomes near-superhuman after putting on a pair of near-all-black Nike Air More Uptempos, one of the more blatant product placements in cinema history. Jerry Seinfeld donned Nikes throughout *Seinfeld*'s run, from Air Trainer SC Highs to Jordan 6s to Nike Air Huaraches. Darius McCrary's character, Eddie Winslow, regularly wore Jordan 3s and Jordan 6s on *Family Matters.* And we probably sold a million pairs of those old Nike Cortezes after Tom Hanks's Forrest Gump ran across America in them.

In hip-hop and music, the Puma Suede dominated the breaking scene in the Bronx. LL Cool J wore Jordans in the early '90s, and on Nas's song "Halftime" he raps about being "a Nike head." The old Converse Chuck Taylors enjoyed multiple resurgences, especially with grunge bands like Nirvana and ska bands like The Mighty Mighty Bosstones sporting them. Kurt Cobain famously scrawled *ENDORSEMENT* on the rubber toe of his Chucks. We carried all of them.

Even in pop culture, sneakers moved after celebrities were seen donning them in paparazzi photos. Princess Diana was often photographed in sneakers, and this would start a frenzy of buyers looking for her styles.

All of this made sneakers a fashion statement, and we sensed *something* going on, a nexus of athletes, music, fashion, and pop culture, but we couldn't, as Dick Johnson recalls, "put our arms around and define what it was yet. I think, subconsciously, we probably knew that we were fueling something, but I don't think we knew what."

We knew that a lot of the shoes we sold were bought for fashion and not performance, but we figured they were bought by athletes who also wanted to buy shoes to wear just because they thought they looked good. Maybe some of their friends ordered some, too.

We now know that we had an entirely separate fan base made up of grown men and women who didn't play sports, who geeked out on sneakers as fashion staples as much as we geeked out on shoes for performance. Sneakerheads were walking around staring down at people's feet to see what they were wearing just like we were, only for different reasons. They liked that they could get hard-to-find styles and colors from us. They liked that they could find the shoes their favorite rapper or grunge band wore. They were *collectors*, who prized unique finds they'd never, ever, get in a store. The chase was part of the fun, and we were part of the chase (they collected *Eastbay* along with the sneakers), and the vibe we created in the magazine perfectly matched the sneakerhead vibe. Inspiring, playful, full of comic energy.

More practically we also had the right cadence. New model rollouts were happening all the time, almost monthly. Retail stores couldn't match that cadence, but our catalog was monthly, and we always made it a point to have something new in every catalog, so we became a natural place to find all these new shoe debuts.

To sneakerheads we'd become like a global boutique sneaker shop that did not exist in brick-and-mortar, or if it did, existed in one or two shops in New York or LA. Bobbito Garcia's writing in hip-hop magazine *Source* "made a lot of people realize, *Hey, I'm not alone in this,*" said sneaker journalist Russ Bengtson, author of *A History of Basketball in Fifteen Sneakers*.[2]

That sense of a community—we're not alone in this—is what we were unwittingly providing to Garcia himself and other early sneakerheads. "I don't remember how I got ahold of it," Garcia says of *Eastbay*. "But once I did, it was like, *This is gold*... Being someone who really appreciated design, and appreciated out-of-left-field, unavailable colors that I couldn't search for in a physical store, mom-and-pop shops . . . *Eastbay* was a welcome alternative. And it was brilliant. Really brilliant."

For Garcia and sneakerheads, *Eastbay* wasn't just about finding cool new sneakers to buy—it was also about gaining access to a world they longed to see but felt excluded from. "We didn't have access to the catalogs the brands were sharing with retailers whatsoever," Garcia says. "That was unheard of. So, it was like, to have a magazine, a catalog with page after page after page of shoes—it was mind-blowing. It was *mind-blowing*—like, *Look at all this!* You know? Like, I'm not sharing this with just anybody."

He laughs. "*Eastbay*, for me, was not to be shared," Garcia says. "It was kind of like this clandestine movement of ballplayers and sneaker fiends who I was down with that knew about it, but we didn't want to tell that many people about it. Because if we ordered the white-orange Nike college team-issue sneaker that season, it's not like we wanted to see a lot of other people with the white-orange, you know? You just kind of kept it on your hip, and just a very small circle of people you would mention it to."

We had started to notice something similar among athletes who got the catalog. As it reached this apex of design and attitude and just sheer volume of products, kids were becoming possessive of the catalog itself. It was a signifier. A status symbol. You were part of some club that *got it.* Kids remember wasting away a study hall just getting through the football section. Circling all the shoes they wanted. Ripping pages out. We often had coaches and teachers complain about kids sneaking in *Eastbay* reading time, literally pulling the old trick of putting it inside the textbook. "*Eastbay* held me down during my school days," one person wrote to a discussion board, remembering the catalog. "Getting dope sneakers at their regular price, or even just trying to be different and unique, you went there."

We didn't know this parallel audience was feeling the same way about *Eastbay* that we did, and the athletes did. Without even realizing it, we'd been serving two different cultures with different dreams about the same products. These original sneaker fiends got just as excited about *Eastbay* arriving in their mailboxes as did the kids who wanted new shoes for a new season. "Back then," Garcia says, "you didn't have fifteen inboxes like nowadays. Back then, it was one mailbox. You had bills, you had junk mail, and then you had the *Eastbay* catalog. Opening the mailbox and seeing that was like a ray of sunshine."

In more ways than we even knew during that time, *Eastbay* became the dream book for kids that we always hoped it could be.

And everyone seemed to get it, except Nike.

34

Lighter Than Air

Nike remained engaged but evasive, or at least careful.

Everything kept coming back to that word *trust*. Nike had every reason to trust that we could sell its premium shoes, but still, it wouldn't. Even the sales reps who worked with us on other Nike products were frustrated they couldn't place Nike Air shoes in *Eastbay*. They knew we could sell them.

We believed Nike still worried about *how* we'd sell them, but we weren't sure why. At some point, we formed a theory. We realized that one of the great strengths of *Eastbay*—the sheer volume of products, the massive variety—was working against us with Nike. Even if Nike got a prime spread for some model, we generally packed as many shoes onto a page as we could.

Analytics had told us that that was the way to go. While our operation was still overly complicated in some ways, it didn't mean we weren't sophisticated about what we were doing. We did "square-inch analysis" on the catalog, measuring the value of a square inch on any given page in terms of sales of the product that took up those square inches. We worked hard on these metrics, and the square-inch analysis told us it would be bad for sales if we made any one product too big—took square inches away from variety in favor of hyping one product line. That helped reinforce our philosophy not to favor one product over many others. So that overstuffed aesthetic of the catalog—so many shoes, so many colorways on a page—was in part a business decision, but it was driven by the fact that the variety and volume were a virtue for athletes and sneakerheads, and something that is even today immediately recognizable. Instagram accounts still post old pages of *Eastbay*, and even without zooming in you know you're looking at an *Eastbay* catalog page. Fans still love poring over those pages and reminiscing about what it was like when they got the catalog.

Nike didn't seem to love it, though. It didn't want the Air lumped in with everything else. Nike wanted it to stand out. It didn't want to be with the crowd, or even above the crowd, even if it was the cool crowd. It wanted to be in an echelon all its own. Nike Air needed to be *separate* from other shoes. If we were going to get Nike back, we needed to figure out how to do *that*.

Whoever had that insight was right, because once we started approaching discussions from that perspective, the pace picked up. By early June 1994, three of Nike's top executives made the excursion from Beaverton through a couple of layovers to land in Wausau.

We had been working with them on a new plan for Nike Air that set the shoes apart, and this presentation could finalize a deal. They wanted to go over the details.

We laid out the plan one more time. We would produce a Nike "beauty book"—a coffee-table-style book full of Nike products given gorgeous photography, shoes and apparel together with minimal text highlighting a few technical specs, but not in a way that distracted from the visual spectacle of the shoe itself. High-gloss, heavy paper stock. It was in many ways the antithesis of the *Eastbay* catalog. Restrained. Elegant. Minimalist. Serious.

The beauty book would be a joint venture—*Nike x Eastbay*. Nike liked this idea. The execs said that was something they'd love to see.

But they wanted something else, too, the same thing that Reebok had wanted: our mailing list. We said that we wouldn't just hand over our mailing list, for reasons given before, but we had an idea for how we could meet in the middle.

We would send the beauty book to our list of known Nike buyers. Nike would send it to its list, and we would share names with each other of anyone who bought from the coffee-table masterpiece. This was a compromise, but one we felt was worth it as it was not just a mass handover of every name. We were happy to get Nike's list of names, but we were quietly confident that it wasn't that valuable to us. We figured that our list would be much more effective than Nike's. Ours was full of Nike buyers from *Eastbay*. Nike's was full of addresses collected through various promotional tactics, of people who may or may not have been buyers.

Nike agreed to the approach. We were getting so close. Six years after losing Nike Air, after all the meetings, the tours, the presentations, the courting, the dating, the stalling, it seemed we were on the verge of getting back together.

We told Nike that in *Eastbay*, we'd position Nike Air with premium space, and would sell at suggested retail, though we'd still offer team discounts.

This was an excruciating decision that hit Rick hard. Even now, three decades later, Rick gets visibly upset talking about it. The logic was sound—we wanted to make sure that the Air products were positioned as premium, that Nike was seen as separate. But suggested retail cut through the soul of why Eastbay was started in the first place. And Rick always fought for the lowest possible price. We remember times when we'd argue over changing a price from $29.95 to $29.99—four cents. But that four cents on the right product could be a million dollars over a year.

Rick battled the rest of the team on the Nike pricing. We get Air back, sure, but now we're doing something that goes against why we went into business in the first place, and what's made us so successful. On our runs he'd hang back to state his piece and when we countered, he'd get frustrated with our reasoning for compromising on price and he'd speed ahead of the pack, putting the rest of the team in oxygen deficit as we raced to catch up with him. (He was always the fastest runner among us.)

Rick wasn't wrong. It was a sea change for the business, and his fear was that this was a concerted move away from being a friend of the athlete to being a vessel for the vendor. All to get Nike Air back when we'd been growing at an absurd pace without that line.

On the other hand, while pricing was important, it wasn't the only pillar Eastbay was built on. Accessibility and variety of products were just as crucial as the team-discount pricing.

This was one of the hardest choices to that point for us as a team, as businessmen and as friends. It was emotional, passionate, filled with anger and screaming. Rick ranted at the rest of the team for days. Because Art knew him so well, he knew not to take any of it personally, that Rick's heart would beat so hard for what he believed in and his mind would race so much, lightning in a skull, that sometimes it simply had to spill out, and all that you could do was absorb it.

Art, in his usual Mickey-Mantle-baseball-card-great-idea way, had an idea for a compromise, saying we could keep the spirit of discounting by bringing the prices and energy of the tent sale to a new catalog—one that we'd eventually call "Final Score." Great prices on great product all the time.

Rick smiled.

So that's what we did. Rick accepted Nikes being sold at suggested retail because it was good for the business and the business was still on its mission to do what we had set out to do. And sometimes, growing and building a business means making hard choices and changing the way you do things, even if they challenge your core vision. This is just another part of maturing as a business and growing up as businessmen. Maybe growing up also means giving up some things.

The execs left saying that they just needed to confer with everyone back at Nike headquarters, but that they felt we had reached the agreements we needed to, and the rest was bureaucracy. We knew better than to believe anything until we saw a signed contract, but we felt, for the first time in six years, a tense optimism about Nike.

On their way out the door, one of the execs started complaining again. There were some raucous patrons in his hotel that had kept him up all night. And he was dreading the flights and layovers to get home.

"Don't screw this up," he said. "Because I'm never coming back to Wausau."

While we waited for word from Beaverton, we were completely surprised to find out that we were being recognized as Wisconsin Entrepreneurs of the Year, throwing a bright light on just how much we had done since losing Nike Air. My God, had we worked hard, and changed, and grown. Doing the interviews for the award, we found ourselves connecting the loss of Nike to so many positive outcomes. Just before Nike pulled Air, Eastbay was the two of us and Trebs, and a team of fewer than a hundred. We shipped out sixteen-page catalogs to a few dozen states and made around $17 million that year.

Six years later, without Nike Air, we grew to more than six hundred employees, we were sending millions of catalogs a year to all fifty states, and we were projected to bring in $80 million in revenue.

If we had kept Nike, would we have grown our product base the way we did? Eventually, maybe. The team was growing the catalog after we lost Jordans. But would we have pushed in so many new, unknown directions so quickly to find new growth if we'd never lost the Air line? We wouldn't have been so pressed to find more product, to expand the catalog, to reach more kids with all the products they wanted. Nike's move had pushed us to new levels as entrepreneurs, as leaders, and pushed the team to work its magic—and they did it.

And the more we grew, the more we knew that we wanted to think longer term and bigger picture. Whether or not Nike came through with the Air shoes now, if we wanted to keep growing this dream, the number one issue we faced was financing. We would need to explore options for raising more money soon, whether through private investors or, maybe, by taking our company public.

A few weeks after Nike left Wausau, we were in Boston with Harry and Dick for meetings with New Balance, getting ready to go on a run.

We had a message waiting for us at the desk. It was from Wausau. Nike, finally, had sent an executed contract, and they wanted us to sign and put together an order for Air products for next season.

That was one of the best runs of our lives. So much stress, so much hard work, so much uncertainty and thinking and rethinking and reinventing and negotiating and compromising and fighting and persevering. It had worked. It had finally, really worked. We kept smiling and laughing as we ran, and we just kept running for miles, effortlessly, cherishing the moment, feeling—we're gonna say it—lighter than air.

35

Testing Limits

New cover: A lone man running down a long road, a big red Nike swoosh under the image. In the bottom right in white: *Just do it.* And in the top left, under the yellow *Eastbay* logo against a purple splash, a simple statement from us to our customers, and a tacit acknowledgment of the six-year effort to get Nike back: *Winning always starts with a dream . . .*

This was an exclusive Nike catalog and an early iteration of the beauty book, sixteen pages dedicated to nothing but Nike running shoes and apparel, a blatant love letter to show our gratitude, and to signal that Nike Air products stood apart. But we still managed to bring hints of the *Eastbay* vibe.

Page two featured the brand-new *teal* Air Max and below it, the Air Structure II, and on page three, the Air Max Triax and Air Huarache Triax. We covered the bottom half of page three with an homage to Phil Knight, a big picture of him smiling under sunglasses and a Nike cap, juxtaposed with an image of the goddess Nike to the left. It accompanied an essay telling Knight's story of how he started Blue Ribbon Sports out of the back of his car, selling shoes at track meets, using his mom's laundry room as a warehouse while he worked as an accountant and professor, struggling to get the business off the ground. It was a story we could relate to. "Phil Knight continues to define sports culture through Nike," we wrote. "It will be the guiding force of the future. For at Nike, there is no finish line."

We had an essay about the Greek legend of Pheidippides and his impassioned run from Marathon to Athens to declare victory for the Greek army. We connected that to Nike, the Greek goddess of victory. "Set your sights high," we wrote. "Run with purpose and test your limits. The rewards will follow."

We included stories about where the shoes came from, about Knight's former coach turned business partner Bill Bowerman's visions for perfect running shoes. We wrote about Steve Prefontaine, the legendary runner and the first to ever compete in Nike shoes, and about other great runners like Joan Benoit Samuelson, Cosmas Ndeti, Bob Kempainen, and Lynn Jennings.

"Winning is personal," we wrote. "Just do it."

Producing that catalog and having Nike Air back in the mix in this way felt like finishing a marathon for us, too. The joy, the dreamlike sense of peace, the sheer relief of crossing the finish line, felt damn near heavenly.

At least for a few minutes. We had celebrated getting Nike back with a catered dinner (probably that meant we ordered a hundred Angelo's pizzas), and our call-center employees gleefully tossed their Nike Air tally notepads like graduation caps. "The first feeling was euphoria," Dick Johnson recalls. "And then, fairly soon after, the feeling was, 'Holy s—, we have a lot of work to do.'"

The first regular *Eastbay* issue with Air Jordans—we knew our catalog, not the beauty book, was where the real money would be made on these shoes—went out on a Friday, and our entire Jordan inventory was sold out by Monday. *That* was it! That's what we'd been waiting for. A new era had begun for the company, one encapsulated by what we wrote in that first *Nike x Eastbay* catalog. We tested our limits. Tested the hell out of them.

Suddenly we'd hit another spate of accelerated growth. Nike Air was gas on a fire for Eastbay. It was beautiful and precarious. And, we were learning, when you hit this scale, it creates new problems that come at you from new angles. The size of the problems grows with your success.

We were getting big enough that fraud was becoming prevalent—analog versions of what you get on online shopping sites today: fake catalogs or phone numbers for taking orders. Credit-card fraud led to inventory going out the door on fake payments. Our dedicated fraud department grew to deal with it, something we never imagined we'd have to do. Soon we had eight to ten people per shift doing nothing but calling banks all day to verify credit-card numbers. We had to train call-center agents on detecting signs of fraud on calls.

Some of the fraud came from inside the house—a call center supervisor threatened to report her manager Maddie Opal, who ran the call center, to the Equal Employment Opportunity Commission for paying her less than promised. She even presented a letter apparently signed by Maddie proving as much, sending poor Maddie into hysterics. A quick look showed it was obvious forgery. We hired a detective, and the shady employee quickly broke down and confessed.

Then there was the time that someone called us accusing Trebs of stealing shoes and company money and using them to pay off debts to the mob. They demanded money in exchange for providing us with the details. Trebs? The mob? Come on. We ignored that one. Still, we were astonished to think that someone would find shoes so valuable that they could be used to pay off mob debts.

Around the same time, UPS kept calling us to report its drivers getting mugged. We were still taking cash-on-delivery (COD) orders, a major part of our business at one point that served customers without credit cards. But criminals had figured that out, so they were robbing the UPS drivers. UPS stopped accepting COD orders from Eastbay, and we moved away from that business model.

Even non-COD orders were in peril. We saw a steadily rising wave of customers calling to complain about not receiving packages for which UPS confirmed delivery. It didn't take long to figure out that their packages were being stolen right off their porches, long before doorbell cameras could catch that.

So instead of shipping the products with Nike Air or Reebok or whatever branding visible on the packaging, we switched to more generic boxes with a shipping label that had the Eastbay logo on it. If anything, that made the problem worse, so we switched again to plain brown cardboard boxes and plain plastic bags that we got from a potato farm near Wausau.

Break-ins continued to be a problem at all our warehouses, especially older ones. One Christmas Eve, Art ended up at the Murray Machinery warehouse at midnight, helping police catch some kids who'd broken and entered, and were rifling through all the shoes.

Meanwhile, we put Polly in charge of managing our private-label Eastbay-signature product line, sending her regularly to work with our manufacturing partners in the United States and abroad to see how things were going. And this was a time when women were very much not making these kinds of trips. "I never thought about it," she says, "because I'm thinking, well, there's nothing I can do to change it."

She recalls one evening visiting the factory in mainland China that was producing our windsuits. The factory owner/manager invited her back to his home for a traditional tea service with his family. She rode with this man up into the mountains to his home, where his wife and half-dozen children waited, dressed in their formal ceremonial attire and lined up by age. She was introduced to all of them. Once inside, she was met by bolts upon bolts of green nylon fabric, in a green hue that she knew instantly we'd rejected from his factory because of bad dye-lot match. She said it was everywhere; the foyer, the hallways, rooms, bathrooms. It a was tacit message, *Look what you've done. I'm stuck with these bolts of fabric you rejected.* "He was showing me how decisions we were making were affecting his life personally," she says. "And I realized I had naively gotten myself into a position where things could go not so great for me at that moment."

The tea ceremony lasted about an hour, and then his driver returned Polly to her hotel, and all was well. "But I felt kind of shaken up by it," she says. "I grew up a lot that night."

Growth was again testing our ability to manage it. We'd started sending catalogs to Japan, with a Japanese-language cover wrap, and suddenly orders from Japan began pouring in, our fax machines just spitting out a continuous feed of them overnight until the fax machines ran out of paper. When someone added paper in the morning, the machines just picked up where they had left off, spitting out what turned into thousands of orders per week. We eventually learned that we were the second-most-popular catalog in Japan behind only *Victoria's Secret.* It caught on in Australia, too. Fast-pitch softball players from Australia discovered

Eastbay when they had come to play in summer leagues in Wisconsin. They brought it home, where the same viral spread occurred that we'd seen in the United States. *What's that you're looking at?* Eastbay*? Can I see? Where can I get that?*

We put out fourteen *Eastbay* catalogs in '94 with a circulation topping ten million, a big leap from just a couple years prior when we sent smaller catalogs seven times a year to half as many people.

Managing all the demand became a relentless, ever-changing science. Planning call center staffing was especially difficult. Say there was a snowstorm in the Northeast, and those catalogs arrived in mailboxes a day or two late. Suddenly there's a surge in orders two days later than typical. Pandemonium on the understaffed phones.

Even as we were shipping out inventory as fast as we could, all the warehouses were overflowing, too. New shipments would sit on trucks until we could load an outgoing shipment and make room in the warehouse for the incoming trucks' cargo.

The warehouses themselves were nightmares, aging relics with wobbling old staircases that didn't feel particularly sturdy. We needed to deal with that, too.

With Nike Air products back, we were again growing at a pace—40 percent—that drew down our cash as we spent and spent to keep up.

Intriguingly, the company growth, as astonishing as it was, wasn't quite as much as we had anticipated—though in fairness we thought sales might double, which was a giddy forecast. Still, the Nike growth was robust, and a tide that lifted all boats. Having Nike in the catalog brought more people to the catalog. As we expected, the Nike beauty book didn't convert sales like the *Eastbay* flagship catalog did, and we'd phase it out over time. Our list always crushed Nike's, because it was full of buyers, and your best next buyers are your last buyers.

We were surprised to learn just how valuable that organic growth of the Eastbay mailing list had been, and we got a good sense of it once when Harry Colcord and John Schaefer met with Bill End, the CEO of Lands' End. Harry was carefully exploring a possible business deal with Lands' End, but Schaefer, to Harry's annoyance, kept peppering End with questions about mail order. End revealed in the conversation that his company's goal was a 2 percent conversion rate—it wanted 2 percent of the catalogs it sent out to generate an order. "With all respect to Bill End," Schaefer says, "I was like, *Holy s—*. We're already blowing that out of the water." Our conversion rate was around 7 or 8 percent. That sounds amazing. Dick and John would tell you—he told us—it meant we weren't sending enough catalogs. We could mail more. Maybe millions more.

The upshot of all this is that growth was creating massive new challenges, and we were on the verge of losing any sort of financial cushion as we bought and bought and invested and invested to keep up. "Just going nuts," says Schaefer, who was maxing out our lines of credit. We were paying merchandising employees tons of overtime to keep up with demand. "We were over-ordering everything," Schaefer says, "because we were afraid of running out."

Then those bills came due. Our $6 million line of credit was supposed to be paid to zero every April. John Schaefer did that, only to immediately realize that $9 million more we'd drawn was due by August. "I absolutely s—a brick," he says. "I thought, *Oh, s—. I killed this company.*"

He called a guy he knew named Randy at a local branch of a Milwaukee bank and told him the situation. Schaefer said, "We need more than nine million bucks." We sent the bank numbers, and it did a bit of due diligence.

Randy came back to John: "Okay," he said. "Our bank can do a credit line up to twenty million. Will that work?"

"Hell yeah, that'll work."

In two weeks, we had our $20 million cushion. "He told me they all looked at our numbers and projections," Schaefer recalls, "and to them, it was just obvious. In their words, this was a rocket about to launch. Apparently, you can't hide success."

PART SIX

Getting Out

36

Eastbay World Tour

Every time we added money, we grew faster and needed more money to keep up. Even with a new $20 million credit line to underwrite the rocket ride, we were again outgrowing everything. We needed a new office. Creative needed more space. The call center needed more space. We were thinking how we also might fix our warehouse problem, consolidating into one big, new space.

We wanted to do these things and keep growing without taking on more debt. We explored getting the kind of money we'd need through private equity. We flirted with some firms; some dangled around $40 million for 40 percent of the company. None of us really liked that idea, though—getting in bed with soulless finance sharks who lived for numbers and spreadsheets and had no feel for what Eastbay was about. We cared about more than building the business; we wanted to enjoy building it.

Another option was to sell to a bigger company. Foot Locker came around asking about that, and threw at us a number around $60 million. It also told us that if we didn't sell, it could just start its own catalog and put us out of business. "Foot Locker kind of scared us a little bit," John Schaefer recalls. "We kind of figured well, sure, maybe they *could* start their own catalog, but if they could, why hadn't they already?"

Nike got into the mix for a hot second. But those conversations didn't go far. If Nike bought Eastbay, why would Adidas or Reebok or New Balance or anyone try to compete with Nike in a catalog that Nike owned? They'd all pull out. That would erase more than half the revenue from the catalog. Nike never made a formal offer.

We were still young, barely in our forties. And looking at the industry landscape, we felt like we still had lots of room for Eastbay to grow running it our way. That sense that *Eastbay* was connected to something larger only continued to grow as we got further into the '90s. We weren't ready to give that up.

We were also working to grow in another way, by finding more products to sell. That included meeting with leagues like the NFL and the NBA about becoming exclusive marketers of their licensed products.

Harry remembers sitting down in Toronto with Detroit Pistons legend Isiah Thomas and other athletes as part of a meeting with the NBA. During a similar meeting with the NFL in Atlanta, Harry remembers Herschel Walker getting excited about meeting "the *Eastbay* guys," and then asking for a picture with Harry. When it came to *Eastbay,* athletes just *got it.* They were all fans, and they knew it was special. "They seemed like people who understood that Eastbay was a company that respected the young athlete that they had once been," Harry says. "There was no trickery involved, it was just straightforward, get you the product."

There was a third option for getting the money we needed: going public, and we'd started taking steps in that direction. We'd been kicking the idea around ever since we hired Harry, and he said one of his major priorities was to get us acting more like a public company. When Harry hired Dick Johnson, he told him that when we got to $100 million in revenue, that was the time. And at this moment, as we looked at the need for a new warehouse and a new HQ, we were there, inching up on $100 million in revenue.

There was something very Eastbay about the idea of an IPO, too. If we were going to look for capital, what better way than by offering the opportunity to the people we started this business for in the first place—the employees, the customers, the coaches, the athletes, the people who knew and loved and understood what Eastbay was about—to be part of it.

We floated the IPO idea during the spring of 1995, and it didn't stay secret for long. Merrill Lynch approached us. Harry recalls, "They said that if we were looking to go public, they could wrap up our story so that you will look like the most significant thing to ever hit the sporting goods market." Meetings with other firms in New York, Chicago, and Los Angeles generated similar promises. It was deeply flattering and a bit intimidating. The way they talked about it, we didn't know if we could live up to what they were selling.

We liked a firm called R.W. Baird, based out of Milwaukee.

It sent a guy named Brent Rupple to meet us in Wausau in late April '95. He arrived in white shorts, a $500 sportscoat, and Gucci loafers. Harry brought him in and then swung by our offices. "Rupple's here," he said. "We might be able to work *with* this guy, but he could never work *for* us."

Gucci loafers aside, Rupple seemed more down-to-earth about the IPO process than the larger firms, and we liked that he was local. He understood us. We felt comfortable with him and thought the process would be more fun with him than it would if we were swallowed into a massive New York firm, where we'd be a small play. If we're going to raise capital, we thought, we might as well enjoy the dog-and-pony show, which we were warned could be grueling.

Baird it was. We would offer shares for 30 percent of the company, likely starting around $12 per share, with a goal of raising $20 to $30 million. Harry would retain his 12.53 percent stake, with the two of us splitting the remaining 57.47 percent.

We went to Piper Jaffray in Minneapolis to secure a second partner, and right away Rupple made us feel good about choosing Baird. When two of the investors there expressed doubt that Eastbay was going to be able to open at $12 per share, Rupple jumped in. "C'mon," we remember him complaining to the Piper Jaffray skeptics. "I've spent my whole life trying to put whipped cream on turds. Eastbay is the real deal." The rest of the meeting went well enough that Piper Jaffray joined us and Baird for the roadshow.

In early September, we started a month-long Eastbay national tour with Peter Kies from Baird. At first it was legitimately thrilling for a couple of guys who still sometimes felt like kids from Wausau. Here we were, gallivanting around the country with bankers.

Baird made it comfortable. Every flight was private. We just parked at the airport, walked onto the tarmac, climbed into the jet, took our places in the recliner seats, and then ate and drank to our stomachs' and livers' content. When we landed, a car awaited us. We felt absolutely spoiled, and a little embarrassed.

Boston, Chicago, Denver, Baltimore, San Francisco, La Jolla, San Diego, Los Angeles, and of course, scheduled for the last leg, New York. We had next to no time to enjoy any of these places that looked like they'd be fun to visit but which felt so far from Wausau. Some cities we saw only through the window of the car shuttling us from airport to conference room to airport. We landed in San Diego at night, went straight to our presentation, then a hotel for a nap, then back to the plane before the sun came up. We never saw the city in daylight.

We hit Europe, too, where we had a bit more time. In London, we made like proper tourists at Abbey Road. In Edinburgh, we ate haggis, which tasted pretty good if you didn't think too hard about what it was. Couldn't be less healthy than the cheese curds and brats we grew up on.

But mostly, it was meetings.

We told our story fifty-seven times on that tour, and it never got old, the impression that it left. It felt good to be able to tell our story, though we're not entirely sure why it felt so good. We certainly weren't trying to brag or show off, but maybe it felt good to prove to people that we really knew this business, maybe better than anyone. Certainly, anyone in the athletic shoe business.

We'd get pointed questions. "Okay, so you've had five years of compounded annual growth rate of 39 percent in sales, 43 percent in profits. That's ridiculous. How can you maintain that? How do you know you can maintain that?"

And we had answers. We had a decade-plus head start on mail order, and we did mail order better than anyone in shoe retail. It was our sole focus. We were the only direct marketer in America that offered all premier products from all major athletic manufacturers, and we were the only direct marketer selling the full line of Nike Air. We were working with the NFL and the NBA on potential deals. We were Nike's only catalog provider—that one always got their attention.

Why couldn't others enter the market, they'd ask us. And we'd hit them with the litany of things competitors had no idea they'd have to do to get it right, all the time, like we did. Timing inventory, understanding demand cycles and how weather affected regional demand, knowing the cash you needed available to cover for mistakes, knowing how to do same-day shipping, working with all the shoe companies.

Others could try, we told them, but it would take a while.

And even though they never asked, we pointed out that we were ahead of everyone online as the first sporting goods seller with that new thing called a website. At the time it was only for collecting names for the mailing list. Amazon existed then, but it was a small bookstore. Zappos wouldn't even be around for four more years. We remember that nobody at these meetings asked us about the internet or cared much about it; back then they didn't see much value in it.

Our mailing list always piqued their interest. They seemed to want to know, *How are these guys getting millions of catalog requests every year from kids who nobody else knew how to reach?*

The other rote talking points seemed to get their attention, though, especially the last one we'd bring up, if they hadn't asked yet: the loyalty from and connection with our customers, the millions of young people between the ages of twelve and twenty-four. We said it again and again and again: *Eastbay*'s spirit, its vibe, its specialness to the athletes, would be hard to copy. If it weren't, someone would have copied us by now. Plus, we'd say, "How many kids get mail? Almost none."

We got good at figuring out which of the bankers had kids who got *Eastbay* and which didn't. Those who didn't wanted to know who we'd gotten to know at companies like Nike and Reebok, or what professional athletes we knew. But they were mostly buried in spreadsheets and asked the financial questions.

Those who'd seen *Eastbay* in their house were more engaged and personal. They'd talk about how their kids ordered all their favorite gear from the catalog. They marveled at the inventory, wondering how we could get so many pairs of Air Jordans. One woman in Denver was excited to meet us because her son, a high-school junior, was a massive young man with a size 14 and they couldn't find sneakers for him anywhere except in *Eastbay*.

Those firms who knew about us usually requested a small percentage of shares.

The bigger firms, including the biggest in the world, Fidelity, in Boston, immediately asked Baird to set aside up to 10 percent of the shares for them.

Not everyone got it. Some institutional investors, John Schaefer remembers, were saying, *We understand Lands' End. We understand Foot Locker. Who the hell are you guys? You're not selling your own brand of stuff. Foot Locker's this juggernaut. Who are you?*

We tried explaining to them that we *did* have a private label, too, that was a steady source of revenue. But this only seemed to confuse them more. Were we a clothing company or a sporting goods company? And how could we sell so much stuff? How did we manage to fill a 128-page catalog?

We were stumped over how to turn them around until Schaefer got an idea. Once when he was in Chicago, he saw the CFO for Snap-On Tools give a presentation where he poured out a bunch of nuts and bolts and tools onto a table and said to the crowd, "This is what we sell."

So, Schaefer decided to try that. He ran upstairs to our hotel room, rummaged through a bag and found shoes, and ran back down to the conference room. "I said, 'These are baseball shoes,'" Schaefer recalls. "Now, they weren't baseballs shoes. I don't know why I said baseball. But not a single person called me out on it. And I said, 'This is what we sell. These are Ken Griffey, Junior, spikes.'"

The skeptics sort of got it, and the meeting went better after that. Once they were gone, Harry almost died laughing, pointing at the shoes. "Those are Art's golf shoes!"

In the end, there were more advocates than skeptics. During the tour, the initial IPO price kept rising, from $12 to $14 to $16 per share.

In New York City, one of our last stops, Bill DeVries invited us to dinner. He was CEO of the AFAD group—Athletic Footwear and Apparel Division—within the F.W. Woolworth Company, which owned Foot Locker. And here luck was playing its game again, because in his younger years, DeVries had oversight of the Kinney Shoe Store that had once sat right next door to our downtown Wausau headquarters (he didn't manage it or work there, but it was part of his purview). That shoe store later became our phone center.

He had come to Wausau to check out our operation prior to this dinner, on a hot summer day when our AC-less offices were being "cooled" by big barn fans. And yet now here we were going to Sparks on 46th, one of New York's finest steakhouses, and the same place where just a decade prior, John Gotti's men had gunned down mob boss Paul Castellano.

Prior to the dinner, Harry said, "They're courting us, and it's a full-court press."

They'd already offered $60 million to snap us up previously, and Harry was right, dinner was one last bid to buy Eastbay and stave off an IPO. But they stayed at $60 million. And we again declined. Emboldened by the road show, we thought Eastbay was worth more than that already and would become worth significantly more after we went public and had the capital to keep building the dream.

Seemingly feeling slighted by our answer, one of the Foot Locker executives at the dinner sneered and said, "All right, you go ahead with your little IPO. We'll talk later." By later, we knew, he meant when the IPO went bust and our company value would halve.

After dinner, John Schaefer looked at us and said, "Screw them. We're going public. And we're going to make it."

Maybe that crankiness was part John Schaefer and partly a result of the tour. We were at the end of it, and we were dog tired. Dick remembers us being cranky jerks for a while when we got home.

We still had one final presentation to do, though, for the people of Wausau, who would have an opportunity to become retail investors in Eastbay. We held a public meeting—we even wore suits—where we explained what we were doing and answered questions, many of which were still about what the hell we did. As the presentation wound down, a couple of women approached us and introduced themselves as Sharon and Jan. They'd been classmates of ours way back in grade school. "We just had to see this," Sharon said. "Because we remember how the nuns would always tell you guys you would never amount to anything."

On September 29, 1995, we stood on the trading floor at Baird in Milwaukee as our IPO launched at $17 per share. Then we flew one last charter jet home to Wausau, where we threw a party for all of Eastbay. We made bottles of wine with our pictures on them and labels that declared us corporate stooges.

It was thrilling to see our company become suddenly visible to anyone in the world who cared to look. We'd set out to raise some $26 million with the IPO, but we raised closer to $40 million.

By market close, the stock was up to $19 per share. A couple of days later, it was at $22.

We were happy that the plan worked. We'd raised the cash we needed. The existential stress we'd felt all those years was finally, finally gone, replaced with a financial stability that meant Eastbay would continue to build this dream, and that also meant our team knew this was a company they could stick with. We had trusted our guts, and it worked. We'd chosen the path we believed in, turned down Foot Locker and others. We'd gone our own way, inviting the world to buy into what we had built and help us continue to build it. The world had done just that. And now it had given Eastbay everything it needed and more to keep going.

What we weren't thinking about in that moment, something that Harry Colcord and John Schaefer and Dick Johnson were probably thinking about more, because they knew, was that 30 percent of Eastbay wasn't ours anymore. And those owners were represented by a board of directors that we'd need to work with. And now there was a scoreboard for everyone to see, every day, next to our stock symbol, EBAY. We'd always been stooges dreaming big, but now we were corporate stooges, dreaming big with other people's money.

37

Welcome to the Club

By 1996, we'd shipped more than thirty-seven million copies of the catalog around the world. We didn't think about it much, because we were so busy trying to keep up, but when we allowed ourselves to, on a noon run, or just looking out over the sprawling, busy office, we struggled to comprehend what Eastbay had become and marveled at what it could become now that we were public.

With the cash from the IPO, we began planning for a new warehouse and distribution center. We could buy a space along the Wisconsin River, on South 1st Ave., for a new headquarters. It was even more massive than the J.C. Penney building, big enough to house operations, an outlet store, and the call center, the pulse of the business, which now employed seven hundred people in various capacities. Actually, it was up to a thousand people, but we'd run out of people to hire in Wausau, so we added three hundred more in offices in Green Bay and Oshkosh. The call center was staffed with kids working after school, athletes coming in after practice, moms picking up shifts to build Christmas funds—all of them working on our updated computer system, which allowed them all to leave notes on certain shoes or common complaints they were hearing. This was reasonably cool stuff at the time, and we're certain it helped us keep returns down and increased our customer loyalty.

Still, we knew it could be a stressful job. In the new call center, we hung pictures of athletes who we knew had bought from us and who knew of us. Gwen Torrence. Roger Clemens. Shaquille O'Neal. Isiah Thomas. Frank Thomas. We had a replica of sprinter Michael Johnson's golden shoe from the Olympics on display. The idea was to remind the phone agents during tired and stressed moments how they could be helping the next great athlete who would eventually hang on the wall next to these legends, and even if the customer wasn't the next Ken Griffey, Jr., the agents were still helping someone who dreamed of becoming that.

And it was happening. The next generation of great athletes growing up in the late '90s and early 2000s *were Eastbay* kids. One day, in Raleigh, North Carolina, a kid brought an *Eastbay* to his AAU basketball practice. "Yo!" said a teammate, in a scene of the sort we've heard described to us countless times. "What *is* that?" The second kid, and all their teammates, crowded around the first kid, peering over his shoulder.

"It's *Eastbay*," the first kid said. "It's where you get shoes from."

The second kid was mesmerized, took down the phone number in the catalog, and called to get a subscription as soon as he could. "Mind blown," NBA star P.J. Tucker, the second kid, would say years later. "Crazy. I would wait for that magazine to come in and just circle stuff. I couldn't even get everything in there, but I'd probably get one pair, like, every quarter or so. But it was planning out which ones I was going to get, if I got the chance. I would have it in my backpack. I would be in school just looking at my *Eastbay* all the time. That catalog was a real moment in my life. A big chunk of my life."[1]

Across the country, in L.A.'s Compton neighborhood, fellow NBA star DeMar DeRozan would a few years later do the same thing. "*Eastbay* was my whole childhood," he says now. "That's all it was. Let me tell it: I wanted everything, and I had to have everything out of *Eastbay*. It was always just that motivation of seeing what new shoes were coming out, just seeing if they had my size, seeing unique kicks."[2]

We always loved hearing these stories. We loved to hear how *Eastbay* brought kids together and bridged cultures. We started hearing more such stories after we went public, because we were just more visible to the world. We didn't expect that. Nor did we anticipate other ways that the IPO would change our lives. Suddenly, Nike, Rebook, Adidas, and New Balance were letting us into their world in a way they hadn't before. Art remembers being at Nike after we went public and Phil Knight coming to congratulate us, smiling, saying something like, *Isn't this better than suing each other?*

Before, we were suspect, breaking unwritten rules and showing up at trade shows looking amateurish. Now, we were VIP guests at the Summer Olympics in Atlanta. We watched Muhammad Ali light the torch and sat with Nike brass. During the opening ceremony, when they got to country number 168, Art turned to Rick and Harry and said, "They've gotta be making some of these countries up."

Come to think of it, that's kind of how we're starting to feel about this book now that we're writing it all down. Somebody's gotta be making some of this up. The Super Bowl, the NBA Finals, the World Series, the Masters. Eastbay had standing invitations from one vendor or another to all of them. All expenses paid. Private flights or first-class. Meeting athletes. Taking pictures. Getting on the field.

But it wasn't made up. For two kids who grew up broke in Wausau, isolated from the rest of the world, it always felt unreal.

And the more the industry got to know us, the more it wanted to work with us. One after another, the NFL, the NBA, Adidas, they all asked us to help them develop their own catalogs. Just a couple of years before, it felt like nobody wanted us around—they certainly loathed coming to Wausau. Now, *everybody* was coming to us.

We like to think this new attention didn't go to our heads too much. In fact, it never quite felt natural to us. Sometimes it made us miss flying under the radar.

We wanted to spend time with our own families even more than we wanted to go to these amazing sporting events. Those were fun; meeting superstars was fun. We saw in them a parallel to us—they were people who liked to work hard and dream big, too. A big part of the thrill of meeting them was sharing that feeling with them.

But with Eastbay finally, for the first time, in a relatively safe place, we also wanted to coach our kids' sports teams, enjoy a slow morning with our wives. Do things we could finally afford to do that we'd put aside while we worked for fifteen years to keep Eastbay going and growing.

We started holding massive cookouts along the river, with executives grilling up thousands of burgers and brats. We held carnivals as part of United Way drives, competing to collect the most coins. Employees got to decide the "reward" for the exec who collected the most coins. One year, it was a dunk tank, and the executives were told, bring your suits, because you'll get wet. Dick Johnson brought his suit, all right—a business suit. He committed to the bit, climbing right in and telling everyone to bring it on. They may seem like small, ordinary moments, but they're what we remember most fondly. We just wanted to make sure we took care of what we'd built with everyone.

There are so many names and faces we remember—our head of HR, Carrie Reif, estimates maybe 8,000 people were part of the Eastbay family over the years, maybe more. We considered putting a running list of credits like they do at the end of movies, but that would've added so many pages our publisher wouldn't have approved the cost of printing them, especially since we would want every name in big type. We understand, but we've done our best to include as many as we could in our extensive acknowledgments.

After we moved into the new headquarters, Rick remembers sitting out alongside the Wisconsin River that ran by it, savoring rare quiet moments. He'd watch the water flow south, thinking about how it always kept rolling. It never stopped. He remembers thinking that that's what he wanted for Eastbay, for it to keep rolling. Keep moving forward, forever.

38

Corporate Stooges

Woolworth, Foot Locker's parent company, wouldn't quit. Within months of going public, it sent someone to Wausau again. We'd heard that due to the small size of Foot Locker stores, mostly in malls, the company was struggling to manage the inventory it needed. If it could snag Eastbay, it would give Woolworth much more flexibility for shipping to stores, and individuals. It wanted us as a distribution channel. "My number one objective is to buy you guys," we remember Foot Locker's Jeff Branman telling us in Wausau. "We *have* to buy you guys."

When we went public, we thought it was the thing that would allow us to keep building Eastbay for years to come. But in the year since the IPO, we'd started to wonder.

Maybe we'd been naive, or just willfully ignored what it meant to be a public company. We'd failed to fully account for how it would turn us into public figures. People *knew* us now—not just appreciative athletes, but everyone. We had to think about what we said in public, as we represented a company being traded on the stock market. We were inundated with requests. Team sponsorships. Help with expanding a stadium. So many charities reached out that we set up a dedicated group for it. Anyone with a passion and a need for funding came calling, and as a public company, you need discipline and formal processes to manage all that.

And while plenty of people in town were fans of what we were doing, there was a surprising number of people who were not. We would be out to dinner, and someone would come up to our table and ask how things were going.

Fine, fine. Working hard.

Well, I hope the stock keeps going up, they'd snort. At the Y, getting out of the shower after a run, we'd be ambushed in an awkward, half-naked encounter as someone demanded to know why the stock price had dropped thirty cents that morning. We rarely knew what to tell them. We could explain that some analysts were lumping us into the retail category, which has different economic cycles to deal with compared to those of mail order, but they weren't really looking for market analysis. So, we usually left it at a *sorry, we're sure it'll iron out soon, thanks, we're going to get dressed and get back to work now.* It never felt good.

We had to cut back on the warehouse squirt-gun battles, and we had to make management start wearing proper shirts. At quarterly board meetings with the board of directors, we found ourselves forced to wear pants. That might have been the worst part.

At the IPO party we had joked about becoming corporate stooges. That wasn't funny anymore. It took surprisingly little time from the IPO for us to realize that while we were perfectly comfortable being idiots in private, we worried constantly about being public idiots. Turns out being the first kind of idiot is more fun. The second kind not only has to change how they do business but also change how they live in the community.

To cope with the strictures of governance, we had to think twice about going out for a drink with coworkers after work. One night we did go out after work and enjoyed a few, only to realize that people, shareholders, could think that we were being too careless. Word could spread. Investors could get upset. The company could suffer. So, we stopped doing that. On our runs, the conversations had to change depending on who we were running with. Once, out to dinner with Harry, we started in on a strategy discussion only to realize someone may be eavesdropping. "We can't talk about this here," one of us would say. After a while, when we went out to eat, even with our families, we found ourselves staying close to our neighborhood and not venturing out. We weren't in hiding, but we just didn't want to go into town. Thank God, we think now, that this was before social media.

Dick Johnson remembers that Art was anxious and tired, and Rick felt penned in. "But the realities," Dick observes, "are that it's not just five board members sitting down having breakfast and saying, 'Hey, we should invest in this, or we should do this.' Even though they're the majority shareholders, they still must present their ideas to all the shareholders. And the local pressure, they would just sort of laugh it off, make some smartass comment, but I think in their heart of hearts, it started to impact them. They saw that the decisions they made impacted the people around them, and not just those in the company, and it was a lot to worry about."

In fact, the whole shoe industry was changing. The sneaker wars had turned many of the shoe companies into multibillion-dollar businesses. None was transformed more than Nike. When Reebok took over the number one position from Nike back in the late '80s, Nike's sales were $877 million. A decade later, Nike sold more than $9 *billion* and its profits were more than $750 million, almost as much as its sales from ten years before.

But with that growth came increasing scrutiny and much more professionalism. This manifested itself at the annual National Sports Goods Association (NSGA) Show in Atlanta, once the site of massive, legendary parties hosted by the shoe companies. These lavish functions became—in the old days—a kind of battle for cultural currency in the sneaker wars, to see who had the coolest party with the coolest guests. Adidas rented a mansion for one of its parties, where Roberta Flack performed. Avia brought in Hall and Oates, who at the time were probably bigger than Avia. Nike once rented out an airplane hangar and booked the Temptations. Reebok rented out an entire high school, assigned everyone a locker, and booked Chubby Checker for an old-fashioned sock hop. Companies would fly in top athletes, including Michael Jordan, to make appearances.

Those days were fading. That kind of cool factor was expensive to create, and skeptical investors saw little evidence of revenue generated from those parties. The shoe vendors were facing the same scrutiny we did—more in fact, as all the manufacturers were in contentious battles over their factory working conditions.

The shoe business had become a behemoth under constant pressure and scrutiny.

And so had we, even if some of it was against our will. The hardest part for us was how public companies simply couldn't follow gut instincts. We felt suffocated by all the restrictions on what we could *try*. We had quarterly numbers to hit, and that meant we couldn't impulsively pour millions of dollars into an idea because we were dreaming of what it *could* mean a year or two later. There's no doubt in our minds that the quarterly number made us stop looking to the future the way we had when we were growing the business. The obligation is to the shareholders, not to the dream.

Take the internet. We were well positioned to dream big with it, having been the first shoe retailer online. We were the second company on the internet with real-time inventory lookup, after only Lands' End. Inspired by many early e-commerce pioneers, we were emboldened to continue to grow that business.

Seeing Eastbay online, rows of color pictures of shoes and apparel and gear, knowing anyone in the world could come and buy merchandise there and have it shipped right away, we felt as amazed as we had the first time we stepped back and looked at one of those big boards with a catalog page cut-and-pasted on it fifteen years prior.

But we soon learned that to scale it the way we imagined, the way we scaled the catalog, we would have to pay internet hosting companies somewhere north of $30 million per year.

Even if we were still private, we probably wouldn't have made that bet. But the simpler fact was that as part of a public company, we couldn't even entertain the notion.

Or any other notion. Rick had big ideas about turning *Eastbay* into a magazine with extensive journalism. He made it sound, as his ideas always did, compelling and inevitable.

And even if we couldn't build a full online store, he still wanted badly to find a way to make the most of Eastbay.com. *There's just something there,* he would say. We groped around the internet and tried coming up with other ideas for growth. We wondered about going back to retail: open more Eastbay stores. If the shareholders think the internet is too risky (oops), maybe they'd support more brick-and-mortar stores, married to mail order. *It's the best of both worlds!* Rick would exclaim. Of course, there was a big problem with this idea, which was that we knew we really sucked at brick-and-mortar retail.

The limitations were frustrating in a way that even the most anxiety-ridden moments of building the business pre-IPO weren't. At least then we were anxious about dreams we were putting into action. For all the worrying over the years as we built the business—*How do we get a storefront? What happens if they pull their shoes? What if all this inventory isn't sold?*—we now realized that one thing that had driven us, that had kept us sane, was the fact that we could come up with an idea for how to set things right and then throw everything we had at that idea. We could always *do* something. Now there was only so much we could do.

We understood why it had to be this way, but we craved that freedom to take chances we believed in. The creative risks that had built Eastbay now had to be channeled into something safer and more predictable. Something incremental. It felt like part of Eastbay's soul was evaporating. The sense of loss was palpable. There was some grief in it.

All of it made us question how much more we could do for the business as a couple of corporate stooges.

So, when Jeff Branman of Foot Locker's parent company, Woolworth, came to Wausau and said to us "We *have* to buy you guys," we found ourselves more open to the idea than we had been in the run-up to the IPO. And this time, he brought a much more aggressive offer.

39

Heads or Tails

We went to visit Foot Locker. Its reps wined and dined us. They loved what we did, they said. They saw how valuable we were to people. They told us about their customer preference surveys, and how we came in at number two, behind only Foot Locker. Woolworth CEO Roger Farah took that to mean that Foot Locker absolutely needed us. We floated the idea of a partnership. No, Farah told us. They wanted to buy us.

But they'd told us all this before and had never changed their offer of $60 million. Now they had a new pitch. They wanted to give us Foot Locker stock.

Art wasn't having it. He would invoke his Uncle Bob in situations like this, and he did in this situation as well: Cash was king. "You want to give us stock?" Art protested. "How much is that worth? When can we sell it?"

Farah said we could sell in a year or so. Art said: "We are definitely not selling this company for stock. If you want Eastbay, you're going to give us cash." Admittedly, we can't remember if he said this to Farah's face or waited 'til we were back at the hotel to declare it, but that's where Art stood.

While golfing the next day, Woolworth COO, Dale Hilpert, pulled John Schaefer off the course and interrogated him about our IT infrastructure, organizational structure, and other internal operations, a sure sign that they had gotten our message about a stock offer and were sizing an offer that included cash. By the end of the trip, they made an offer: $19 per share, $2 more than Eastbay's current price.

John Schaefer, who had cursed the idea of Foot Locker buying us in the run-up to the IPO, says, "That's when 'Eff you, Foot Locker' became 'Well, thank you, Foot Locker.'"

We'd consider it, we told them and went back to Wausau. (We learned that one from Nike.)

Personally, we were torn.

Art felt it was a good offer, and he felt some relief to be getting an offer like this. He was deeply stressed, putting so much energy into finding new ways to make this public-company situation work. Art remembers that at the time another large local company, Wausau Insurance, had gone through some extremely bad times (it would eventually be sold to Liberty Mutual). He didn't want to see that happen to Eastbay.

And we had growing concerns about emerging threats to our business model. Vendors were starting to dabble in direct marketing themselves; some manufacturers were doing their own retail. That scared us. We thought what we were doing was so simple that if they had the real desire to, they could waltz in with their wads of cash and take over mail order. It might take some time, but they could do it. Although we'd curried enough favor to be a preferred retailer for Nike, Harry remembers, "There were so many reasons to believe that Nike was going to continue working toward going direct."

The internet was causing us angst, too, probably more than it was causing the market analysts. We could see the potential for a living catalog online, even if we couldn't afford to make one. (Everyone else would feel this angst soon enough.)

Rick, though, felt convinced that we could do more. He saw the threats, but he also saw opportunities. The industry was going through another tech revolution. The shoes had never been of better quality or cooler design. There was another round of explosive market growth that we could miss if we sold, and we had dreams of capturing the next wave the way we'd captured the big one in the '80s.

Harry said we should go to New York and have some meetings with other investors just to see what the interest in Eastbay was more broadly, and to get a sense of whether the offer we had was a good one. Baird flew us out on a Tuesday, and our stock was trading somewhere between $16 and $17. By the time we got back to Wausau on Friday, it had hit $20.

Jeff Branman at Woolworth/Foot Locker called Harry angry, saying Harry did it on purpose. Negotiations continued, usually by phone. Branman occasionally screamed at Harry; Harry generally let him. Talks reached a contentious apex when Harry asked for $24 per share. After he let Branman rant, Harry countered by saying we needed $24 per share for our public shareholders, but he would be willing to accept $22 per share for the portion that the three of us still owned. "That makes us bulletproof," Harry recalls. "Our fiduciary responsibilities will be fulfilled. Nobody will be able to say that we were somehow taking unfair advantage of our shareholders, because we are selling theirs at a higher level."

Branman yelled some more, so Harry told him to think it over, and then he hung up. "When you're negotiating something highly volatile," Harry says, "the best thing to do is walk away and then see what the other party will do."

An hour later, Branman called Harry back and said they'd do it.

Harry thanked him for his cooperation and said that he needed to consult with us, and he'd be in touch soon.

This was it. If we accepted this deal, that would mean Woolworth—Foot Locker's parent company—was going to buy Eastbay for $146 million (north of a quarter-billion today). Harry didn't think we could get a better offer, and he was ready to take it. Art thought it was a good offer, too. But Rick was torn. He was still dreaming. *Eastbay could still be so much more,* he said. *The magazine idea. The internet. The retail stores. The possibilities are endless.*

Art countered to the effect that, *All the possibilities cost a lot of money and investment after going through the Nike thing and surviving—did we want to risk it all again? And what about the last year as a public company? They won't let us chase those endless possibilities.*

Rick knew Art had thought it through, but Rick was still feeling flummoxed and maybe outvoted. Art assured him that wasn't what was happening, and part of him still wanted to keep going, too. He just didn't see how they could recapture the old lightning in this new corporate bottle.

We kept talking. As business partners. As friends.

We had so many difficult heart-to-heart conversations, sometimes with Harry and Dick and Schaefer, sometimes just the two of us, exploring every angle of either decision. And the longer we talked, the more we could see how badly each of us wanted the decision to go a different way than the other.

Always right there at this time was that desire, that need, to preserve the friendship. A fight that caused irreparable harm would have devastated both of us. All of us. It was as delicate and fraught as anything we can remember in our lives.

It's important to us to point out that, for the two of us, this decision was never about the price. We might have, as a public company, worked to make sure we got the best price possible, but the decision to sell didn't rest on that. When you are entrepreneurs at heart, your business becomes almost like one of your kids. You do whatever you think is best for your child, but what's best isn't always immediately obvious. Or you have different opinions about what's best for the long run. So, you discuss it. You argue about it.

We realized that we kept coming back to something other than money. Partnering with Foot Locker, gaining its expertise in retail and its clout in the industry and marrying its stores with our catalog, could become unbelievably compelling. But we wondered—Rick wondered—if Foot Locker would, or could, preserve Eastbay's culture and *Eastbay*. We would be setting our kid up for life, but was it what our kid really wanted or needed?

Thank God for our noon runs to let off steam. There were at least two noon runs we remember when we had to tell the group to stay behind so we could talk this through with Dick, John, and Harry. And we'd run hard and repeatedly go over the same points in different words. Rick remained convinced we could do more with Eastbay than Woolworth would allow us to. Art thought a sale would ensure Eastbay's future. Those runs ebbed and flowed with the conversation. Rick would feel frustrated and speed up, and we'd labor to catch up, then slow the pace, and Art would put in his point. Speed up. Pull back. Keep running. Slow down. For miles.

All our lives, we'd always found our way to the middle, and now, right now, on the biggest business decision of our lives, no matter how much we talked about it, we couldn't find the middle. We didn't know what to do.

Finally, one afternoon in the office, exhausted, two immovable objects just pushing up against each other, we made a decision.

In hindsight, it seems absurdly impulsive.

What the hell, let's just flip for it.

Rick pulled a quarter out of his pocket.

Heads we sell. Tails we don't.

This wasn't a movie, so there was no real fanfare to the moment. No dramatic buildup. No slow motion. No swelling music, as the world went quiet. Rick just flicked the quarter up off his thumb as both of us prayed it would somehow land on its edge.

The quarter bounced down on the table and then wobbled for a hundred years before the clanging accelerated into that familiar ring that becomes a shiver, and then finally it went quiet. Flat and still, it looked back at us with our future on its face.

Heads.

PART SEVEN

Letting Go

40

Passing the Baton

The deal was announced on December 3, 1996, and it was the biggest thing to happen in sports.

We're kidding. You'd be forgiven for having missed the news. It happened shortly after the Summer Olympics in Atlanta. Shaq had made his Lakers debut the previous month. Pat Riley had become the fastest NBA coach to win eight hundred games, and Wayne Gretzky had made it to three thousand points. Bill Clinton had just been reelected, and a bunch of tech companies were going public, pushing air into the dot-com bubble. Roger Clemens had signed with the Blue Jays, and a movie pertinent to our business had been released: *Space Jam*. What a time to be alive!

For Eastbay, the Foot Locker deal was monumental, and once again, our timing couldn't have been better. Within months, there'd be a strike at UPS, right during Eastbay's busiest shipping season. The heft and backing of the new parent company, Woolworth, helped us endure what would have been another enormously stressful moment in the Eastbay annals.

As kids, we used to scrounge change to get these amazing banana splits at Woolworth's in Wausau. Now, we'd really sold the little shoe company we started with a few thousand bucks to Woolworth for nine figures, a fact that didn't seem quite real.

As part of the deal, the two of us would stay on board with Eastbay for two and a half years through June 1999, a time when we'd get to reflect on what we'd done and what selling meant. "I don't think any one of us gauged it exactly right," Harry says now.

With Foot Locker we gained even more direct access to the athletes and coaches. We couldn't get pro athletes on the cover before this. Now we had many landing there, and we expanded the profiles of them in the pages of the catalog and online. A '99 edition of the catalog shows Terrell Davis cutting through the line. If you looked quickly, you might think it's a cover of *Sports Illustrated*.

It's a beautiful photo, more contemporary and less zany than what we'd done before. Still inspiring as ever. So many other iconic athletes would grace the cover in the 2000s and 2010s, a testament to the power of Foot Locker to create access for *Eastbay*.

The combination of *Eastbay* and Foot Locker in many ways did just what it was supposed to, bringing our energy and that magic relationship with the catalog to an even bigger audience in sports, and opening up access to the athletes. The company grew. A whole new generation of young athletes were growing up with the catalog.

Sneakerheads were there in ever greater numbers, too. In some ways, sneakerheads didn't need us anymore in places like New York City, where that culture was alive and well and growing and more connected through the internet and new media emerging to support it. Bobbito Garcia says that by the late '90s, he'd mostly moved on from *Eastbay*. He'd gotten a job with Nike, he traveled the world, finding sneakers that even we didn't have.

But *Eastbay* was still enabling that culture to spread and thrive in places it wouldn't have otherwise. For a fleeting moment between the pre-internet days and the days after it took over everything, *Eastbay* was still providing access—access was always so key to *Eastbay*'s success—to this vast, seemingly endless world of sneakers and gear to athletes and sneakerheads in far-flung places.

Drew Hammell, a forty-two-year-old regional manager for a global jewelry retailer who grew up in New Jersey, launched the @eastbay.archive Instagram page a few years ago. He started getting *Eastbay* catalogs in 1996, right before we sold. Even for someone that close to New York City, the catalogs "were the way we learned about sneakers," he says. "That's where we were seeing these shoes for the first time."

Steve Mulholland, one of the cofounders of *Sole Collector* magazine in the early 2000s, says, "*Eastbay* was the conduit to the sneaker world for the person in the middle of nowhere."

Gerald Flores, a thirty-nine-year-old creative director for Foot Locker and the former editor in chief of *Sole Collector*, from New Jersey, said to us, "Pre-internet, *Eastbay* put a sneaker store in your hands, so you didn't have to go get on an hour bus ride to go to the mall to see all these products. That was a void that it filled. Especially if you're like me. I love sneakers, because I look at them as beautiful pieces of art."

He points to the Air Jordan XI, the iconic sneaker that Nike designed for Michael Jordan to wear during his first season back with the Chicago Bulls in 1995 after a brief retirement and stint with minor-league baseball's Birmingham Barons. This was right before we sold.

Here's what *Eastbay* said about the shoe:

NIKE AIR JORDAN XI MID

> The best performance basketball shoe for the best player on earth—Michael Jordan. A lightweight, supportive and breath able combination of ballistic mesh, full-grain leather and reinforced patent leather with a nylon strap Speed Lacing system. Phylon midsole with a full-length Air Sole unit supported by a carbon fiber spring plate to encourage elevation. The outsole is a combination of clear gum rubber and solid rubber herringbone traction inserts.
>
> **EBay: $124.99**
> Sz: 6–13, 14,15,16,17,18
> Wt. 16.3 oz.

It just sounds cool. Ballistic mesh. Speed Lacing. Spring plate. Encouraging elevation. Flores loved all that, but more than that, the pictures were the thing. When sneakerheads, especially, saw a shoe like the XI for the first time, in *Eastbay*, it was captivating. "I look at that," Flores says, "and it's not just a sneaker. It's like, look at how beautifully this is designed, and look at the story behind it, and look at the patent leather on it that was never seen on a Jordan before, and how revolutionary this is, this beautiful piece of innovation. And you wouldn't know anything about that shoe unless you watched a lot of basketball or went all the way to a store and heard about it from your friends. *Eastbay* made something like that tangible—where, you may not be able to pay $125 or however much it was in 1995, but you can have the picture of it in your hand, like you can have a poster of a Porsche Carrera—you can pull the pages out and put it up on your wall."

Now, with Foot Locker's heft behind it, we were building this connection even further. *Eastbay* was still much in demand, and we were basking in the Foot Locker effect, which came with all kinds of new attention. The upshot was the validation for Eastbay as a company—everyone knew who we were and wanted to tell us how great we were, even more than when we went public.

Paul Fireman, the Reebok CEO, invited us out to Cape Cod every year to join him for a golf tournament where we met pros like Ian Baker-Finch and John Daly (who on one hole teed off with a shovel and still hit the ball two hundred yards), along with plenty of other athletes and celebrities. We played a round with Bobby Orr, who was absurdly down to earth and raved about the catalog and wrote us a nice thank-you note.

And when NFL linebacker Jevon Kearse was drafted by the Tennessee Titans in 1999, Reebok had him stop in Wausau to do an autograph signing during our annual tent sale. Dick remembers that Kearse seemed genuinely thrilled to meet the *Eastbay* guys and went on about how much he had loved "that magazine" when he was a kid. We had also just put him on the cover. "I mean, he was stunned that we would put him on the cover," Dick Johnson says, "and that we would bring him to Wausau."

Kearse asked Dick to grab dinner after the autograph signing so that they could talk about *Eastbay*. He joked that the signing probably wouldn't take long anyway, because he didn't expect a lot of fans to wait for the Tennessee Titans' top draft pick in Green Bay Packers country. But when the doors opened, Kearse was stunned by the full house. It took a couple of hours to get through the line of autograph-seekers, many of whom brought copies of *Eastbay* with Kearse on the cover for him to sign.

It seemed like there was no end to the number of people who wanted to get to know us and who wanted to work with us now that we were part of Foot Locker. Adidas offered us $25,000 to create feature spreads for its top shoes. New Balance followed by offering $40,000 to expand its presence, our first forays into partner marketing.

Going public brought validation. Being part of Foot Locker brought clout. For years we'd worked so hard to get these brands on board with *Eastbay. Please work with us. Please don't pull your shoes from the catalog.*

Now they were paying us to get real estate in *Eastbay*, and were thrilled to connect us with athletes like Jevon Kearse.

It was exciting and it also felt a bit odd and uncomfortable. Rick looks back now and wonders if maybe we should have been schmoozing more all along, trying to be part of the club. Would that have accelerated our trajectory? We'll never know. What we did know then, though, is we weren't used to the attention, and we weren't entirely sure we loved it.

But no question the Foot Locker effect amped up the star power in *Eastbay*. Even our clinics got a celebrity makeover. We began bringing in some of the nation's preeminent professional and college basketball coaches for Eastbay-sponsored clinics, hosted at Wausau East High. Utah coach Rick Majerus flew in in '98, shortly after he had led the underdog Utah Utes on a Cinderella run through the NCAA tournament, where they upset number one seeded North Carolina in the Alamodome, ultimately losing the National Championship Game against number five Kentucky. Majerus could (and did) recite the last six minutes of the game, play by play, from memory.

At the airport, Dick picked up Majerus, who was exhausted and jet-lagged from being shuttled around the country on a whirlwind tour of talk shows and meet and greets. Despite his wearied state, Majerus raved about *Eastbay* and how much his players loved it.

Majerus was flagging, though, and told Dick he'd just go to the locker room and lie down for a bit. But first, Dick remembers, Majerus noticed a Culver's on the drive to the clinic—this is a burger joint that started in Wisconsin but has grown to hundreds of locations, best known for its "butter burgers," frozen custard, and fried cheese curds. Majerus asked if someone could run over to Culver's, and get him two double burgers, some cheese curds, an order of fries, and a thick chocolate shake. Then, he said, he'd be good.

"So here he is," Dick remembers, "this massive man, and he wolfs this stuff down. He lays down. He wakes up a half hour before his session. And he puts on the most incredible basketball clinic ever. He's pulling coaches out of the audience; he's got them on the floor running the sets that Utah ran. Just incredible."

On the way back to the airport, Majerus thanked Dick and told him that whatever we were doing with *Eastbay*, keep doing it. "All the coaches talked about the same thing," Dick remembers, "how Eastbay did such a great job of serving the athletes. The team-colored shoes, the large sizes, and they all talked about helping athletes identify what was important to their progression, and becoming a better athlete, and then being able to find it at Eastbay."

And while we focus mostly on basketball in many of these stories, this connection was true across all sports and all kinds of equipment. Whatever the sport, coaches always got it, which made sense. We had started out serving coaches. All through those years, if a coach needed a twelve-pound shotput, we'd ship them a twelve-pound shotput. Some coach out in Seattle called in a panic because his star hundred-meter sprinter blew out some spikes, and we'd next-day air them. "Coaches and athletes remembered that sort of thing, even years later," Dick says.

And now with Foot Locker we deepened the connection. Improved our capabilities. Scaled the catalog. Being part of Foot Locker brought the company to a new level and with it, some fame. During a trip to New York, Harry mentioned he worked for Eastbay to a cab driver, who was so excited he pulled out a camera to take a picture with him. Harry autographed a Best Buy receipt once for a fan who worked the registers there.

Polly recalls wearing her Eastbay jacket on flights or pulling out a catalog to do some work on the plane only to end up fielding eager questions from a fan sitting nearby. "They'd tap me from across the aisle, 'Hey, can I look at that catalog when you're done?'" she says. "Or, 'Do you have an extra one?' Or, 'Can I get on the mailing list?' All that. I had people writing their name and address on napkins. It started happening enough that I kept a Ziploc bag full of customer registration cards in my briefcase for them to fill out. I'd get back to the office and find Maddie and just dump a pile of them on her desk."

41

Last Call

For those first couple of years after selling, we tried to stay involved, each in our usual roles, Art working on inventory and merchandising operations while Rick continued working with the creative team on cover designs and catalog layouts.

The Eastbay team began doing even more interviews with the stars that we featured on the cover and inside the catalog. (We put them online, too.) We hired writers and editors to help with the burgeoning content. When one of those writers, Keith Roerdnik, interviewed Allen Iverson after AI's Answer 3 shoe debuted, he remembers Iverson smiling big and going on about how much he loved *Eastbay* and how exciting it was for him to have his own shoes in the catalog. Keith remembers many athletes asking—persistently—if we could send some boxes of catalog copies to their locker rooms so they could pass them out and show all their teammates they had made it in *Eastbay*.

Kevin Durant told Keith a story that he'd told others, about how his mom would wait for the *Eastbay* sale catalog (called Final Score) to come out and order shoes from that. One time when he was playing AAU, she got him the only pair she could find in his size, Sheryl Swoopes's signature Nikes. Everyone made fun of him for wearing girls' shoes. Keith remembers Durant telling him, "I don't care. I got new shoes." Later, Durant told ESPN, "I played well in those."

John Schaefer would leave the company shortly after the sale. One of the last things John did while working at Eastbay was to convince Dick to go through with an idea that they'd kicked around ever since we'd sold to Woolworth: order Eastbay championship rings. We passed on the idea—but they went ahead and got massive gold rings with *EASTBAY* engraved on the face along with a wreath encircling it. The sides had *RUNNING* engraved above a shoe with wings, and below that, *1980*. Nestled in the wreath were five diamonds, one each for Art, Rick, Harry, John, and Dick. It was a symbol of their commitment to Eastbay, maybe a way to feel that magic again. "We blew two thousand bucks," Schaefer says. "Then I left, Harry got the invoice, and Dick had to explain it."

John Schaefer went on to work for Bill End. End asked him to help him run a catalog company called Cornerstone Brands, which Schaefer pulled from the brink of bankruptcy, then turned around and sold for $760 million five years later.

The Foot Locker deal also finally afforded us the opportunity to fix our warehouse situation. The group that financed it was led by our friend Paul Gassner, who was also our first accountant. Back in '81 with the business struggling to get off the ground, when we asked Gassner how we could make more money, he told us, "You could get jobs." Now he was leading us in the building of a gorgeous 250,000-square-foot work of distribution-center art, where we could finally consolidate 70,000 SKUs that had been scattered across seven dingy old buildings.

Before it was done, but after the massive concrete slab had been poured, Rick visited the site. He had brought along a single pair of Nike Air shoes in their iconic orange Nike box. He placed the box at one corner of this endless concrete floor and stepped back to stare in wonder, admiring the vastness. He was thinking back to his parents' basement, the first warehouse, overstuffed with a few hundred boxes, and now trying to imagine how many boxes would fit in *this* space.

We continued to get invited to major sporting events, and we even went to a few, because it was like walking through the same dream that we knew kids flipping through *Eastbay*, tacking our posters on the wall, were dreaming.

But we weren't big schmoozers. We'd spent so long doing all that we could to curry favor with people throughout this industry, and it had worked, but we were never naturals at it. It was fun for a while to watch the Masters or play golf with Bobby Orr, but sooner than you might imagine, we started passing along most of those invitations to other folks at Eastbay. Harry and Dick and John and Polly and many others would get to experience big games and major events. We felt as much joy for them getting those experiences as we'd felt for ourselves. John Schaefer went to a Nike party in Atlanta where he met Gail Devers and Michael Johnson, "and they all knew who we were," he says, "which kind of surprised me."

Harry made it to the World Cup in Paris in 1998, where he sat at midfield with Adidas CEO Robert Louis-Dreyfus to watch France beat Brazil 3-0, "and then we got drunk and sang 'Viva La France' until five in the morning," Harry recalls, smiling.

We gave our invitations to them because they had given so much to us. But also, we were tired. We'd run our business with razor-thin margins, being pulled along by growth that we barely managed for nearly twenty years, and now that we had done away with that sort of stress, we didn't want to add new stress by creating thinner margins with our families. Larger financial margins couldn't hold a candle to gaining wider margins of time.

Once, at dinner with the baseball Hall of Famer Harold Baines and his wife, Art asked Baines how cool it must have been to travel everywhere as part of a baseball team. It was everybody's dream, right? Baines looked at his wife. Yeah, he'd been blessed to be a good baseball player, but, he said, the travel is hard. He said he really missed his wife and his kids.

We had to agree with him. Steak dinners at Sparks were great to experience, like New York is a great city to visit, but that wasn't somewhere that felt like home.

We didn't want to be on the road. We wanted to be with our wives. We wanted to be with our kids. To thank them. We wanted to be home.

That didn't mean we wanted to be done with the business for good, however. Both of us hoped that we could work something out with Woolworth that would allow us to stay around even longer than our contracts laid out, even if only in a limited capacity. We remembered the experience of Art's Uncle Bob, who himself had sold a couple of companies and who'd stayed on a long time afterward. (We didn't realize then that he might have taken a stock position in the company, giving him more reason to stay, whereas we took cash.) We were naive; we had thought Foot Locker would want us more involved. But it didn't take long for us to realize that there wasn't a hell of a lot that Foot Locker really needed us to do. We found ourselves consulting some, but mostly edged out of decision-making, and that was a strange new feeling for us.

It was never cold or deliberate; the business needed to evolve and become part of something bigger. Woolworth's people were ready for us to see ourselves out the door. We later learned that it's normal for the acquired leaders to quietly, but quickly, step back and slip out. Here was another unwritten rule of business we didn't know that we were accidentally breaking. But we weren't businessmen the way the folks at Foot Locker were, or even the way Harry and Dick and John were. They all knew it was time, too, even if everyone was being polite about it.

As well as the merging of Eastbay into Foot Locker went, it was harder to merge two entrepreneurs and creative spirits into that big machine. Big, publicly traded companies and professional dreamers go together like track spikes on a basketball court.

We weren't prepared, and no one had told us when we sold Eastbay that at some point sooner than you believe, you'll have to let it go completely. We didn't know if we were ready. The end felt sudden.

We decided we'd share a few last rounds of drinks in the days and weeks that followed and throw one last big party for the office. By June 1999, the contract was up, and so was our time at Eastbay.

42

Wausau + New York

There's a lot more to the Eastbay story. In fact, it went on a couple of years longer without us than it had with us, and it continued to grow into a business that reached billions in revenue. And for a long time, it was massively successful and grew and grew. We're proud to say that so many of the Eastbay family stayed on for so long after we left, including Tom and Jim Gering, who both worked there up until they both retired in the 2020s. Many who started in the '80s and '90s finished their careers there or are still there working for Foot Locker today. (Actually, as we're writing this, Foot Locker was sold to Dick's Sporting Goods—the industry continues to evolve.)

But we weren't there for it. It's not our story, and it feels somewhat distant to us. But we owe it to you, and to those who stayed on for all those years at Eastbay, to tell the story. To that end, we spoke with many of those who stayed on and enjoyed many more years at the company and who worked to keep the spirit of what we'd built alive, and we feel it's crucial to finish the Eastbay story with their help.

Technically, Woolworth became Venator Group—that change happened in 1998—and in 2001 Venator became Foot Locker, Inc. And the upshot was that, even as the acquisition brought new access to athletes and increased *Eastbay*'s reach, a bit more quickly than expected, the people at the parent company who had that vision for Eastbay as part of Foot Locker, they began to disappear.

Harry was working as co-CEO of Eastbay in Wausau. His job was to work with Jeff Branman, the dealmaker who'd become co-CEO in New

York. Harry was optimistic going into this arrangement. "I thought it was all going to work. I really did," he says. When you pay what Woolworth did, Harry says, "you have to believe that *they* believe that the expertise that has been developed, inclusive of all the people in the business, was going to be something that they would count on, build on, and respect."

As part of the effort to bridge Eastbay and Foot Locker, Harry asked Polly to work in New York as a liaison, someone the New York contingent understood represented the talent in Wausau. Rick made a few trips there with her before her move. On those trips, Rick felt some misalignment, like there was one team with two different game plans. There were strategic advantages for Foot Locker acquiring Eastbay, and the company was buying both the brand and the operation, but it felt to Rick like there was less of a cohesive vision of what to do with Eastbay the brand than the operation. There was what Eastbay thought it could provide—an immediate impact on the whole company, and what Foot Locker was focused on, managing a big, diverse business in which Eastbay's revenue was just a small piece.

For Polly, her eventual move to New York was, "The worst thing that ever happened to me in my career." In the beginning, she was the only Eastbay employee who moved to New York. Her job was to help Foot Locker bring catalogs into retail stores. She recalls the first vision was to create catalogs for Foot Locker and Champs Sports, another brand the company owned. But New York also wanted to use Eastbay's inventory and resources to fulfill orders in Foot Locker stores. Polly says, "They wanted a red *Eastbay* bat phone in the Foot Locker at the mall."

It would work like this: A kid comes into a Foot Locker, intent on getting the Nike Air Max in a size 13. It's not in stock, but instead of losing the customer, the associate at the store picks up the bat phone and calls Eastbay.

This wasn't ideal. Kids want to walk out of the store with the sneakers. They don't want to pay and go home empty-handed, but at least *some* would make the purchase, whereas before the order was 100 percent lost if the shoes weren't in stock. Also, it was operationally complex. Eastbay had to package shoes differently depending on if the order was a Foot Locker order or an *Eastbay* order. There were sales tax complications between in-store sales and mail order. It was also hard to give the store credit for the sales Eastbay was fulfilling, and those stores ran on commission, so the person selling the shoes didn't really want to pick up that bat phone.

"It was a systems problem, and it was an accounting problem," Polly says. "It became this big cluster."

Eastbay was learning a new and different company culture, too. When Dick and John Schaefer and Polly proposed how they might use the catalog and phone combination in stores, they were schooled by Bill DeVries, CEO of the company's biggest division, the Athletic Footwear and Apparel Division. DeVries, Dick recalls, "quickly and with great pomp annihilated us," making the team walk through the math of their proposal, which he tore apart in front of the entire leadership team. At Woolworth, economics beat vibes.

Culture clashes are inevitable in mergers and acquisitions. Everyone wanted this acquisition to succeed, and by nearly all measures it did. Foot Locker poured a lot of time, energy, and money into Wausau. It committed to the business there. Thousands of people working for the company benefitted from the acquisition for years and kept Eastbay's culture going in Wausau. But it was hard on a few, especially for those who'd worked at Eastbay the longest. "New York had visions for how they wanted Eastbay to operate," Polly says. "And Eastbay very much had visions about how they should continue to operate, and I was very much stuck in the middle. And all my friends from Eastbay treated me like I was a traitor for going. And everybody in New York was like, *Who does this catalog girl think she is? Why is she here thinking that we should start doing stuff that she wants us to do?*

Soon, DeVries left the company, along with more people who had championed Eastbay, and those who replaced them weren't shy about their less enthusiastic view of the company. When one new executive crossed paths with Polly, she remembers him saying: "Oh, you must be one of those hayseeds from Wisconsin that we foolishly spent $140 million on."

Polly laughs now. "He really called us 'hayseeds.' He just thought that they had grossly overpaid."

Polly was also negotiating tension between Harry and his Eastbay co-CEO, Jeff Branman. "They hated each other," Polly says. "I had dueling co-CEOs, and all they did was try to pump me for information about the other one. It was like being between fighting brothers." For her, it wasn't working. "I was in my early thirties. I was in what felt like a hostile environment. It was also very much a boys' club back then. It was nothing I was prepared for."

Harry didn't see his co-CEO situation getting better and was planning next steps. He suggested to Dick Johnson that he look around for other jobs. Dick quickly found an opportunity and submitted a resignation letter to Harry, who was floored. Yes, he had told Dick to look around, but he didn't think it would happen so quickly.

Harry pleaded with Dick to stay on at Eastbay and said he'd make him president. Dick consulted Art, who thought having *president* on his résumé would help Dick get his next gig. So, Dick agreed to stay.

Polly couldn't do it anymore. "I was officially burned out," she says "The emotional highs involved in chasing a dream are very different than the emotional lows of defending a dream. I was so tired. So, I left, and I went and sat on a beach in L.A. for two months."

Harry wasn't far behind. His contractual time was up in January 2000. Venator's then-CEO invited Harry to talk about a job in New York, but Harry didn't want to join Foot Locker in New York. "That was pretty much the end of my Eastbay career. But I realized I was no longer needed," Harry says now.

For us, watching and hearing about all this as it unfolded surprised us. We thought the Eastbay team would move up with Foot Locker, but it hadn't worked that way. What did happen was a perfectly ordinary outcome of the sale of a small company to a big one, just businesses doing what businesses do, but it was all new to us. We were probably naive about some of these things at the time.

Despite these shifts, in Wausau it was business as normal for virtually the whole staff, including Tom and Jim Gering and so many others who stayed on. Eastbay grew, and Art couldn't believe all the athletes that were getting featured on the cover and inside the catalog. *Eastbay* was something Foot Locker invested in. The operation kept getting better, and bigger. But the *specific* magic we had created, we guess that's what felt like it was changing. Everything that seemed to be working after the acquisition, the infusion of more athletes and more editorial into the catalog, helped Eastbay continue to grow and reinforce that special bond with athletes and sneakerheads. It was just *changed*, and we weren't driving that change, and that was new for us and not entirely comfortable. Even looking back on it now, it feels a little unsettling. It's like a Super Bowl winning coach stepping down, then watching as a new staff installs a different system and continues to win, in a different way. You're happy they're winning. But you'd do it differently.

There was one constant through all this that always gave us comfort, and that was Dick Johnson. He always fought for Eastbay. He always made it better when we were there and long, long after we were gone. "God bless him," says John Schaefer. "He ended up running the damn thing."

43

No More Vaulting Poles

After becoming president of Eastbay, Dick remembers when one of Venator's execs came to Wausau. Walking through the gorgeous new warehouse, they saw some vaulting poles on one wall. The exec asked how many Eastbay sold per year.

Dick rattled off some modest number. "We lost money on every vaulting pole we had to ship," Dick says "I mean, that's just the way it is with things that are fifteen feet long. They don't ship easily."

The exec said, "Well, we're going to stop that now."

Back in the day, vaulting poles were part of our track-and-field budget. It was okay if one product lost a little money in the portfolio. Foot Locker, though, had bought the Eastbay platform, not just (and maybe not primarily) the brand, and the company measured profitability on every product. Vaulting poles were bad business.

"It became less about the athletes," Dick says, "and more about the business model." And it had to. Dick knew that, and he was expert at balancing the Eastbay culture and the demands of a multibillion-dollar business.

To us it was different. At the old Eastbay, we *had* vaulting poles. And maybe we couldn't quantify it well, but there was *value* to having vaulting poles beyond how much you made (or lost) on each sale. It counted for something. It was a droplet of that magic in the brand, that sense of endless possibility we'd created. But again, Foot Locker didn't just buy a brand.

Leadership changed again. A new CEO from Foot Locker moved to Wausau. Dick became Eastbay's President and COO. Around the same time, Foot Locker officially changed the division name to footlocker.com/Eastbay, which represented the platform it had bought and was integrating into the bigger brand.

By 2003, Dick himself was named CEO of footlocker.com/Eastbay. We were happy to see Eastbay headed by someone who really knew what it was all about.

The political wrangling with New York had settled down, and *Eastbay* managed to thrive as a catalog. Athletes still coveted it, and it still brought that massive selection and some attitude to those who loved shoes and who loved to feel part of the tribe that *got it* when it came to performance and excellence. Years after we left, Stephen Curry, the Golden State Warriors' legend and personification of an underdog transforming himself into an icon, would tell Dick that he *really* knew he'd made it when he made the cover of *Eastbay*.

"We never had to pay them," says Dowe Tillema, who joined Eastbay in January 1994 as assistant controller and was by this point CFO. "They just did it because they had a lot of gratitude over the history of the catalog. And they wanted to be on the cover. They were like groupies for *Eastbay*." They were customers, too.

We watched shoes in the early 2000s take on more original and unique designs than ever. The Nike Shox line from 2000 had blown us away, and in 2003, Nike released a young LeBron James's first Air Zoom Generation signature shoe. *Eastbay* put him on the cover in April 2004 wearing King-branded shirt and shorts. (That cover also advertised eastbay.com as "your million-square-foot cyber warehouse.")

The catalog had taken on a sleeker and more modern look. Rick's imagination wasn't there, but the team continued to play with some creative ideas that reminded us of the "old *Eastbay*." The September 2001 edition showed Allen Iverson floating through space to finger-roll a layup into a net high above Earth, with a space shuttle in flight in the background.

But now the draw was athletes on the cover, sometimes mid-action, sometimes working hard at practice. Some were stylized shots. It was often beautiful. Randy Moss, Allen Iverson, David Eckstein, Calvin Johnson. Legends like Kobe and LeBron and Durant. Track stars like Boris Berian and Allyson Felix. WNBA star Skylar Diggins. The list goes on and on. Terrell Suggs. James Harden. Xander Bogaerts. Odell

Beckham, Jr. Peyton Manning. Ichiro. One great cover with five of the best WNBA players together. The company had an unwritten rule that rookies didn't make the cover, but longtime Eastbay employee Sean Cummings, who's still there today, told us that in 2010 they met Devin McCourty at the NFL combine and were so impressed by him as a person, they broke their own rule and featured him.

Art always loved these covers and marveled at the stars *Eastbay* was getting. Still, it was different.

Much of the catalog's success at this time could be attributed to the full and deliberate embracing of sneakerheads in addition to athletes (and more athletes themselves were becoming sneakerheads), and how they, as shoe fanatics and collectors, made *Eastbay* culturally significant to that audience. You could see it in covers like the 2009 edition that featured a beautiful shot of the classic Nike Cortez placed on a track, drenched in golden-hour light, nothing else, the unmistakable profile of those razor cuts in the sole. Or one from 2013 that showed a pair of new all-black Jordan XX9s with majestic black wings spreading from them—Jordans in flight. These were the kinds of covers an athlete *and* a collector would drool over.

The time was right for this. In fashion, some Nike sneakers reached iconic status after Nelly's hit single "Air Force Ones" debuted in 2002. The same year saw Nike roll out the Nike SB Dunk, a low-top skateboarding shoe modeled after and remixed with the Dunk that the company first released in 1985, a shoe that some say launched modern streetwear.

"*Eastbay* was like our encyclopedia," Drew Hammell said to us. He's the forty-two-year-old from the Philly area who runs the @eastbay.archive on Instagram. "They had great, thorough descriptions that explained all the technology in the sneakers, from the cushioning to the upper materials, to the way the laces were designed, to the weight of the shoe. So much information in each catalog." And that was something that carried over from the old *Eastbay*—we had always seen the value in detailed descriptions and giving information about fit. That continued.

Sneakers were special. Limited-release editions increased, the trading market for sneakers grew and grew. (It is estimated to reach $30 billion by 2030, and at least one bank classifies collectible sneakers as an alternative asset class.) *Eastbay*—Dream Big, Dream Often—always *connected* with the kids who loved sneakers in a way that others didn't, and couldn't, in a store at the mall.

In 2004, ESPN journalist Tim Keown published a column in which he called *Eastbay* "the most influential sports publication on the market" and "consumer porn at its very best."[1] The point of his column was to shine a light on Reebok's publicity stunt in that year's *Eastbay* Christmas wish book. "The Allen Iverson Question" from that catalog featured a pair of $65,000 black Reebok basketball shoes with diamond-encrusted laces designed by Jacob Arabo, better known as "Jacob the Jeweler," along with a few other outrageous offerings. Pure Sneakerhead bliss.

Dick was still fighting for Eastbay as it became one division of many looking for investment and capital from the parent company. He sometimes got frustrated having to prove, now to his own parent company, the same things that we had proven to Nike, and Reebok, and Asics, and Saucony, and the other brands a decade before—that Eastbay wasn't a threat to retail. Dick usually was persuasive in those battles for investment, at least in the beginning. At dinner, he'd tell us how he had to, again, explain that *Eastbay* was different than retail and could reach different customers in different markets and retain them better, and we swear when he told us that it felt like time travel, like Eastbay was back in 1992 begging Phil Knight to trust us.

44

Still Running

You know what happened to the world next. The internet, e-commerce, social media. Smartphones. Disruption.

It was a strange time for us, and a strange feeling. We stayed close to our friends. There would be golfing, and dinners, and noon runs, though fewer of them. Someone might show us something they were doing on the website or talk about a new market they were exploring. They couldn't always talk freely about the business—public company and all—and sometimes we felt uncomfortable asking. We were curious, of course, but it could feel like prying. And we weren't always sure we wanted to know.

Sometimes we'd go to the retail store—after a lifetime in mail-order, we'd become store shoppers—and people working the floor wouldn't know us.

We didn't see much of the catalog after we left, because we never had copies shipped to our homes. We weren't on the mailing list. We may have been at one point, but Dick points out that we most likely fell off due to Eastbay's own equation for keeping a name on the list. We weren't the target demo, and we didn't buy enough to warrant the mailing cost.

Rick certainly retreated from Eastbay, and from *Eastbay,* even more than Art, but we both made a concerted effort to stay away and let them go forward in the direction they wanted to go. We didn't want to be looking over their shoulders.

There was one story during this time that we learned about and that we think is worth sharing, because it shows how *Eastbay,* to the end, kept chasing that magic.

It starts with Steve Mulholland, who grew up on a horse farm in rural Columbus, Indiana, "far enough out we didn't get cable." His first encounter with the catalog in the '90s was like so many others we've heard about. He saw a friend thumbing through *Eastbay* and snatched it from him. "What *is* this?"

It was, he remembers now, "just row upon row of this heat. People don't understand now—*Eastbay* was heat. There weren't websites, so kids funneled their passion through that magazine. *Eastbay* did such a good job. *Eastbay* was the only way that kids knew when something new was going on, and it made it to where we could buy Jordans in high school, and nobody else has them, because we're the ones getting *Eastbay.*"

A few years later, Mulholland's parents lucked into some Indiana Pacers tickets. Michael Jordan was in town and took the floor wearing the brand-new Air Jordan 11s. "It was really inspiring," Mulholland says. "You just *felt* it." He wanted to take something with him from the experience to remember it by. "I'm not a jersey guy," he says. "The piece I wanted to take from that were those 11s. And I could buy those in *Eastbay.*"

Eventually Mulholland turned sneakers into a career, first selling some on eBay, then on his own site, instyleshoes.com, which became a gathering place for sneakerheads from around the world. After that he created *Sole Collector* magazine, which exploded in a way not that different from how *Eastbay* had a couple of decades before.

To do *Sole Collector* right, Mulholland felt like he had to involve *Eastbay,* so he schlepped to Wausau hoping to beg into some meetings. Like all pilgrims before him, he didn't love the journey. "Getting there is a big, big pain in the ass," he says. Getting Eastbay's attention was just as hard. "I was trying to get them to understand," he says, "that there's a whole sneaker universe out there and *Eastbay* was the conduit to that world for the person on a horse farm in Indiana, anywhere that's the middle of nowhere. I've seen it with my own eyes."

Mulholland had the stories to prove it. He'd done a project where he interviewed one sneakerhead in every state. In Wyoming, he pulled his rented Dodge Durango down a dusty dirt road where he saw a cowboy waving at him, wearing black-and-silver Jordan 5s. "Where the hell did you get those?" Mulholland asked. "*Eastbay,*" the cowboy said.

Eventually, Eastbay's chief marketing officer, Dave Lokes, saw *Sole Collector,* and he got it. *Eastbay* went all in on this market that we'd always sensed was there but never quite captured. "We gotta leverage this," Mulholland remembers Lokes saying. "This, this, this. This is the market we want to speak to."

Mulholland began traveling to Wausau regularly to work with Lokes and the team on various *Eastbay x Sole Collector* projects, leaving the warmth of his home in Key Largo for Wausau. Once, he forgot gloves and thought he'd get frostbite driving from the hotel to the office. At the office he said to Lokes, "Dave, how the hell do you live out here?"

"I know, isn't it great?" Dave said, beaming. "Let me tell you about the motorcycle riding, especially around the lake."

Eastbay x Sole Collector became a nationwide tour with Mulholland interviewing people previously featured in *Eastbay*. Mulholland says that without those early *Eastbay* collaborations, he can't see *Sole Collector* growing into what it eventually did. "They really helped sculpt part of *Sole Collector.*"

It was a kind of passing of the baton. *Sole Collector* was becoming *Eastbay*'s heir. Mulholland was creating the same kind of magic connection with his audience that we had with ours, and he was sharing that magic back with *Eastbay*. Mulholland helped the Eastbay crew build out a blog. He once spent a day or two combing through the *Eastbay* archives, feeling like a kid all over again. That led to an issue of *Sole Collector* that featured beautiful spreads of just vintage *Eastbay* covers. It was a beautiful collaboration that we think captured some of the old *Eastbay* spirit for sneakerheads.

But Eastbay still faced long odds as the world and the market continued to change, a world full of new media and online retail. Dick's Sporting Goods was a rising force with millions and millions of square feet of retail space across the country. Competitors could grab talent that didn't want to come work in Wausau. And Eastbay's parent company had a small, special brand, but a huge thriving fulfillment business.

Mulholland noticed tension between Eastbay and Foot Locker. "They did not have the same culture," he says. "The guys [at Foot Locker] were difficult to work with. They thought they were above us. Never gave *Sole Collector* the time of day. Everybody just snubbed me and was really kind of jerky. But Eastbay, they were on top of it, and it was cool."

Dick did what he could to fight for resources for Eastbay from within Foot Locker, but in the summer of 2007, Foot Locker dispatched him to

Amsterdam to run the company's European region, carving him out of Eastbay completely.

Mulholland continued working with Dave Lokes on *Eastbay x Sole Collector* collaborations. Eastbay was about to get an exclusive on the release of an important new Nike shoe. Nobody will say what shoe, but somebody at Foot Locker HQ found out about the collaboration, and then, Mulholland says, "There was an explosion in those offices." This person apparently went straight to Nike's top executives demanding to know how Eastbay got access.

They killed the collaboration, and *Eastbay* lost the exclusive.

Maybe that shoe launch would have reignited *Eastbay* for the new era, kept it culturally relevant, and injected a new round of growth and magic. Probably not, though. So much had already changed.

There was another leadership change at Foot Locker, which resulted in Dick moving to New York to become president and CEO of Foot Locker US, which also included Lady Foot Locker, Kids Foot Locker, and Footaction.

By then, online commerce was ascendant. It was easy to find information about sneakers, even rare ones. Even *Sole Collector*, just seven years old, wasn't so unique anymore. The sneaker-centric media and online retail scene was crowded. *Complex* magazine. The Hypebeast sneaker blog. The Nice Kicks website. There were discussion boards like niketalk.com. There was eBay, and there was Amazon. Retailers themselves were in the game with their own online retail stores.

Eastbay did its part to join the fray. Its online store did well enough. But according to Dowe Tillema, who'd been named Eastbay's CEO in 2008, catalog circulation crested in about 2010 before starting a steady yearly descent as the world fully shifted to online and mobile.

The Eastbay team tried a lot of things to keep the brand going. More *Eastbay x Sole Collector* sneaker launches, like the Nike Air Max 95 360 in gray and volt, that bright green-yellow seen in safety vests, in 2012, and the Nike Sportswear Olympic Dream Team Pack, which featured five different shoes worn by different members of Team USA.

Eastbay expanded into league-branded catalogs for the NFL, Major League Baseball, and the NBA. It launched "The Most" marketing campaign in 2010, to show off Eastbay's vast inventory and its breadth of sizes. *Eastbay* still offered sizes up to 23.

It expanded the editorial, running full magazine-style feature stories and using QR codes to get people to the website.

It tried getting into education with an Athlete Resource Center, an online library of tips and advice and training strategies for athletes ranging from high school to the pros. Condensed versions made their way into the catalog, efforts to deepen connection with the kids.

Then there was "The Truck"—a full-sized semi covered in Eastbay branding that roamed the country visiting tournaments and competitions to drive team sales. Inside it contained the Eastbay Experience: merchandise, catalogs, touch screens for people to peruse and through which to buy anything they could imagine from eastbay.com—a far cry from Trebs's Gremlin and the Beast!

As we write it down now, we can see Eastbay's original spark, its DNA, in many of these efforts, thanks to Dick Johnson and the corporate support of Dowe Tillema, David Lokes, and the team on the ground in Wausau. The Most campaign reflected something the company had always been proud of—having it all. That was something that never went away and always left an impression on people like Steve Mulholland and Drew Hammell. The Athlete Resource Center was focused on education, and education was, from the very first clinic, a core part of what made Eastbay special. The Truck was bringing the store to the athletes, like the Beast, only much cooler and with a suspension. Eastbay also began aggressively expanding its physical presence of team-sales reps, especially at AAU basketball events, which also seemed to us an effort to return to the company's roots with teams, its first and most loyal customer base.

But even *Eastbay's* team sales began to flag as new, deep discounters gained ground. Eastbay.com, while it produced some great content, never broke through. "You have *Sole Collector,* you have the Hypebeast, you've got *Complex,* and they have *tons* of traction," Mulholland says.

The brand contracted. *Eastbay* faded, surpassed by the media it had inspired, and in the case of *Sole Collector,* media it helped to create. *Sole*

Collector reached vaunted heights. On its ten-year anniversary, legendary Nike designer Tinker Hatfield gifted Mulholland a gorgeous custom pair of Mulholland's beloved Jordan 11s.

Dick helped guide Foot Locker from $4.9 billion in sales in 2009 to $6.5 billion in 2013. The Wausau operation thrived as part of this. He became CEO in 2014. We couldn't have been prouder of the man who'd once applied for an assistant controller job with Eastbay out of curiosity.

"From our little company in Wausau," John Schaefer says, laughing. "Our head merchant, and he ends up running the whole damn company. That's pretty cool."

Even as he managed his endless array of responsibilities as a global CEO, Dick found himself regularly getting back to Wausau. "I was really trying to figure out how we could stimulate the brand," he says. "We would do all that we could to try to promote it and rekindle that athlete connection."

He supported an ambitious nine-part video series in partnership with LeBron James's media company. He tried to merge *Eastbay* with retail brand Champs. The merged brand got a new logo and new slogan: *We Know Game.* Vendors didn't get it. They'd ask, *Why do you need Eastbay? Why not just call it all Champs?*

In hindsight, the Eastbay brand's greatest strength was our instinct to focus solely on making the catalog as great and as special as we could, without trying to also make retail work. In the new world, that strength had become a weakness. *Eastbay* still didn't mesh with retail, but the catalog expertise was less and less relevant in a world with an endless digital catalog: the internet, social media, and phones.

And the way we'd unwittingly helped build sneakerhead culture worked against Eastbay too, eventually. That culture got so big that it found the internet and retail itself. The proliferation of boutique sneaker retailers didn't help *Eastbay,* Mulholland says, as they started getting the rare finds that *Eastbay* used to. "All of a sudden, you're getting Huff, Supreme, *they* were doing the collaborations," Mulholland observes.

"And for sure everybody wants the Jordan 11 or the latest Jordan that's coming out in the colorway that *Eastbay* has, but to get something unique—*Eastbay* wasn't getting that anymore."

The world had changed, and Eastbay couldn't. It needed to become more of a magazine, maybe, or more of a media company, possibly. Or perhaps it needed to become a chain of larger athletic stores. Whatever the case, it had to happen quickly. And the team, we could see, was trying everything it could.

"We tried all sorts of things," Dick says. "None of them ever really worked."

Year by year, Eastbay's return slipped, from 12 percent down to 8 percent, to 6 percent, to 4 percent. "I battled for a while," Dick says. "I probably protected Eastbay longer than I should have. The guys running it were still passionate. But as we evaluate each of the business segments in a $9 billion business, they're all competing for finite resources, and there were more people around the table arguing that Eastbay shouldn't continue to receive the funding it did. It's a math exercise at some point. Why would you invest where you only get four percent back? We just didn't have it anymore."

Dick had a legendary run in the business, including nearly a decade as Foot Locker's CEO. One website named Dick the third-most-influential person in the shoe industry in 2015, behind only the Nordstrom brothers at number two and Mr. Shoe Dog himself, Phil Knight, at number one.

He did all he could and more for *Eastbay*. But by the end of 2021, Dick had run out of ways to talk himself into keeping it alive. Rather than push the board into forcing the issue on him, he thought it better to handle things with some dignity and grace and make the decision himself.

After staring out the window at the Midtown Manhattan office, taking an extra moment, remembering, holding on to the gratitude, Dick sighed his heavy sigh and then strode to a conference room, where he told his team they were shutting down *Eastbay*.

Epilogue

Dreaming Together

For a long time, even as we saw it fading, we wouldn't look back on Eastbay the way we have here.

That was the Eastbay way—do the work, solve the problem, always look ahead. Keep dreaming big. We feel lucky that we don't think we're terribly ego-driven and that we have families who kept us grounded as Eastbay soared to extraordinary heights. We always used to call ourselves business *typhoons,* which is maybe more apt than we even thought at the time, because often that's what Eastbay's success felt like.

We were so detached from any sense of posterity that, between the two of us, we didn't even save copies of all the catalogs. We didn't save Eastbay-branded products or our favorite sneakers. No Eastbay backpacks. No Attaqs. No Adidas Top Tens. Art may have taken a case of Asics Tiger Epirus. To this day he regrets he didn't hang on to the original Air Jordans.

But it was still a hard transition for us. Athletes often talk about struggling after retirement to find something to fill the vacant space, and we probably had some of that to deal with.

After we left Eastbay, we did open an office, taking administrative assistant Lisa Walkush with us. Our venture was called Head Groovy Cats. We would help local boards run foundations and charities, and we looked at doing small-business investments.

We got involved with some charitable boards and with a charity party, started by a group of individuals who raised money at dinners by auctioning off somebody's services—shoveling a sidewalk, say, or taking a dog for a walk. Everything was provided anonymously.

The more we got involved and brought our Eastbay energy to this effort, the more it grew. The charity parties evolved to include auctions for big-ticket items like vacation trips, washing machines, back-to-school clothes and shoes (we knew a place where we could get a discount), and other items for families in need. Once, we auctioned a minivan for a struggling single mother.

Our one group became multiple committees, each trying to outdo, outraise, outgive, the others at their parties. We formed a committee to find families in need. It was all going so well until it became clear that we had never registered as a public charity and the IRS wouldn't look too keenly on it. Some attorneys said best to shut it down, and the operation disbanded. Or as we like to say, we got shut down for *doing too much good.* At least we knew that we still had that magic touch and, even now, could stumble into breaking rules.

We had our run at vigilante charity work. We invested in a handful of companies and served on some boards, but nothing fueled us quite the way that Eastbay had. The connection with athletes, the sense of giving people something special, the joy of knowing the joy you were providing others—nothing else ever came close.

In private moments each of us may have reminisced, quietly. We certainly didn't care to muddy those memories by trying to bring it all back in detail. But for several years our wives and our sons and daughters told us that maybe it was time to stop and look back. Maybe we should write a book.

We considered it a few times, but it never really went anywhere. We put them off for a long time.

After Dick called and gave us the news that Eastbay had been shuttered, we thought that was that, and we continued our walk with Barb and Susie. Our retired lives weren't going to change. We all live in the same neighborhood in Florida. Rick and Susie's house has the same layout as Art and Barb's, only possibly it's one square foot larger. Dick moved in nearby after he fully retired from Foot Locker in 2023. Our running days are past us. Art has navigated various surgeries; Rick kicked prostate cancer's ass. Time is undefeated, but we stay active. Art golfs. Rick rides his bike. Every summer we return to our cabins nearby each other in northern Wisconsin and spend our homeland's handful of warm months with our kids and our thirteen grandkids and our friends.

Eastbay was gone, but we were content in the knowledge that we'd proven the nuns wrong and in the knowledge that, ultimately, the sale to Woolworth had worked. Foot Locker's presence in Wausau was maintained, and so many of the Eastbay family continued to thrive in the operation there—so many still do. The brand was shuttered, but the spirit of Eastbay never really left the Wausau Foot Locker operation.

But then, shortly after Dick called us, something started to happen. We started to get texts and calls from friends. They'd read some story or heard a rumor. Someone told them. Was it true? They couldn't believe it. Something was happening online, they told us, we should check it out.

Surprising to us, the story of Eastbay's closing was trending. The country's largest media outlets were talking about it, from NPR to the *New York Times* to *Sports Illustrated.* SI published a tweet about the news alongside a crying emoji.

Eastbay fans were sharing their love.

NBA icon LeBron James:
We used to love getting those magazines.

NBA superstar Kevin Durant:
End of an era.

NPR producer Gus Contreras:
Growing up in the 1990s, I was obsessed with the *Eastbay* catalog. I spent hours and hours poring over the latest catalogs like a detective combing through evidence . . . [looking for] the newest sneakers worn by Ken Griffey Jr. and Deion Sanders.

Barstool Sports:
iconic memories.

Former NBA player Lance Stephenson:
When that book would come out and you could see all the sneakers before they even came out, it was like you were seeing [the future].

And it just wasn't stopping. It felt surreal.

ESPN business reporter Darren Rovell:
Hard to believe *Eastbay* is closing. They were the ultimate catalog us kids of the 90s looked forward to.

Nick DePaula, ESPN journalist and host of *The Sneaker Game*:
I grew up reading *Eastbay* with my cereal *every* morning—and it's how I learned all about the sneaker industry. For everyone growing up in the 90s, we owe a huge thanks to *Eastbay* for sparking that love for sneakers early on.

NBATV broadcaster Alexis Morgan:
Eastbay was the window shopping of my youth.

Comedian and broadcast commentator C.J. Toledano:
RIP *Eastbay*. Without you, what would I have done my book reports on in middle school?

Chris Weber, former NBA star and current TV analyst:
It was the internet before the internet.

Memories of *Eastbay*, love for the catalog, came flooding out. It was like a global online wake. There was so much nostalgia and affection.

Brendan Schaub, a former pro MMA fighter turned comedian:
my all time favorite sneaker mag as a kid.

***The Athletic* culture writer Jason Jones:**
Kids will never understand how big a deal *Eastbay* was in the 90s.

Writer and ESPN *College Basketball Gameday* host Myron Medcalf:
These kids don't understand the feeling of flipping through *Eastbay*, picking out a pair of shoes, waiting for them to arrive, and then putting them on . . . *Eastbay* changed lives.

Mike Vorkunov, an NBA and business journalist for *The Athletic*:
Eastbay would take out like an hour of my day whenever it arrived . . . even though we never ordered anything.

To be considered tastemakers, to be considered some sort of icon of culture, to be considered sneakerheads—we never even thought of what we did like this.

> ***Sole Collector* journalist and *Complex* writer/host Rich "MaZe" Lopez:**
> [*Eastbay* had] immeasurable impact on the culture long before the culture was defined.
>
> **Bleacher Report personality and podcast host Jeff J:**
> *Eastbay* was *Time* magazine for sneakerheads in the 90s. So many kicks dreams were sparked from its pages.
>
> **The NBA's head of design, Ced Funches:**
> carrying a copy of *Eastbay* to school gave you power comparable only to Thanos collecting all the Infinity Stones.

To have *Eastbay* remembered like this? By so many athletes and sneakerheads, some well-known, others ordinary people like us who loved to dream? As we scrolled through it all we were overwhelmed. We legitimately struggled to comprehend what was happening. And it just kept happening.

> a treasure chest
>
> the holy grail of sneakers
>
> pure nostalgia
>
> [we would] gather around an *Eastbay* magazine like a campfire
>
> you weren't cool until you had your *Eastbay* magazine confiscated
>
> Eastbay held me down during my school days. Getting dope sneakers at their regular price, or even just trying to be different and unique, you went there.
>
> I remember when I got my first real job after college, I ordered a bunch of basketball shorts from them because they had colors I never saw in the stores. I thought I made it.

> Eastbay catalogs were dream material. I would stare at those shoes and track outfits for hours
>
> man I used to order so much stuff from the Eastbay mag back in the day, def held me down, RIP to one of the goats
>
> Eastbay was revolutionary man.
>
> Nothing like getting this right before baseball season.
>
> **Music industry executive Ibrahim "Ib" Hamad said it all:**
> Legendary . . . Long live *Eastbay*.

It was only *then*, watching all of this happen online in real time more than forty years after we started with a car full of sneakers—it was only then that we felt the years rush back into us.

And how lucky we felt, to have been there during the golden era of the athletic shoe industry, its version of the '60s British Invasion—a time of new energy and ideas that changed forever how we all view sneakers in sports, music, and culture, and how those things merged. To be present as this new generation of athletes chased their dreams, grew up working hard and then succeeded. To be even a small part of it was such a privilege.

The internet might've helped make *Eastbay* obsolete, but now that's where people were sharing their love. Talk about beautiful. We remembered that feeling, the feeling that we had never just been selling shoes. We'd been giving people what a good pair of sneakers can give to anyone. We knew from all the way back at the clinics that it just takes putting on a new pair of shoes to feel like a new kind of person. We'd been giving people the same experience that we'd been having the whole time. We'd all been dreaming together.

> **Dan Woike, *Los Angeles Times* Lakers beat writer:**
> My mom told me that we ordered some stuff from the catalog. I don't remember. I just remember looking and wanting and wishing. Maybe that's what matters most.

Our wives and kids saw another opening and suggested, again, that we should write a book about this. This time, we felt ready. And once we were convinced, we tackled that with the same what-the-hell-let's-do-this attitude we had when we drove the Gremlin to the first clinics.

The choice to look back turned out to be a gift, because the act of retrieving all the details from the past meant we found ourselves at dinner with people we hadn't seen in years, talking for hours. We got to read others' memories in interview transcripts and in notes they'd taken the time to write down about what they remembered. We found ourselves in disbelief at the details of the memories that came back and were overcome with the happiness the memories brought us.

We found ourselves feeling deeply emotional about Eastbay again, several times, and feeling so grateful to everyone who made Eastbay what it was. Any business can be built on talent, but we were lucky because we found people with talent and passion. So much passion, so much love. Maybe your business isn't like that. Ours was.

As part of making the book, we revisited downtown Wausau, which has changed. The Washington Street buildings are gone or remodeled, and it's hard to picture the old storefront. No smell of gas from the garage. There's a building on the lot where we used to play catch. Wally's is long gone, and so is Market Square, but we could retrace some old running routes.

The old J.C. Penney building, our second headquarters, was razed and is now a park, where every Wednesday night there's live music on the lawn. The crowds there reminded us of the old tent sale. Joe from the Mint Café, who used to run food over to our center staff, was still there. The massive distribution center where Rick placed the orange Nike box on the corner of the slab is there and somehow feels even bigger now. The third headquarters, next to where the Wisconsin River flows south and Rick used to stare out, is still going strong, branded with *footlocker.com* above its entrances. Near the far end of the long building, an Eastbay logo still hangs above the old retail store door, faded. Hard to make out.

Inside, we were unnerved, and a bit sad, by how quiet the office had become—in part due to post-Covid-19 work-from-home arrangements. This was not a place for squirt-gun fights.

We spent a couple of days in the offices, going through the old *Eastbay* archives, time traveling and remembering the sound of the place. The laughs, the high-fives, the faxes buzzing, the squirt-gun fights, and the phones constantly ringing.

As we pored over the past, we couldn't help but wonder what would have happened if that coin had landed on tails. We still wonder what Eastbay would have become, and we wonder what else we might have done.

It's hard to believe that once upon a time we were sitting in a bar across from an empty shoe store, drinking beer on a tab we didn't know how to pay, wondering if we'd ever make any sales. Sometimes it doesn't seem like all that long ago, and other times it feels like that was a whole different lifetime. Sometimes it's hard to believe any of this happened.

It's an odd thing—childhood dreams come true, and then become memories we miss. Memories of cold days in Wausau when we were just kids, walking down the street in one of the only pairs of shoes we could find, let alone afford. We remember what it felt like the first time we drove a carload of shoes to a school and showed them to kids, who just lit up. They'd never had anyone come to them with so many styles before; so many *possibilities*. The feeling it created was palpable, and we followed that feeling all the way, as far as we could. For that to have given Eastbay the run that it had is the luckiest damn thing ever.

And if you're reading this, there's a good chance that you are part of the reason why, too. If you ever bought some shoes from *Eastbay*, or even just subscribed to the catalog, or, heck, stole it from your classmate, then you helped make this happen, too. You helped two kids become men who lived, who are *still* living, big dreams.

We are proud of many things, but the thing that makes us proudest is that, for more than seven decades now, we've stayed friends. Starting a business. Growing a business. Dealing with catastrophic setbacks. These are hard, hard, things that have ripped apart more than their fair share of friendships. They didn't get us. And our five kids who urged us on to write this—Barb and Art's kids Jessica, James, and Jenna, and Susie and Rick's kids Elizabeth and Tommy—are all friends as well. They stood up for each other in their weddings. Tommy and James even started a business together.

Our kids asked us to write a book. We thought, well, that's impossible. But we were pushed on by them and by our deep desire to create an artifact that honored the spirit of Eastbay. If we were going to do a book, we said, it would have to include the Eastbay family—the employees and the customers. We'd make their voices heard. We'd let them tell their stories, too. We'd honor them. As we did the research, we realized that while we've always struggled to feel like we've said thank you well enough to everyone who made Eastbay great, this book is that thank you.

And now, here we are, at the end of it, saying it again. Thank you. Thank you for being part of it. From our hearts, thank you for everything.

We hope we helped you in some small way, too, even if it was as simple as helping you get some shoes that made you feel good about yourself, that reminded you of your heroes, or that made you feel like you could do anything. We hope we helped you dream, too. We hope you never stop.

Dream Big. Dream Often.

Art + Rick

Notes

Chapter 9

1. Bobbito Garcia, *Where'd You Get Those? New York City's Sneaker Culture, 1960–1987* (New York: Testify Books, 2003), 13.

Chapter 11

1. Justin Tinsley, "The Players' Anthem: When Marvin Gaye Sang 'The Star-Spangled Banner' at the 1983 All-Star Game," Andscape, February 13, 2018, https://andscape.com/features/marvin-gaye-the-star-spangled-banner-1983-nba-all-star-game-players-anthem/.

Chapter 15

1. Russ Bengtson and David Cabrera, "Shipwrecked: The Untold Story behind Michael Jordan's Banned Sneakers," *Complex*, August 31, 2016, https://www.complex.com/sneakers/a/russ-bengtson/nike-air-ship-history.
2. Bobbito Garcia, *Where'd You Get Those? New York City's Sneaker Culture, 1960–1987* (New York: Testify Books, 2003), 12.

Chapter 16

1. Bobbito Garcia, *Where'd You Get Those? New York City's Sneaker Culture, 1960–1987* (New York: Testify Books, 2003), 12.

Chapter 20

1. Andrew Evan Serwer, "Nike Hits Its Stride," *Fortune*, August 31, 1987, p. 97.
2. Joseph P. Wright, "Understanding the Wisconsin Fair Dealership Law in Tough Economic Times," *Wisconsin Lawyer*, November 5, 2009, https://www.wisbar.org/NewsPublications/WisconsinLawyer/Pages/Article.aspx?ArticleID=1858.

Chapter 33

1. Nick DePaula and Aaron Dodson, "The 30 Best Sneakers Worn on 'The Fresh Prince of Bel-Air,'" Andscape, September 10, 2020, https://andscape.com/features/best-sneakers-worn-on-the-fresh-prince-of-bel-air/.
2. Russ Bengtson, *A History of Basketball in Fifteen Sneakers* (New York: Workman, 2023).

Chapter 37

1. Ohm Youngmisuk and Nick DePaula, "Eastbay Was More Than Just a Magazine for Basketball Players," ESPN, March 20, 2023, https://www.espn.com/nba/story/_/id/35830420/eastbay-was-more-just-magazine-basketball-players.
2. Youngmisuk and DePaula, "Eastbay Was More Than Just a Magazine for Basketball Players."

Chapter 43

1. Tim Keown, "The Shoes for the Serious Player," ESPN, November 9, 2004, https://www.espn.com/espn/page2/story?page=keown/041109.

Index

The Team behind the Team

Whether you call it a cool-down, a recovery period, or a time to decompress, every athlete knows you need time to slow down and absorb what you've just done. You've got to let your lungs and your heart catch up with what your muscles already know—that you need to rest and reflect.

That's what this book has been for us: the chance to look back, breathe deeply, and realize what an incredible race it's been. And of course, we couldn't have done it without our team of supporters. We'd like to take time to acknowledge all those who made this book possible.

To the greater Wausau community and the Frozen Tundra in general: thank you for supporting us in ways we didn't even know we needed. It was a wonderful community to grow up in; it made us who we are and was vital in building a company that people throughout our country trusted.

To our coaches, who taught us so much that helped us in building our business: get up when you're knocked down; momentum is better than perfection; attention to detail matters; showing up every day builds discipline; and practice matters. We thank you for teaching us sports lessons that turned into life and business lessons for us and for our teammates.

To the coaches around the county who impact so many athletes every day: thank you for getting us started and for spreading the word about Eastbay. When folks were telling us we wouldn't make it, your phone orders gave us the courage to keep going. But our biggest thank you is for your asking us early on, "Do you have pictures of the shoes?"

Thank you to our noon running buddies, who allowed us to step out of the chaos, even for an hour, for a restorative and productive lunchtime run. We're thankful to running friends like Brett Miller, a neighbor and close friend, and Pete Kerswell, who loved the Vikings, which allowed us to hate him on a daily basis. Thanks to Chris Evans, our life insurance agent, who kept us in good hands. To Paul Gassner, our first accountant, who somehow managed to teach us how to read financial reports. We wouldn't have made it without you.

Thank you to Trebs and to Harry Colcord for your special contributions to Eastbay.

To all the former teammates at Eastbay who gathered with us in Wausau early in this book-writing process to help spark our memories and reignite the Eastbay magic, thank you. You may not have realized it, but your words picked us up and carried us to the finish line. Thank you, Don Baptist, Sally Barwick, Tammy Brewer, Jim Carlson, Sean Cummings, Lisa Day, Stephanie Grauden, Brian Haack, Renee Hodell, Nancy Janz, Michelle Korman, Brian Krenz, Paul LaPree, Jimmy Olafson, Maddie Opal, Susan Peloquin, Dina Rasmussen, Carrie Reif, Keith Roerdink, Pat Schmidt, Jim Sisko, Johnathan and Mari Stein, Dowe Tillema, Karla Turzinski, Lisa Walkush, and Keith Wolfgram.

To each and every Eastbay teammate—the thousands of you—who took a call from a customer, proofed a page while buying the right shoes at the right time, stayed a couple extra hours to answer a phone that just wouldn't quit ringing, helped us gain customers' trust, laughed instead of cried when a rack of shoes fell over, made (for the twelfth time) just one more edit to the cover of the *Eastbay* catalog, took photos of shoes day after day, unloaded a semi while dodging traffic, searched high and low in dusty, cold warehouses for the last size 8 Nike Waffle Racer SKU 2227, manned a tape gun, held up a tent pole during our annual tent sale as a windstorm whipped around us, and found a way to work during blizzards. To all of you, we say thank you for being part of the best team in the world and for bringing a good attitude and a tremendous work ethic to the job each and every day. As Coach Herb Brooks said in the movie *Miracle*, "I'm not looking for the best players, I'm looking for the *right* ones." All of you were the right ones.

To our reps and vendors, who got us into the game and taught us how to play it, thank you. The stories of your treks to Wausau were sometimes unimaginable, but you did it time and time again.

Thank you to our customers, big and small, who started with us as starry-eyed kids but who stayed with us as adults, parents, and even storied athletes. To the parents who took a second job so their kid could get a better shoe, thank you. To the three-sport athletes who came back to us every season, thank you. You were right there with us, soaking up the team colors, telling players in need that size 16s were just a phone call away or that women looking for a great *women's* shoe would also find what they wanted. Thank you for opening your mailboxes to us and for trusting us with your names and addresses. We were always amazed that, simply by word of mouth, we reached two million unsolicited catalog requests a year from young athletes, without ads and before the internet even existed. Thank you for giving us insights into your lives and for telling us what products you desperately wanted but couldn't find in your local store: you gave us the knowledge to buy the right products at the right times.

To Brandon Sneed, our writer, thank you for slogging through a lifetime of memories with us, capturing our stories, and putting them down on paper. Your narrative craftwork and deep belief in our story—and the story of sneakers in general—helped bring the past back to life. And thank you to Jonah and Nolan for having great taste in shoes!

To Scott Berinato, our editor and former Badger, thank you for helping us find our voices and for bringing a flow and clarity to our story that captured what we lived. And thanks to his family, even though they're not all Badgers, for sharing him with us. You were the coach that got us over the finish line. Thank you, Leah Spiro of Riverside Creative, who was with us from the beginning to the end. And thank you to the entire Harvard Business Review Press team led by Melinda Merino and including Emily Lang, Anne Starr, Allison Peter, Julie Devoll, Felicia Sinusas, Alex Kephardt, Lindsey Dietrich, and Stephani Finks.

A big thank you to the Footlocker.com crew, and especially Dorothy Haggerty, for your hospitality and for helping us find the *Eastbay* archives and spending hours sorting through the memories.

Thank you to Bob Becker and Ben Clark of the Marathon County Historical Society for helping us track down some ancient pictures of old Wausau.

To good friends and family members who patiently listened to us these past two years as we rode the roller coaster of book writing for the first time: Jim and BJ Behnke, Tyler Galeazzi, Dr. Eric Hartwig, Bill Kraus, Mike LaBarbera, Matt Mirchin, Andy and Ellen Rolling, Kathy and Mino Spada, Jere Trudeau, Joe Urcavich, and Joel Wissmueller.

An extra-special thank you to Polly James, for bringing the same enthusiasm and hard work to helping us with the book as she did every day at Eastbay. To John Schaefer for his always-valued sage advice and insights, and his ability to help us make two plus two equal six. And to Dick Johnson, our friend and former CEO, who brought his memories, his incredible industry experience, and a perseverance for keeping us in line and on task.

Our families mean everything to us. Thank you to Rick's brothers, Tom, Jim, and John, all three of whom started early, gave us the confidence to keep going, and spent many late nights at the office for many, many years. Tom and Jim served with Eastbay and Footlocker for forty years each!

Endless love and gratitude to our children and their spouses, Elizabeth and Aaron, Tommy and Laura, Jessica and Pete, James and Bryna, and Jenna and Alex. We are so proud of the people you've become and the parents you are, and we are deeply grateful for your love, support, and encouragement.

To our dearest wives, Susie and Barb . . . there are no words. You kept faith in the dark, early days. You were a safe harbor in stormy seas. We would be nothing without you.

Although the Friday night lights are long gone, the stories never end. Somewhere out there, a young athlete is lacing up a pair of shoes, not knowing that decades ago, two guys in Wausau dreamed of helping that happen and are cheering from the sidelines.

If you've read this far, you've been running with us the whole way. Maybe you laughed, maybe you remembered your own team, maybe you recalled your own dreams. Maybe you remember that special pair of shoes that helped your dreams take off. Maybe you saw yourself in these pages.

If you did, our dreams have come true.

Thanks for looking back with us. It was the race of a lifetime.

Art + Rick

About the Authors

RICK GERING and **ART JUEDES** are entrepreneurs, business leaders, and lifelong best friends who built Eastbay, the athletic shoe and sporting goods mail-order company. They became a global reseller of sneakers and all things sports through the release of the iconic *Eastbay* catalog, which reached millions of people around the world and helped spark today's thriving sneakerhead culture. After starting with $4,000 and a carload of sneakers, Gering and Juedes grew the company, took it public, and eventually sold Eastbay to Foot Locker in 1997 for a nine-figure sum. From there it went on for two more successful decades. They now split their time between Naples, Florida, and Manitowish Waters, Wisconsin, where they spend as much time as possible with their wives, children, and grandchildren.

BRANDON SNEED is an author and journalist who writes for *Rolling Stone*, the *New York Times*, and *Sports Illustrated*. His book *Sooner* was described by *Kirkus Reviews* as "elegantly written . . . vigorous and smart." In addition, it was labeled "the sports book of the year" by the Pulitzer Prize–winning author and journalist Don Van Natta Jr., of ESPN. Van Natta also described Sneed's book *Head in the Game* "a thrilling manifesto."